DEATH VALLEY LORE

DEATH VALLEY LORE

CLASSIC TALES OF FANTASY, ADVENTURE, AND MYSTERY

edited by Richard E. Lingenfelter
and Richard A. Dwyer

University of Nevada Press
Reno and Las Vegas

Library of Congress Cataloging-in-Publication Data
Death Valley lore.
Bibliography: p.
1. Death Valley (Calif. and Nev.)—History.
2. Folklore—Death Valley (Calif. and Nev.)
I. Lingenfelter, Richard E. II. Dwyer, Richard A.
F868.D2D43   1988   979.4'87   88-17277
ISBN 0-87417-136-9 (alk. paper)

"Half a Century Chasing Rainbows," by Frank (Shorty) Harris: Copyright ©
1930 Automobile Club of Southern California, reproduction by permission,
courtesy of *Westways*. "Scotty's Castle," by Edward A. Vandeventer, is from "Death
Valley Scotty": Copyright © 1926 *Sunset Magazine*, used by permission of Lane
Publishing Company.

ILLUSTRATION CREDITS: jacket photo of Shorty Harris, by Dane Coolidge,
ca. 1916 (Courtesy of Bancroft Library); p. xii from Death Valley Hotel Co.
pamphlet, 1931 (Courtesy of Death Valley National Monument Library); p. 14
from *San Francisco Call*, December 25, 1898; p. 76 from *Overland Monthly*, May
1897; p. 138 from *Cosmopolitan*, May 1894; p. 162 from *Mining Investor*, December
4, 1905; p. 192 from *Overland Monthly*, May 1897; p. 244 from Charles Taylor's
The Story of Scotty, 1906 (Courtesy of Automobile Club of Southern California);
p. 284 from *Across Death Valley in a Ford Car*, 1926 (Courtesy of Hugh Tolford);
p. 318 from *Los Angeles Times*, January 19, 1890.

The paper used in this book meets the requirement of American National
Standard for Information Sciences—Permanence of Paper for Printed Library
Materials, ANSI Z39.48-1984. Binding materials were chosen for strength
and durability.

University of Nevada Press, Reno, Nevada 89557 USA
Copyright © 1988 Richard E. Lingenfelter and Richard A. Dwyer
All rights reserved
Designed by Dave Comstock
Printed in the United States of America

CONTENTS

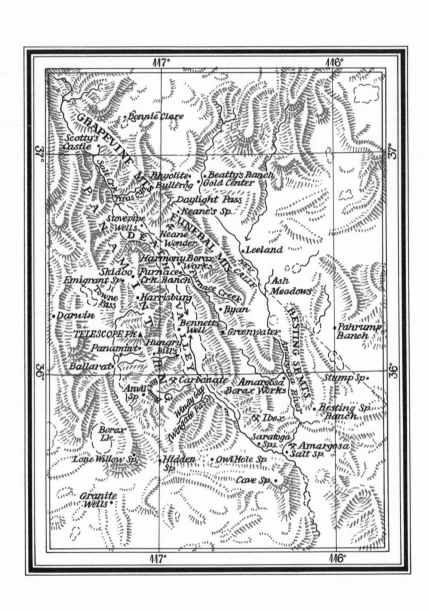

PREFACE

THESE TALES capture much of the rich but elusive spirit of Death Valley—its adventure, its mystery, and its lore. They are the classic tales that have formed the popular image of the valley.

These stories tell firsthand of the ordeal and heroism of the forty-niners, of the hopes and hardships of the perennial prospectors, and of the spellbinding exploits of later adventurers. They evoke also the illusions that shaped the history of the valley. They tell of the illusory shortcut that lured the forty-niners into the valley, the glimpses of death that they saw there, and the awful name they left upon it. These tales speak of the deadly specter that arose from its name and of the very real deaths in its desiccating heat that further fed that vision. They whisper of the mirage of riches that the forty-niners found there, of the lure of lost mines that grew out of those finds, and of the prospectors who braved death in the quest of those elusive riches. They report the real bonanza of borax that was discovered there, and the twenty-mule teams that hauled it out. They follow the mysterious Scotty, who exploited the valley's illusions for all they were worth, to become the personification of its wealth and its mysteries. They tout the adventure-seekers who challenged its death-dealing image just for the sport of it. And lastly they spin some of the tall tales that have been played off against its fatal illusions, stretching credibility beyond the breaking point with yarns of solar armor, water mines, canteen fish, deadly gases, and petrified argonauts.

These stories were written by many sorts of men, by forty-niners—John Brier and William Lewis Manly; by jackass prospectors—Shorty Harris and Milo Page; by mining promoters—George Graham Rice and Standish Rood; by mining camp editors—Clyde McDivitt and M. R. MacLeod; by adventuresome journalists—Paul DeLaney, John Edwin Hogg, Sydney Norman, and John Randolph Spears; by popular poets—Earl Brininstool, Clarence Eddy, and Rufus Steele; and by professional storytellers—J. Ross Browne, Dan De Quille, and Charles A. Taylor.

These tales were selected because they catch the feel of the times and the spirit of the valley in the words of those who were there. They cover the major events of the valley's history, though they are not intended as a history. That has been written elsewhere. Instead these stories express personal perceptions of the valley. They sometimes deliberately misinform; but what they may lack in accuracy they make up for in vitality and naive charm. To retain that flavor no attempt has been made to correct obvious misconceptions or idiosyncratic spellings, such as Armagosa or pignone. Obvious typographical errors, however, have been silently emended, and a couple of gratuitous racial slurs have been deleted. In our own comments on the stories, we indicate some of the less obvious gaps between the legends and the realities of the place.

Although some of these tales have been reprinted, most have lain hidden for half a century or more, all but forgotten, in the yellowing pages of old newspapers, magazines, pamphlets, and rare books. Now at last they can be enjoyed again.

For their generous aid in helping to make this collection of tales available, we would like to thank Irene Moran of the Bancroft Library, University of California, Berkeley; Shirley Harding of the Death Valley National Monument Library, Death Valley; Bill Michael of the Eastern California Museum, Independence; Phillip Earl and Lee Mortensen of the Nevada Historical Society, Reno; Leigh Goddard of the Nevada State Library, Carson City; and Ruth Anthony and Georgina Payton of the University of California, San Diego, Library, La Jolla. For permission to reprint two pieces still under copyright, we are also indebted to the publishers of *Sunset* and *Westways* magazines.

A Place in the Mind

MORE THAN ANYTHING ELSE, Death Valley is a place in the mind—a mirage land—conjured from illusions. And of all its mirages, the most powerful and persistent have been those of its ever-lurking deadliness and its boundless but hidden riches. These illusions have distorted in one way or another the vision of nearly everyone who has ventured into the valley. They have contorted its history for over a century and their influence pervades most of its literature. But nowhere have they found more vivid expression than in the two turn-of-the-century pieces that follow: a horrible catalog of unnatural history, concocted by a New York Sunday supplement writer, and a fantasy of health and wealth, dreamed up by a self-styled poet-prospector. Before such compelling visions of Inferno and Eldorado, the simple truths of the place quickly vanished.

3

THE HORRORS OF

This epitome of Death Valley's horrific lore was the creation of an anonymous Sunday feature writer for the New York World, where it appeared on September 16, 1894. It is a dramatic distillation of the valley's imagined and mythic history. Even the barest facts of the forty-niners' ordeal are grotesquely distorted, despite the publication earlier that year of William Lewis Manly's firsthand account (excerpted in the following section). For the record, the forty-niners actually entered the valley in the winter of 1849–50, not the summer of 1850, and only one was definitely known to have died in the valley itself.

DEATH VALLEY

The Reptile-Inhabited, Sun-Baked, Waterless Desert in California—The Loneliest, Hottest, and Most Desolate Spot in This Country

THE VALLEY OF DEATH, Inyo County, California, is the loneliest, the hottest, the most deadly and dangerous spot in the United States. It is a pit of horrors—the haunt of all that is grim and ghoulish. Such animal and reptile life as infests this pest-hole is of ghastly shape, rancorous nature, and diabolically ugly. It breeds only noxious and venomous things. Its dead do not decompose, but are baked, blistered, and embalmed by the scorching heat through countless ages. It is surely the nearest to a little hell upon earth that the whole wicked world can produce.

Death Valley is situated in the southeast corner of California. It is about eight miles broad by thirty-five long, and comprises some three hundred square miles of the most desolate country on the face of the globe. Its northern extremity is near the boundary line between California and Nevada, and it extends in a southeasterly direction. It is nearly two hundred feet below the level of the sea although within two hundred miles of the Pacific Ocean, and lofty mountain ranges intervene between it and the sea.

The Telescope Mountains tower above it to the height of 11,000 feet on the west, and it is bounded on the east side by the Funeral Mountains, whose peaks are scarcely less high. Still, it is a parched and arid wilderness. It knows no shade. No friendly clouds ever intercept the scorching rays of the sun. No moisture ever falls to cool the burning sand. Hot, suffocating winds sweep down the chasm, laden with blinding sand. Vegetation is unknown save for here and there a sickly cactus.

Of fresh water there is none; but a liquid having the appearance of water oozes in some parts from the salt and lava beds. It is deadly poison. There is no humidity; simply a straightforward, businesslike, independent, sizzling heat which keeps the thermometer in the region of 130 in the shade all the time; and the visitor has to provide his own shade.

This frightful place originally earned its name away back in the days of the Argonauts. In the summer of 1850 a wagon train containing a party of thirty emigrants passed through the Mormon settlements bound for the new Eldorado. They ascended the Funeral Mountains, and went down into the Valley of Death. Only two survived to tell the tale. Twenty-eight were killed by heat and thirst. But these are not the only instruments of death which justify the title of this horrible cañon.

A trackless waste of sand and salt, shimmering by day beneath the rays of a more than tropical sun. On entering there is no escape. Hemmed in on all sides by titanic rocks and majestic mountains, full of treacherous pitfalls, false surfaces, and quivering quicksands, surrounded by a silence that can almost be felt, in its most cheerful aspect Death Valley is enough to appal the stoutest heart.

As if presided over by cunning devils, and to enhance its treachery, the traveler is treated to delusive mirages. Green lands and sparkling springs of water appear temptingly in his path, only to recede or vanish as he advances into the hopeless tomb.

But when night comes, countless lizards squirm out of their burrows, rattlesnakes wriggle across the alkali crust, horned toads creep about, and scorpions and tarantulas of enormous size sharpen their claws and hustle around in search of prey. All these are abnormally armed with weapons artfully contrived to aid their master in this terrible Kingdom of Death. Here are also the headquarters of that most hideous and horrible of American reptiles, the deadly Gila monster.

Of birds there are very few in the neighborhood of Death Valley. Though that funereal fowl, the raven, may be heard in the woods that skirt its edge, crying with mournful notes for the many travelers whose dried and mummified corpses are scattered over the burning plain, he rarely, if ever, ventures down to the fatal torrid level. Some few specimens of animal life contrive to exist in this desert, but they are of unique species and essentially freaks. As if in sympathy with the uncanny nature of the place, they have impish habits and distorted anatomies such as Ingoldsby attributed to the fantastical devil's family conjured up by Satan for the temptation of the good St. Anthony.

There are rats with extraordinary ears, which bulge out at the side to an extent known in no other animals. There are "kangaroo rats" and "kangaroo mice," which get over the ground with a succession of vigorous hops. They live in burrows and have great, powerful hind legs, but no forelegs worth mentioning. Their tails are surprisingly long and strong. Still, according to Dr. C. Hart Merriam, of the Department of Agriculture, who led an exploring expedition

A Place in the Mind

three years ago, they are not in the true sense either rats or mice. They belong to families quite different.

One of the most curious rodents peculiar to Death Valley is the "scorpion mouse," which lives wholly on scorpions, and gets fat at that. By instinct, probably evolved through generations of unpleasant experience, it knows enough not to tackle its prey at the business end. Then there is the "grasshopper mouse," which has a strong taste for centipedes; and "pocket mice," with huge wallets outside their throats to store provisions in. Not for a rainy day, though, for it never rains in these infernal regions.

All these little creatures are in themselves harmless to humanity, yet they play a part in the diabolical scheme for the destruction of life in this den of the destroyer. It seems as if they were merely placed there as food for the terrible reptiles with which the gorge abounds, and which are the true ruling spirits of this valley of desolation and death.

The snakes are not said to grow to any enormous size. They are not the snakes of the conventional storyteller. But they are the most accomplished snakes in their particular line of business that the whole continent can produce. They are sudden-death snakes. A little "rattler" about two feet long is the champion lightweight of the community. It is claimed that he can put a strong man to sleep in one round and less than five minutes, so that you may count him out till doomsday.

During March and April a species of gnat which can give cards and spades to a Jersey mosquito takes a hand in the game. It swarms so thickly that it could probably sting a regiment of soldiers to death before the bugler had time to sound the signal for retreat. After these months the heat kills even these insects off. Scorpions and tarantulas are plentiful as blackberries and very poisonous. Lizards often measure as much as two feet in length. They are eaten and considered a great luxury by the Digger Indians, who live on the mountains adjoining the death pit. Half-starved coyotes prowl around afraid to enter and feast upon the human and animal flesh which fries and frizzles in the sun. . . .

In Death Valley there is no humidity, which, however unpleasant when in profusion, is nevertheless necessary to life. Curious effects of the arid air are recorded. Chairs transported to this region of eternal heat immediately fall to pieces. Water barrels, incautiously left empty, lose their hoops within an hour. One end of a blanket that has been washed will dry while the other end is being manipulated in the tub. A saturated handkerchief held in the sun becomes dry in a flash—quicker than it would before a red-hot stove.

Surveyor McGillivray, attached to the borax company which operates on the brink, says: "The heat is intense. A man cannot go an hour without water, without becoming insane. One man died from the heat while lying still within the adobe house. Another, while riding with a canteen in this hand on top of a load of borax, fell over and expired. He was so parched that his head cracked open over the top."

A Frenchman named Isidore Daunet had a terrible experience in and around the valley. In 1880 he, with six others, attempted to cross, bound for Arizona. He was a strong, vigorous, healthy man, and scouted the idea of danger in so narrow a strip of land. The party started, and before they realized their condition their water was gone. Half wild with suffering, they cut the throats of their pack animals and drank the spurting blood as tigers might have done. Daunet and the strongest of the band escaped with life. Three perished. Some time afterwards the Frenchman tied up his head in a white handkerchief, sat down facing a mirror, and put a bullet in his brain.

The Indians and Piutes who dwell in the woods at the border of Death Valley are restricted to a peculiar diet. Their staple food is lizard flesh. One of these reptiles, called the "Chuckwalla" by the whites and the "Chahwalla" by the Indians, is large enough to weigh three pounds when dressed. The Indians place them as caught between two hot rocks to roast. The whites dress them and broil them on the coals of a sagebrush-root fire or fry them in bacon fat. The meat resembles that of a frog's hind legs.

Perhaps the greatest curiosity of Death Valley vermin life, and at the same time the most deadly, is the "sidewinder" snake. It is peculiar to this one desert region. It is a little "rattler" from fifteen to eighteen inches long, that flops about from side to side instead of crawling, as respectable reptiles do. It has a horn one-eighth inch long over each eye, and the warning ring of its rattlers is so mild and soft as to be rarely heard. The first knowledge of its unfortunate victim is the sting of its teeth. The next thought is that he has but three minutes longer to live.

The record of frightful deaths endured in this desert is appalling. In every instance the victims first become insane. John C. O'Brien, a prospector, reached some coyote holes on the edge of a dry lake. The water there only aggravated his thirst. His brain gave way and he began digging in the sand with his hands. When help reached him he was found dead under a grease-bush, with his fingers worn to the bone from insane efforts to dig for water.

A strange delusion often seizes the sufferers. The dreams of

A Place in the Mind

water become realities to the wanderer. He believes he is at last in the water. More than one man has been found stripped naked and walking about on the burning sand, holding his clothing above his head. As rescuers approach they are warned to be careful for the water was deep, and once they were within reach of the dying man he would clutch them as a drowning man might do. Is it an exaggeration to designate Death Valley as a veritable hell upon this earth?

Death Valley was undoubtedly once a lake of water highly impregnated with various solutions of sodium; hence the deposits of borax and common salt. It is also of volcanic origin, as is proved by the fact that the springs which supplied this lake must have been subject to great heat to produce sodium biborate, or borax. It is now the sink of the Amargosa River, which in itself is quite a marvel. This erratic stream rises in the western Sierras, about two miles from the California boundary, and flows southward for ninety miles, when it disappears from sight in the bed of an ancient lake at the foot of the Resting Spring Mountains.

A little way south it bobs up again and scurries on through another sixty miles of sunshine, then it dives once more into its mysterious subterranean channel. Again it appears on the surface, and flows northward nearly one hundred miles, when it makes its final disappearance on the verge of Death Valley. No one knows what becomes of its buried waters.

The only parallel to this extraordinary place is, perhaps, to be found in the Dead Sea of Europe. Both are of lava, basalt, and granite formation, and both emit poisonous gases from the fissures of their rocks. It is the one foul spot upon the fair face of our land. Population may press forward. Civilization may claim our country bit by bit. The conquering flag of freedom may be planted on every square yard of our continent. The sons of liberty may make their home from pole to zone. They can never enter here.

This is the dominion of death. It is forever destined to stay in its state of primitive desolation and barrenness. By some mysterious decree of nature this pestilential place must remain the resort of venomous reptiles and vermin. It will ever be avoided alike by man and beast. It is the last and a lasting remnant of the world as it probably was, in that pleiocene period ere man was made to dominate and fructify the earth.

TREASURE BASIN

Death Valley's other great illusion was captured by a "poet-prospector" from the Rockies in this rapturous fantasy of boundless riches, published in the February 1908 issue of the Death Valley Magazine *from the booming metropolis, now ghost town, of Rhyolite. Needless to say, young Clarence Eddy was trying to raise money to dredge out all of the riches that he envisioned, but the mirage vanished soon after this piece appeared.*

OF THE WORLD
by Clarence E. Eddy

YOU HAVE HEARD of the boasted treasure vaults of this country and that. In 1849 it was California; in 1898 it was Alaska, in the present year of our Lord it is Nevada. But I have found the real treasure-basin of creation.

You have also heard of the Eldorados, and health resorts of every country upon the globe—the health-restoring, life-giving, balmy breezes, germ-killing atmospheres of different places, but I have found a place where the consumptive may seek refuge from the white plague; where the rheumatic may have the laugh on his departing pains.

And this treasure basin and universal health resort lie within the same bounds. The place is known as the accursed spot of earth; its name carries dread and terror with it; to its desolation and weird wastes hundreds of lives have been charged.

In my many trips across Death Valley I have made discoveries that will, one of these days, bring wealth and comfort to the poor and health to the afflicted.

I am not going to tell you a fairy tale nor spin a thread of theories, but will state facts that are comprehensive to any intelligent being.

I can tell the sick where to get healed and the poor where there is wealth, immeasurable.

It is all in Death Valley!

That place of horror! For all of these years, since the first immigrants wandered into its depths and perished and until the mountains upon its borders could no longer conceal the gold which protruded from the ledges along their sides, avoided by all mankind, has turned out to be the blessed spot of earth for the afflicted, and will, ere long, become a mecca, a haven, a supply point for all those who are financially depressed.

The sufferer from tuberculosis may here feel his lungs heal as if by miracle, see his chest expand with all the power of health, even watch the flesh come upon his emaciated body. The dread white

11

plague vanishes as if by magic, and ruddy, sun-burnt skin replaces the sallow, lifeless covering, while rich red blood fills the wasted veins, and all the pulsations of life are renewed down in this hole in the earth which is a crucible for the segregation of the pure with its furnace for the destruction of the impure ever burning around it.

I saw many examples of its work. There had been no failures. Big, full-chested men with ideal physiques and the pictures of health told their stories while reclining beneath the fig trees and plucking the delicious fruit. They had wandered into the country hopeless invalids, and living here nearly 300 feet below the rest of the lowest portion of the earth, they have found health and life. No wonder they tarry.

I am not able to give theories or scientific reasons for this wonderful phenomena, as I said before. I give the facts. The student of science may figure it out for himself.

I was told that there had been the same results in cases of rheumatism and other chronic and constitutional ailments. Bounded on two sides by mountains that extend so high into the clouds that they are perpetually covered by snow, this sink in the earth, which is nearly 300 feet below the sea, is so different from any other point on the globe that another atmosphere is created, some kind of a refining process is caused which probably has something to do with the miraclelike results.

Death Valley proper contains about 500 square miles. Within this area there is sufficient wealth to make every poor man in the world richer than Croesus; to make King Solomon's mines and Monte Cristo's treasure look like penny savings banks. It is literally composed of gold, silver, copper, and lead.

It only requires the ingenuity of man to secure it. He will do it. The time is not far distant. It is the deepest unoccupied spot on earth. The surging waters of the seas do not, upon an average, go to much greater depth. As to its original depth one can only approximate. It was doubtless at one time, and that not far distant, a lake. It has been filling for centuries and centuries. On the one side is the Panamint range of mountains. On the other are the Funeral and Grapevine ranges. These extend thousands of feet above.

For ages the rains and snows have been beating these mountains down into Death Valley. They are filled with the precious metals. Gold, silver, copper, and lead abound here. The great quartz rocks, on account of their weight, go down. Down, down, down, they have rolled for centuries! The melting snows and rains of winter keep the surface of the basin damp throughout the season. The entire surface of the valley is composed of the highest chemical matter.

A Place in the Mind

There is salt, saltpetre, iron—every chemical known to science, in one form and another. Vats of vast areas have formed which are perfect quagmires of chemicals under constant action.

Well, these highly mineralized rocks, largely impregnated with the precious metals, are constantly rolling down into this cauldron of chemicals. They have been doing it for ages and centuries, as already stated. The dampness of winter sets the processes to work. The hot suns of summer follow. No druggist's graduate nor assayer's crucible ever performed more scientific functions!

The quartz may be seen there in all stages of decomposition. It melts under these processes like the snows in the burning sunshine above. In a few years the ore is a part and parcel of the bed of this great sink—a mixture of strong chemicals in powdered and liquid form that work on and on with the centuries, filling higher and higher the great basin that has become one of the seven wonders of the world.

For time immemorial the ores of the mountains have been rolling down into the valley; the processes have been as busy as nature itself. Gold is indestructible. It may be 100, 1,000, 10,000 feet below, but it is there, and when the process is discovered by which it may be reclaimed, all the world will be rich, and gaunt poverty will cease its weary journey in the land!

The Forty-Niners

*D*EATH VALLEY'S ILLUSIONS OF
deadliness and riches owe their origins to the hapless band of argonauts who
stumbled into the valley in the winter of 1849–50. Eager to get to the gold
fields of California, they had left the known trail to seek a phantom shortcut.
But they wandered for months, divided and demoralized, losing nearly all of
their belongings and some even their lives. They gave the valley its deadly
name, and they got from it only a few pieces of rich ore to fire their
imaginations. Much has been written of their ordeal and heroism, but the
most moving accounts are those of two survivors, John Wells Brier and
William Lewis Manly. Although they started out together and suffered many
of the same hardships, their stories are still quite different. Brier, a boy of only
six at the time, and his family followed a group of Georgians and
Mississippians (known as Bugsmashers) into Death Valley and left with a
party of midwesterners, called Jayhawkers. Meanwhile Manly, an adventure
seeker in his late twenties, guided the Bennett and Arcane families, together
with some stragglers, by a different route. When the families weakened,
Manly made a heroic trek out to the settlements and then
back into Death Valley to rescue them.
These accounts should also serve as an antidote to the often mythical tales of
the forty-niners' trials that embroider some of the stories that follow; yet they
also reflect strong personal bias.

THE ARGONAUTS

In this reminiscence, published in the June 1911 issue of the Grizzly Bear, *John Wells Brier gives a succinct account of the lengthy ordeal of the Death Valley forty-niners. He draws not only on his own recollections, but on those of his parents, the Reverend James and Juliet Brier, and sets the scene by supplying the place-names that the region later acquired.*

OF DEATH VALLEY

by John Wells Brier

Being a Concise but Truthful Account of the Trials and Tribulations of that Pioneer Band Who Came to California by the Southern Route, as Told by One of the Survivors

THE TIME WAS propitious for a long and hazardous journey. The war-like tribes had buried at least the blade of the hatchet, and the Mormon settlement in the valley of the Jordan offered a haven of repose and a market for supplies. Indeed, the saints were glad to profit by the sojourn among them of those who had no wish to quarrel with their views or necessity to become pensioners on their bounty. The fate of the Donner Party conveyed a warning that could not be despised, and the companies were fortunate whose seasonable arrival at Salt Lake made it entirely safe for them to adopt the northern route.

But there were upwards of three hundred emigrants whose belated coming or enforced stay compelled them to choose the alternative of wintering in Utah or entering Southern California by the Spanish trail. It was late even for this, and the prospect discouraged the most sanguine until it was learned that the services of Captain Hunt—a competent Mormon guide—were available. For a thousand dollars, the experienced pathfinder bound himself to conduct a train of one hundred wagons and get them to Los Angeles at the expiration of nine weeks. The chosen rendezvous is now occupied by the city of Provo; and there, on the ninth day of October, the caravan, augmented by five wagons—with whose Mormon community the guide affiliated and domiciled—formed the line of march, steering southward across the wild flax-fields of Utah.

Mutiny and Revolt Invade Camp

It was a splendid train, representing many states, from New York to Iowa and Missouri, as far north as Michigan, and as far south as Mississippi. The wagons had been thoroughly overhauled, the oxen had been recruited in the pastures of the Jordan, and the emigrants were in perfect health. To expedite travel, and by advice

19

of Captain Hunt, provisions had been supplied to correspond with the time limit; and, during those early days of the journey, when the comparative smoothness of the way, the even temperature, and the accommodation of grass and water to the stages of travel kept everyone in a state of optimistic good humor, the food question was not among the topics of conversation—it certainly did not give rise to apprehension. At length, however, the memory of the guide seemed to be at fault; and, while much valuable time was consumed in laying out the course and locating the infrequent springs, the aspect of nature became more and more austere, and the poverty of nature more and more appalling.

When the camp circle was drawn at Iron Buttes, the company had been on the road seven weeks, and less than half the distance had been covered. The more difficult as well as the longer journey lay before; and the proximity of winter was betokened in the shortening days and the chill of the lengthening nights. The drudging teams were becoming lean, dispirited and sore of foot, while, to crown a pyramid of real and imaginary woes, the food question rose out of obscurity, its famished features wearing a goading look of interrogation and fear. Captain Hunt was a guide, but not a leader. He had no power to resolve the doubts and tranquilize the spirits of men, to restore their confidence, inspire their courage, and "grapple them as with hooks of steel"; he listened to complaints with an air of reserve; throughout, he was taciturnity itself.

Very unexpectedly, the camp at Iron Buttes became a scene of mutiny and revolt. It was incident to the arrival of a party of twelve Mormons, avowedly in marching line for the valley of Owen's Lake. These men were instructed by a chart they professed to have procured from the Utah chief, Walker. It defined a trail across the wilderness, located with precision the springs and feeding grounds, and avoided difficulties without a waste of energy or a loss of time. Perhaps no object of nature had presented greater imaginary attractions to the emigrant than Owen's Lake. Fancy had ascribed purity to its waters and invested its surroundings with all the charm of vernal landscape, bright with flowers and vocal with melody; and thitherward led the new, prospective route.

Several of the leading men decided to call a meeting and collect the opinion of the mass. It was evident from the first that a large majority favored the repudiation of Captain Hunt. That gentleman was called out, near the close of the meeting, and responded with characteristic bluntness and brevity. "Gentlemen," he said, "all I have to offer is, if you take that route you will all be landed in Hell."

A vote was taken, and early morning found the camp astir with preparation for the "new departure."

Mountain Meadows, famous in the record of Mormon atrocities, was the first objective point, and the course lay to the southwest. The strangers had already gone their way, never to be seen or heard of thereafter by those who had taken their counsel. It was shrewdly surmised that they were twelve emissaries of the twelve Mormon Apostles, and the reader will find much in these pages for reflection along that line. The entire Gentile force drew away from the guide who, with his five wagons, steered leisurely for the Spanish trail. The requirements of so large a company, in grass and water, were always great; and the satisfaction was complete when, at the close of the first day, the camp was formed in the midst of abundance. Anything short of complete satisfaction, in a host without leadership, implied a state of discontent. Indeed, without leadership there can be neither unity nor continuity; and when the seceders had renounced their leader, they neglected to appoint his successor.

Ax-men Lead the Way

It was difficult to select one for this distinction, where all were equally ignorant of the way; and while men of independent minds might meet in conference, there was no certainty that they would come to an agreement. When, by information of the chart, it was time to bear in a westerly direction, the southerly outlook seemed more inviting. This was enough to detemine the choice of the majority. Without knowing it, they had been traveling on a line nearly parallel with that of Captain Hunt, and it was not long before they were compelled to halt on the profound brink of the Santa Clara, a tributary of the Vegas. The only available water flowed at the base of a thousand-foot declivity, and the only man who could get to it was a French voyageur. His risk and labor were easily worth the dollar collected for every bucketful he brought to the surface. The earth was barren, so that the oxen had neither food nor drink; the way was effectually closed; the desolate aspect of nature quelled the ardor of youth; men began to ascribe the simple effect of reaction to a veritable foreshadowing of doom.

Under these trying circumstances, the major part of the company, following the example of Mr. Rhinierson, abandoned what they had come to regard as a foolhardy and chimerical undertaking and, by a venturesome shortcut, reunited with Captain Hunt. This reduced the train to forty wagons, but it was a winnowing by which the timid and cautious were separated from men whom death alone could vanquish. The situation required immediate and vigorous action. Exploring parties were sent out to find, if possible, a way of escape without additional loss of time. The Rev. Mr. Brier scaled a lofty mountain, where towered a pine, conspicuous for its loneliness. With strenuous effort he climbed to the topmost branch and obtained an expansive view of that wilderness to which distance alone could lend enchantment. Others explored the seemingly impassable range, bristling with dwarf cedars, that closed in upon the west. It was evident that if a roadway could be cut through the jungle, passage would be assured into the open country, whose vast plains the imagination mantled with grass and dotted with the verdure of springs. When the train was once more set in motion, axmen led the way, and the silence of ages was broken by sounds familiar to the logging camps of Maine and the populous clearings of the forest-teeming West. A rough and hazardous track was exposed to follow which tested to the utmost the discipline of the oxen and the will of their drivers. Evening closed about a camp pitched among the bog-lands of the Muddy, a sluggish stream issuing southward from the Mountain Meadows.

I shall here crave the indulgence of the reader for a brief digression. Simultaneously with the departure of the sixty wagons, eleven young men packed their backs for an expedition march to Owen's Lake. Their store of provisions was compact and necessarily inadequate, consisting mostly of bread. Prudence dictated and firmness would have enforced the severest restraint upon appetite, but the sanguine exuberance of youth and the insistent cravings of hunger prevailed over judgment. Before they had sighted the White Mountains, the grim visage of famine rose out of the sagebrush and sternly disputed the way. On the eastern margin of the Amargossa Desert, Funeral Mountain before them and the glittering peaks that exchange salutations with Mt. Whitney and the Minarets just visible above the northwestern horizon, they disputed and separated. Two of their number—Savage and Pinney—steered for the peaks, and the remaining nine passed over into the Valley of Death, there to await the last summons to earth's countless millions. Ten years thereafter, Governor Blaisdel of Nevada discovered their skeletal remains, side by side in the undisturbed composure of the last and painless sleep; for in that land of silence Nature, warring upon all forms of life, has imposing regard for the repose of the dead.

A happier fortune was decreed for Savage and Pinney. Overcome by famine, they had crept into a shadow of the desert scrub, where they were found by a band of Owen's Lake savages. The wild men ministered to their captives and led them to the lodges of their

tribe. They were saved from death by torture or the horrors of pro-
longed slavery by Pinney's red hair and the vigor of his thews.
Having danced himself and his companion into favor, he was hailed
as the "Big Red Chief," and when spring had melted the snow from
Walker's Pass, the Indians consented to the departure of their new
friends, generously conducting them into the Valley of the Kern,
whence they proceeded to the placer mines.

Relief from anxiety assured to the camp a night of perfect rest,
and the oxen, renewed by abundance, were ready for the long climb
and the trackless way inviting to purer air and a wider view. The
grade was easy, however, and near the summit, in an old Indian
cornfield, the camp circle was formed and the cattle were relieved of
their yokes. There was a light fall of snow and the cold was penetrating, but soon great fires, fed by greasewood, shot into lofty
spires, imparting warmth and radiating cheer during the preparation
of the evening meal. Nat Ward played the old tunes on his violin
and they who had music in their souls, though not, perhaps, in their
throats, vexed the air with the old-time songs. Enchantment had
woven about them an iris-tinted web, yet to be torn, shredded, and
dissolved by the stern realities that awaited them in the lone and
silent desert land to which they were hastening.

A Kind Providence Intervenes

Descending to the west and passing northward around a promontory, they entered upon the last of the grassy plains. Its western
boundary was the Timpahute Mountain, whose length was about
fifty miles. Northward the valley expanded indefinitely; southward,
it met the true desert and lost its character, for there the great hill
could no longer protect it from blasting siroccos and encroaching
sands. Traversed by a considerable stream, it was not wanting in fertility, and this impression was confirmed by the shocks of grass seed
that, dotting a wide area, bore a striking likeness to those of grain
on a field of stubble. Prudence would have overcome scruple, and
wisdom would have appropriated enough of the abundant store to
meet a pressing want, but the strangers respected the rights of ownership, leaving the harvest undisturbed. The savages were less scru-
pulous. In the gray of dawn they stole upon the camp, stampeded
two riding animals and drove them to the base of the distant mountain. As the owners vainly pursued the flight, they heard yells of tri-
umph and saw the grand salaam executed in reverse order of dis-
respect and insolent contempt.

It will be here noted that had the train proceeded to Mountain Meadows, distance would have been saved and complications

avoided. In a more open and expansive region, their course would have been cheered and guided by those shining peaks that for more than a hundred miles crown the lofty range on whose bold, marble brows burst the storm-fragments hurled from Mt. Whitney and his kindred heights.

If the wanderers were not fatuously drawn southward by the sun, we may ascribe their seeming folly to the kind intervention of Providence. Had their wish been gratified in entering the valley of Owen's Lake, they would doubtless have suffered all that hostile and implacable savages are able and willing to inflict. In any event of this nature, their course would have been deflected southward by insuperable barriers, so that the outcome may have been practically the same. By accident or preordination, however, they became, after their unfortunate comrades, the discoverers of Death Valley; but more to the purpose, they were permitted to behold California in one of its most highly favored provinces—when spring was trailing her verdant robes amid a captivating bewilderment of flowers.

What direction? This was the question that divided counsel in Timpahute. It was answered by a deflection to the south, with the consequence that not a drop of potable water was found for a period of three days. About mid-afternoon, as the train dragged a weary length through intolerable sand, and billowing horizon suddenly disappeared, earth and sky were blended, and a transparent sea, reflecting vermillion and gold, bounded the desert plain and breasted the distant mountains almost to their topmost peaks. Along the hither shore were stately trees of forest growth, and nearer, the semblance of green meadows and the rich mantling of level field and undulating prairie. This was the mirage, but they who gazed upon it had never known what wondrous power it is capable of exerting within its true zone.

Ignorant of its illusive splendors and its fatal charms, unsuspicious, they hailed with childish rapture the inland sea that had so long engaged fancy with its imaginary charms. The phantasmagoria slowly faded; and when the sun declined to his setting, it was no more. So strong had been the impression of reality that disillusionment did not come until, long after nightfall, the train halted on the margin of a wide basin over whose glazed surface rolled a shallow flood of brine, impelled hither and yonder by the winds. For stately trees there was a jungle of gnarled sage; for meadows and grassy fields the ever-drifting, never-changing wilderness of sand, ungladdened by a spring, unrelieved by a spot of verdure. Far westward, two arms of the desert embraced a high and stony hill; thitherward the emigrants chose their course, with such speed as the difficulties of the way permitted. The sky was overcast with a gray film, and the air was cold enough for snow.

Retreat, the Height of Folly

Early in the afternoon the train approached the mouth of a deep fissure, and the weary oxen were unyoked. A German was first to explore the yawning breach that receded far into the mountain. At its narrow, abruptly closed extremity, he surprised two scantily clad savages who were engaged in ladling the sand out of a slow-pulsing spring. Seizing the terrified natives, he led them into camp. They were treated with all possible kindness, and every effort was made to elicit from them information of value. Comprehending at length that water was the pressing want, they pointed toward a mountain whose baseline marked the confines of the desert some ten miles to the south of west. One of them was chosen for a guide, and a party of young men supplied with canteens was immediately dispatched to the distant spring. Clear and cold it rose in its stony vase, and was found carefully covered by a great, flat rock. The swarthy captive, having quieted suspicion by his willing and faithful service, struck the back trail with a rapid pace, and when advancing night made objects indistinct, he eluded vision at a bound, leaving the panting white men to find their way alone. Guided by the distant camp fires, they experienced little difficulty, and made a timely arrival with the water that had cost them so dearly. The native held in camp had been made the beneficiary of many gifts, but he, too, managed to elude his sleepy guards and was never seen again.

It was now feared that the prediction of Captain Hunt would be verified. Entoiled, bewildered, and depressed, the unorganized mass could not avoid disintegration. In one thing alone was there a perfect agreement: that with worn-out teams and stores almost exhausted it would be the madness of folly to attempt a retreat. The march was continued, but no longer with unbroken ranks. Some found an outlet into the region traversed by the Spanish Trail. The Jayhawks and the Mississippians bore to the southwest and were able to wheel their wagons into Death Valley. Arkane and Bennett forced a more southerly entrance into a veritable cul de sac of that famed Locus Averni, and there dug the pits long known as Bennett's Wells. The Towns, Wards, Mastertons, Briers and others, bound by congenial ties and concurrent judgment, bent their course a little to the north, presently involving themselves in difficulties and intricacies from which there was no escape except by the abandonment of their wagons. The sacrifice was considerable, especially wherein it involved favorite volumes and things of taste or endearment. Discarded comforts and treasures that had preserved to the pilgrims a sense of home life throughout their wanderings were thrown out upon the sand at the base of a wind-beaten hill, where, ten years thereafter, Governor Blaisdel found them, still in a state of remarkable preservation.

As the company thus scattered by dissentient views was destined, in the main, to share a common lot, it may be permitted to anticipate the event and locality of their reunion. The latter may be designated as Salt River camp, a stage northward from the Hot Spring oasis of Death Valley. This camp was visited by the Blaisdel party and, doubtless, by many prospectors and explorers. The wagon tracks leading to it, and also those of human beings who wore shoes, may have suggested that absurd fiction of "The Lost Train," so widely published and implicitly accepted as being true. As a matter of cold fact, until the 25th of December, 1849, Death Valley contained no intimation of the whilom presence of civilized man—no reminder of the near or remote entrance of white men within its borders; and only they who might have been so fortunate were, two years later, the victims of the Mountain Meadows massacre. Pathfinders of widest celebrity avoided even the approaches to a region in which there was nothing to attract and everything to repel, of whose true character they must have heard in Santa Fe; and the hapless mortals with whom this narrative is concerned were not in quest of knowledge or adventures. They drifted, so to speak, on the current of chance, each day leaving them more profoundly involved in a chaotic wild, their escape or deliverance from which can only be ascribed to the season of winter and the Benign care that was always most apparent in the time of deepest trouble.

Journeying afoot over wide and sandy plains is a trying experience at best, even when there is no lack of the things that nourish and every step is ordered by a knowledge of the way. To cross deserts in endless succession; to goad reluctant oxen to their task—skeleton creatures that desire to lie down and die; to mount the rising landscapes of stony mesa and abutting, barren hill; to climb mountains whose formidable escarpments forbid progress and whose sharp and ragged summits pierce or rend the sky; to know the protracted rage of thirst and support life with the diseased flesh cut from marrowless bones; to lie down with alacrity, sleep with troubulous dreams, and rise with languor to renew the hopeless march; to know the frame-sickness of famine and the heartsickness of hope deferred—all this through months that seem as years; to emerge at length, as from a pilgrimage of wars, harmless spectres, clothed in rags and wearing the expression of those who have seen strange vi-

The Forty-Niners

sions and have communed with fears—no fanciful picture, but stern reality here, feeble abridgement of sufferings endured by the "Argonauts of Death Valley."

"The Argonauts of Death Valley"

The complete record of their names is not available at this writing, and personal reference is, for the most part, to those who are still among the living. The survivors of the Jayhawks were young in '49, and now they are old. The Rev. J. W. Brier died in Lodi, California, at the age of eighty-four years. His wife is ninety-eight years of age, and her faculties are unimpaired. Of their three boys, respectively four, six and eight years of age, the author of this narrative alone remains. Col. John B. Colton of Kansas City, and Dow Stephens of San Jose, were mere boys when they shared the experiences of the desert. John Grosscup lives among the Mendocino hills, and has a lively recollection of the events that crowd this brief epitome.

It will be observed that the parties who deferred the inevitable abandonment of their wagons escaped a chapter of woes by beginning a long stage east of the Amargossa. It was a breaking-in stage— the habit of walking was to be acquired, and the habit of eating and drinking was to be disciplined. The evening of arrival at the dry wash of the Amargossa marked the second day of enforced abstinence from water. A cloud had burst on the summit of Funeral Mountain, but no rain had fallen on the intervening plain. Along its margin a multitude of dark and corrugated rocks projecting from the sand obtruded a grotesque feature, but they interested the mother and her children because their concavities held a scant collection of dew. This was industriously ladled out with teaspoons, insufficiently, as the train was well under way and the call for haste was urgent. The day ended at midnight. Far in the rear the lonely family trudged, the oxen moaning and the children crying for drink. When the camp fires began to glimmer at the base of Funeral Mountain, two good Samaritans met the laggards with full canteens of water dipped from a turbid pool left by the recent deluge.

Another day southward, among cobbles, bowlders, and jagged rocks, across dry ravines, and through jungles of greasewood and sage, brought them to a bend of the Amargossa where pools of water were found; and westward from this point a pass invited to the mountainous region beyond. The writer does not recall anything more cheerless and repellant than this gateway to the nether world. The north wind swept over barren hills "in gusts of doleful sound." No good thing could spring from such soil; but a hollow weed, buliform, mottled with pale red and faded blue, rattled an accompaniment to the moaning and whistling of the blast. The place was as parched as the tip of Dives' tongue, and the canteens were empty. Even scrub was denied, so that the oxen were without food or water. Through the still, clear atmosphere of morning, from the summit of a lofty peak, Mr. Brier discovered an oasis. Green and inviting, it lay at the extremity of the winding pass, on the brink of a vast depression three hundred feet below the level of the sea. This was Death Valley.

The abutments of the Funeral Range obstructed vision northward, but that of Panamint, rising to a height of ten thousand feet, increased the apparent depth of the pit and suggested its great extent. It was estimated that two leagues would measure the distance to the springs. In the desert, all atmospheric conditions are deceiving, and in this instance the tortuous trail led the travelers in a march of forty-five miles, consuming the entire day and more than half of the night. It was not remitted for rest or refreshment, and to describe its horrors would be to paint in the colors of the Epic Muse. History must content itself with a bare recital, unless it would invade the realm of poetry and eclipse the Homeric fiction of "the man of woes." Mr. Brier carried his youngest the last six miles of the way, and some of the exhausted men returned to meet and cheer the belated ones in their struggle for life.

Christmas in Death Valley

Midnight gave birth to the anniversary dedicated by Christian nations to festivity and mirth, but no thought of days to come or dreams of former happiness disturbed the sleep that came to the wayworn pilgrims the moment they reclined on the cool and fragrant sward of the oasis. Memories were revived with the dawn. An ox was slaughtered with ostensible regard for the day, but in reality to meet a pressing want; but with some there was a grateful sense of Divine favor, especially in effecting deliverance from the last and greatest peril. Complete relaxation was possible amid surroundings singularly attractive. The spacious green, shaded by blooming willows, made a charming picture, heightened in effect by the blacks and grays predominant in its framing of naked rock and sterile hill. The bubbling and murmuring, the rush and swirl of waters, and the croaking of frogs dissolved the spell silence and mystery had imposed. The day was spent in luxurious repose and many long-deferred ablutions to which the varying temperature of the springs invited. In the evening, by request, Mr. Brier delivered a reminiscent discourse, humorous and pathetic, to which the aborigines may have listened from among the neighboring rocks.

Meantime an exploring party reconnoitered the way into the valley. A short distance from the camp they came upon an old Indian, buried in the sand, only his head visible. Doubtless, his great age and total blindness rendering him incapable of flight, his people, panic stricken by the approach of the strangers, hoped thus to effect his safety. Deep trails, worn or cut through the very rocks and all converging at the springs, marked the region as an Indian resort; but of wigwams, there were none visible, and the buried patriarch was alone.

The trail led by the channel of Furnace Creek—creek by courtesy because, though not of perennial source, after a storm on Funeral Mountain it flowed full to its banks. Fretting and foaming for a space, it sunk from view or poured a slender tribute into the saline swamp beyond. This swamp or, with a better shading, marsh was merely an inlet. The gulf toward which it expanded was fed by rivulets of brine and a considerable stream of much the same character, and was so strong in mineral solutions that all the contributions of winter storm and summer cloudburst could not freshen it. Flowing from under the base of a skirting hill, shallow floods of brine deluged the way and spread over the corruscating plain, there to evaporate and augment the undisturbed accumulations of a thousand years. These floods the travelers waded, leaving at muddy intervals footprints that were not effaced for half a score of years.

At length they approached the Jayhawk camp—a desolate spot with a desolate prospect from every point of outlook. The White Mountains gleamed just above the northern horizon, the Panamints towered in stony might of grandeur westward across the way, while Funeral Mountain, like a huge sarcophagus, loomed solemnly against the altar of the rising sun. Salt River slipped along over its sandy bed, by its seeming virtues aggravating the thirst it could not quench. Browse for the oxen was scanty and here it had an ending. Across twenty miles of naked dunes the way was laid to a mountain pass, above which Telescope Peak stood like a lone sentinel; and it looked towards Mt. Whitney and the Minarets. At this camp a number of the party, headed by Captain Town, announced their determination to pack their backs and push for the Tulare plains. They gave some score of oxen to Mr. Brier, and made the remnant of their flour into bread for the journey. Here it was strongly urged upon the Brier family to remain at the oasis until relief could be obtained from California. The proposition was promptly vetoed by Mrs. Brier, whose gentle and patient spirit was, nevertheless, of the heroic type. More-over, she saw at a glance the fatal consequences of such a choice. Well-meaning men had, after their blundering fashion, overlooked the possible hostility of the natives and the certainty that they would plunder the helpless family of the only means of support. If, how-ever, safety from violence and wrongs had been assured and, as well, the continued health of the family head, climatic conditions were to be reckoned with; for it was entirely certain that within a few months, possibly weeks, an attempt to enter the valley or escape from it would have been attended with the greatest danger.

"The Gun Sight Lode" Legend

On the morning of December 27th the reunited company, now relieved of the cumbrance of wagons, steered their course for Town's Pass, over ever-drifting, never-changing billows of sand. The cold north wind blew quartering across the way, driving the fine crystals forcefully into face and eyes; add to this hunger for bread, raging thirst, and the difficulty of pursuing refractory cattle among the un-dulations of such a surface. No rest short of the snowline, and the desert behind them, it yet remained for the toilers to climb the dark, rock-strewn bluffs and bench lands, pressed out, seemingly, by weight of the superincumbent mountain. Snow lay in patches not far above the spot chosen for a camp, and quantities of it were brought down in sheets to be melted for the oxen. Under other circum-stances, the panoramic view of Death Valley would have kindled in-terest in sluggish minds, and quickened sensibility to enthusiasm or quelled it by a more awful emotion of the sublime. The vale was submerged in shadow, the day flaunted its signal of departure from the crest of Funeral Mountain, night proclaimed its truce to the wind, and the deep, clear heaven of violet, with its myriad lights, bent low over a wilderness at rest; all this unobserved and unheeded by the wanderers, who thought only of the morrow—what rewards it had in store for them or what severities it would inflict.

First of all, they passed over a belt of snow, of which the oxen greedily ate; then opened the winding passageway, walls, high and ever heightening on either side, a footing of sand or jagged rock, often boulder-obstructed, precipitating leaps of difficulty and dan-ger—a long trail of weary longing and rude discouragement of hope! A sudden emergence brought Mt. Whitney and the Minarets into glorious prominence. The former, a pyramid of snow, bourgeoned in sunset's rosy hues; while the latter, like the flues of some vast fur-nace, shot upward to the height of nearly two thousand feet and shone in the yellow splendor of burnished gold.

The bewildered travelers did not know that Wild Rose Canyon opened a little way beyond them, affording a direct route to Walker's Pass. They were about to enter the Panamint Desert, and soon, at its northern extremity, they went into camp, where they had water from a spring and their oxen saw the color and tasted the flavor of grass. There the Town party reappeared, having climbed Telescope Mountain and made a detour involving much labor and loss of time. They had specimens of silver ore, some of virginal purity, and one of which, afterward shaped into a sight by a gunsmith of Mariposa, gave currency to the legend of "The Gun Sight Lode." The remarkable discovery has never been located, though for years the search was unremitting. From this point the Town party proceeded westward, entered the great interior plain by Walker's Pass, and thence made their way to the southern mines. Town himself was killed some years later by the Tulare Indians.

The main party skirted the desert southward, falling into a trail that led them to an Indian village. Situated among mesquites and supplied with water by an abounding spring, this collection of willow-woven, thatch-covered huts had a cheerful outside for eyes long accustomed to look upon an uninhabited waste. With a single exception, the lodges had been vacated in haste. An old squaw alone remained, who, from the doorway of her hut, scolded the intruders with a vehemence that could not be misunderstood. Earthenware, baskets, bridles and hair ropes were much in evidence, while great heaps of offal and the bones of horses betrayed the preferences and predatory habits of the natives. It was their custom to drive animals from the outlying ranges of Southern California and slaughter them in this desert home. A spring-fed pool had been escarped and screened in order that wild fowl, attracted in their flight over a thirsty land, might be easily slain with the silent arrow. This was apparent from the quantity of feathers scattered all about the place.

After a short rest the march was resumed, ending for the day at a spring where no settlement had been made. At this camp another small party decided that the outlook was good for a quick tramp, and forthwith set about their preparations. They alone had hoarded a small quantity of flour, the making of which into bread consumed the early hours of the night. Many remained awake to watch with hungry eyes the interesting process. One young man offered ten dollars for a biscuit and, being curtly denied, turned sorrowfully to his blankets. Certain fag ends were given to Mrs. Brier—all things considered, a very considerable act of self-denial—and these she wrought into thirteen diminutive rolls, reserved against occasion of direst need.

Horrors of the Desert March

The eye was attracted by two depressions of the western range, and Mr. Brier, along with three others, volunteered to investigate them. Two reports following, the company—now numbering something above forty—divided for the passage on grounds of expediency. They who chose the northerly pass encountered great difficulties, but were first in accomplishment, while the others were fortunate in nothing and most unfortunate in the loss of two of their number. Nothing in the annals of desert pilgrimage could greatly exceed the horrors of that march. The first stage—a damp tract of sand covered with the tracks of Indians in flight—was succeeded by a wider area, dry and drifting, upon which the sun burned with a fierce delight. Entrance to the range was by a corridor whose perpendicular walls, separated by a narrow space, rose to the altitude of a thousand feet. It was three miles in extent, and seemingly drove to the bloodless heart of the mountain. Its level floor was paved with sand, and where it ended, a vast slide, formidable for its pitch, foreclosed the view and shut the travelers in for the night.

For some distance a slutchy taint had advised them of the proximity of water, and the oxen were first to take the scent and make the discovery. It proved to be a barely perceptible drip from the base of the closure—enough, after patient waiting, to make coffee for the evening meal of jerk. During the night two of the oxen escaped, and aged Mr. Fish, who had long been an object of solicitude, declared his inability to go farther. Two young men volunteered to go in pursuit of the strays and a third to care for the old man until their return. The larger number, scaling the acclivity, made all possible speed to gain the summit and rejoin their comrades in the plain beyond. At noon they entered a narrow defile that, with ever-changing course and doubtful certainty of way, left no alternative but to follow where the torrent had torn for itself a passage at a time when the summer cloudburst on the mountain had poured a deluge along its declivity. It was a wild and rugged pathway, suggestive of foaming rapids and roaring cataracts, for its descent was frequently abrupt and its windings interminable. Narrows through which an ox could squeeze with difficulty—six- and even ten-foot perpendiculars he would only take by forcing—and vast promontories that persisted in infinite succession to shut away the prospect and obscure the light are features that are vividly recalled and, along with them, the hunger and thirst that made them intolerable.

When the end was reached in open day, the sun had nearly finished his course, but the glory of his setting was not on mountain summit and pinnacles of snow, but rather on the bosom of a vast, uplifted sea, whose farther horizon was of carmine and vermillion, passing by insensible degrees into orange and gold, the hither shore washed by transparency of cerulean and a margin of glittering white. There, too, was the silvan border of blue, tipped with ashes of roses, its back-lands faintly suggestive of emerald. The desert itself was transformed almost to the foot line of the slope on which the travelers stood. The first lesson of enchantment had been forgotten, and the eyes that had seen a vision of equal splendor fade, expressed the joy a conviction of reality alone can inspire.

One tires of writing about yielding sand and impeding scrub, so effectual in stretching distance and consuming strength and time. The waterless, desolate plain upon which the pilgrims entered lay in the gloaming, but half of the night was gone when they halted on the shore of a shallow, briny pool, now dignified by the name of "Borax Lake." While yet trekking the desert, they were cheered by the camp fires of the men from whom they had parted two days before; but the greeting was saddened by the report that no water had been found. Early in the day the search was renewed and prosecuted for miles in every direction, but with no success. One by one the tired men returned to await the inevitable. While some were distracted, the greater number tried manfully to conceal their distress. Mrs. Brier retired to the shadow of a great rock to pray, and when she returned, upbraided them for their want of faith. While she was yet declaring her certainty that deliverance would come, "Deacon" Richards bounded into the circle, shouting, "Water! Water! I have found water!" Four miles away, hidden close in at the base of the mountain, was a clear brook that ran for a space and sank out of view in the desert sand. The heroic discoverer had not been willing to spare time for the slaking of his own thirst, or even to look upon the stream. He heard the music of its flow, and remembered the woman and her children. There was bustle in that camp, and within the hour men who had resigned themselves to die found a new joy in living—so quickly do fading images renew themselves, so certainly does Hope revive and weave threads of gold into the melancholy texture of her song!

Long Journey Nearing End

It had been noted that young Isham was not of the number who arrived during the night. Dead or alive, he was still on the desert, and a search party was immediately dispatched. His lifeless body was found by following the impressions left by his hands and knees for a distance of four miles. For the second time, the desert enforced its claim on the Culverwell party, the Captain himself having surrendered far back, beyond the Amargossa. Isham was buried where he lay, and his watch, with articles likely to be prized by his relatives, were given in trust to Mr. Brier, who afterwards delivered them to the brother of the deceased. In the meantime, the men who had remained with Mr. Fish came into camp, more dead than alive, reporting that they had left him on the trail, almost immediately at the point of starting. By clinging to the tail of an ox, he had managed to scale the acclivity, but there he fell, his spirit broken and his strength utterly expended. Succor reached the spot too late to avail; indeed, it is probable that the old man had passed with the day. He, too, was of the Culverwell mess and, like his comrades of kindred, melancholy fate, was held in mournful memory by all who knew him. Stones were piled about him for a coffin, and raised above him for a monument; and thus he was left alone—none more so—not likely to be disturbed, by man or beast, in the deep silence of his stony sleep.

The stream so opportunely discovered by "Deacon" Richards had its rise in a spring not far above the camp. There, on a level of inconsiderable area, the Indians had built their huts, but to the same enterprising Richards, who treated himself and them with a genuine surprise, they were only visible in flight. It is worthwhile to record that the water to which the Jayhawks owed their lives is now known by the suggestive name of "Providence Springs."

The range that separated Borax Lake from the Mojave Desert was not formidable, as it was traversed by a branching pass long used by the natives in their plundering expeditions coastward. Well-worn trails made going easy, and a sufficient spring awaited on the Mojave side. The only sensation of the passage was occasioned by the temporary loss of a boy who had taken the wrong trail where the canyon divided. He corrected his mistake in time, and was met by his agitated parents, driving his oxen and whistling in absolute unconcern.

The Mojave Desert is wide, and even bladders were put in requisition for the transportation of water. For a space, the course lay through a forest of dagger palms, attaining great altitude for their kind and displaying an unusual wealth of foliage, but, singularly, did not impart that cheer to the landscape their color, at least, would seem to animate. To the traveler in a weary land, there can be nothing to engage the mind in pleasing contemplation, nothing to bring content, where water does not spring or flow. There is no joy in plants that spring where there is no water. They only confirm the impression of sterility, and are hateful because they flourish where life-sustaining vegetation cannot live. The march across the Mojave Desert was attended with great suffering and, after eleven months of pilgrimage, all must have perished but for the fortunate location of Indian Wells. From this point southward it is fifty miles to the Mojave Station. Thitherward, over a trackless, arid waste the journey was renewed, but far east from the present line of travel, and by deviating courses that greatly increased the distance. No water was found in all the way. Famine and fatigue had nearly done their work. The oxen were mere skeletons; once-vigorous men, young, inured to hardship, and disciplined by toil and danger, had no more strength than the pale, attenuated woman and the three shadows of childhood who plodded at her side.

The outcome was precisely where the Southern Pacific enters the inlet of approach to its mountain crossing. There muddy pools were encountered, and presently a remarkable well of the desert, whose depth could not be ascertained. The long journey was nearing its end. Nature had heaved a mighty breastwork against the encroaching sand, and it was touched with green. This complexion of renewing youth, "soft amenity" of the air, and the faint, though certain intimation of fragrance, must have been convincing to men who were not enfeebled in intellect and benumbed in sensibility. The "Argonauts of Death Valley," aroused to enthusiasm by an optical illusion, always awaiting the improbable and calculating upon surprises, either failed to recognize the tokens of deliverance or noted them with apathy. Only when they were received to native hospitality, amid charms that bewildered judgment and captivated sense, did the current of true feeling begin to surge in its customary channels.

At the last camp on the desert side, two events, sudden and unexpected, added grief and horror to depression. As the travelers advanced toward the hill line that curved with the spacious inlet of the plain, they saw wild men of the regions already traversed in the act of rounding up horses for one of their customary drives. The whirlwind activity of the drivers and the frenzied efforts of the herd threw the oxen into a panic, causing them to stampede in every direction. Some of them were not recovered, and presumably were taken by the savages, who also surrounded and captured a Frenchman in ardent pursuit of the ox that was loaded with his effects. The unfortunate captive was not released from a most unhappy servitude before the expiration of fourteen years. The same day, Mr. Robinson was assisted from his horse and borne to a pallet, where he presently expired. Like the Prophet of Israel, he was claimed by the wilderness on the very threshold of the Promised Land, and the men at whose hands he received burial could not be certain of an entrance, as they were all afflicted with the malady that suddenly—as in his case—reaches its fatal stage.

Hospitable Welcome at Rancho de San Francisquito

Before closing a long chapter of woes, it may be well to note in general the effect of so protracted a journey—a journey in which no manna lay like hoar frost about the camps; no timely bevies afforded delicious repast and quelled the rage of famine; no rod-smitten rock yielded miraculous waters to quench the fever of thirst. Thirty-eight men reduced to skeleton weight, afflicted with dysentery, still wearing their rags with much of dignity and self-respect, the great courage native to them in no jot or tittle abated; one woman clad in garments worn, torn, and tattered, gentle, resolute, and brave, devoutly loved and cherished by her own, idolized by all, for whom few in that company would not have cheerfully laid down their lives; three children, wan, large-eyed, and patient, whose shreds bore witness to the cruelty of the desert scrub and whose patches attested the self-sacrificing care of watchful, tender motherhood; some two score of oxen—Mr. Brier's herd had been reduced from twenty-three to seven—in whose bones blood and water had taken the place of marrow, and whose fibrous flesh had been wrung of the substance that nourishes and the flavor that satisfies. Such was the spectacle destined shortly to appear like an apparition before the wondering eyes of the natives of California.

It was the first day of February when the travelers, near the headwaters of the Santa Clara, began their descent to the lands that border on the sea. Their trail followed the winding course of that stream into prospects that visibly brightened with every league. Grass became plentiful and the cattle began to lick their sides and give voice to their newfound happiness. It was delightful once more to look upon trees native to a better soil and a more genial atmosphere. About noon of the second day three horses were shot, whose flesh was greatly relished. To preserve so great a treat, racks were built and a slow fire applied, thus quickly curing it for future use. The packs were stored with slugs of hide, still husbanded with miserly care—this in a land of plenty, by signs not only of horses but of deer. At length the stream so often waded began to flow in a straighter channel, emerging presently where a narrow, grassy dell expanded to the wider lands not yet visible for clumps of live oaks and a point of emerald hill.

Here the camp was chosen and an abundance of acorns suggested the feasibility of bread. The experiment proved a wretched

The Forty-Niners

failure, but the greater wonder may be expressed that it was attempted. When morning dawned the air was misty, but when travel was resumed it began to clear. A deep trail led the way for the file, and soon the foremost cleared the vale and beheld, to their amazement, "sweet fields arrayed in living green," over which roamed countless herds of long-horned cattle. They at once opened fire, and two of the animals fell to their bullets. A light breeze sprang up, the thin vapor began to wreathe about the hilltops, and in a glorious burst of sunshine, a cavalcade bore swiftly down upon the scene. The old ranchero, accompanied by his vaqueros, had been running down coyotes, one of which he dragged at the end of his lariat. When the horsemen approached and reined in before the trespassers, Mr. Brier and his family had just arrived, and fortunately, Mr. Patrick—who was in service as an assistant—was able to explain the situation. As a soldier in the Mexican war, he had acquired a rudimentary skill in the vernacular which, on this occasion, he turned to a diplomatic purpose.

The silent natives were evidently moved to compassion by the ragged and emaciated appearance of the strangers—their woeful countenances unshaven; their hair unshorn beneath torn and slouching hats; their feet wrapped in bandages of hide; their lean oxen under burdens of refuse; the evident extremity of their plight. It only remained for Patrick to designate Mr. Brier as "un padre," a hint supplementary to an appeal more eloquent than words. The simple mind of the old Spaniard, vacant of controversial rubbish, was visibly affected by the great misfortune that had befallen a priest. He reverently removed his sombrero and exclaimed with broken utterance, "Padre, padre, pobrecito padre!"

A warm welcome was instantly extended to the hospitalities of the Rancho de San Francisquito. Vaqueros caught up the children and swiftly bore them to the hacienda, a league distant across the level plain. There they were set down by a clear runnel to await the coming of their friends; and there the camp was located, to which supplies were rushed with generous, though inconsiderate haste. A fat bullock was immediately led to the ground and slaughtered, while meal, torteas, beans, squashes, and milk followed in profusion. Mrs. Brier was met on the brow of the hill on which stood the old adobe, and embraced by the matron with loud cries and convulsive sobbing. Lavish entertainment was distinguished by delicacy of attention and marked respect, and nothing was wanting to the conditions that make for happiness and peace. It was a new world, a varied prospect of illuminated green, over whose hills and vales the rarest sunshine played, through which the purest waters flowed, the whole embalmed in the atmosphere of a perfect spring. More than twenty thousand cattle wandered at will over the rich pastures, with horses, mules and burros numberless. With the reports of such a teeming population borne in from every horizon, it was impossible to have a lonesome thought; and with anticipation wrought to ecstasy, there was relief from agonizing memories and the too poignant sense of wrongs.

GOOD-BYE

William Lewis Manly's dramatic story is one of the truly great tales of heroism in the epic of the westward movement. Yet it also provides an intimate view of the struggles and sufferings of the argonauts. Manly told the story best in 1894 in his now classic book Death Valley in '49, *subtitled* The Autobiography of a Pioneer, Detailing His Life From a Humble Home in the Green Mountains to the Gold Mines of California. *The Death Valley chapters of his adventure are given here. We pick up Manly's party shortly before they reach the Amargosa. Leaving the Bennett and Arcane families and others at a spring, Manly climbed a spur of the Spring Mountains to scout ahead.*

DEATH VALLEY!
by *William Lewis Manly*

NEXT MORNING I reached the summit about nine o'clock, and had the grandest view I ever saw. I could see north and south almost forever. The surrounding region seemed lower, but much of it black, mountainous, and barren. On the west the snow peak shut out the view in that direction. To the south the mountains seemed to descend for more than twenty miles, and near the base, perhaps ten miles away, were several smokes, apparently from camp fires, and as I could see no animals or camp wagons anywhere I presumed them to be Indians. A few miles to the north and east of where I stood, and somewhat higher, was the roughest piece of ground I ever saw. It stood in sharp peaks and was of many colors, some of them so red that the mountain looked red hot, I imagined it to be a true volcanic point, and had never been so near one before, and the most wonderful picture of grand desolation one could ever see.

Toward the north I could see the desert the Jayhawkers and their comrades had undertaken to cross, and if their journey was as troublesome as ours and very much longer, they might by this time be all dead of thirst. I remained on this summit an hour or so, bringing my glass to bear on all points within my view and scanning closely for everything that might help us or prove an obstacle to our progress. The more I looked the more I satisfied myself that we were yet a long way from California and the serious question of our ever living to get there presented itself to me as I tramped along down the grade to camp. I put down at least another month of heavy, weary travel before we could hope to make the land of gold, and our stock of strength and provisions were both pretty small for so great a tax upon them. I thought so little about anything else that the Indians might have captured me easily, for I jogged along without a thought of them. I thought of the bounteous stock of bread and beans upon my father's table, to say nothing about all the other good things, and here was I, the oldest son, away out in the center of the Great American Desert, with an empty stomach and a dry and parched throat and clothes fast wearing out with constant wear. And perhaps I had not yet seen the worst of it. I might be forced to see men, and the women and children of our party, choke and die, powerless to help them. It was a darker, gloomier day than I had ever known could be, and alone I wept aloud, for I believed I could see the future, and the results were bitter to contemplate. I hope no reader of this history may ever be placed in a position to be thus tried, for I am not ashamed to say that I have a weak point to show under such circumstances. It is not in my power to tell how much I suffered in my lonely trips, lasting sometimes days and nights, that I might give the best advice to those of my party. I believed that I could escape at any time myself, but all must be brought through or perish, and with this all I knew I must not discourage the others. I could tell them the truth, but I must keep my worst apprehensions to myself lest they lose heart and hope and faith needlessly.

I reached the camp on the third day, where I found the boys who went partway with me and whom I had out-walked. I related to the whole camp what I had seen, and when all was told it appeared that the route from the mountains westerly was the only route that could be taken. They told me of a discovery they had made of a pile of squashes, probably raised upon the place and sufficient in number so that every person could have one. I did not approve of this, for we had no title to this produce and might be depriving the rightful owner of the means of life. I told them not only was it wrong to rob them of their food, but they could easily revenge themselves on us by shooting our cattle, or scalp us, by gathering a company of their own people together. They had no experience with red men and were slow to see the results I spoke of as possible.

During my absence an ox had been killed, for some were nearly out of provisions, and flesh was the only means to prevent starvation. The meat was distributed amongst the entire camp, with the understanding that when it became necessary to kill another it should be divided in the same way. Some one of the wagons would have to be left for lack of animals to draw it. Our animals were so poor that one would not last long as food. No fat could be found on the entire carcass, and the marrow of the great bones was a thick liquid, streaked with blood resembling corruption.

Our road led us around the base of the mountain. There were many large rocks in our way, some as large as houses, but we wound around among them in a very crooked way and managed to get along. The feet of the oxen became so sore that we made moccasins for them from the hide of the ox that was killed, and with this protection they got along very well. Our trains now consisted of seven wagons. Bennett had two; Arcane two; Earhart Bros. one; Culverwell, Fish and others one; and there was one other, the owners of which I have forgotten. The second night we had a fair camp with water and pretty fair grass and brush for the oxen. We were not very far from the snow line and this had some effect on the country. When Bennett retired that night he put on a camp kettle of the fresh beef and so arranged the fire that it would cook slowly and be done by daylight for breakfast. After an hour or so Mr. Bennett went out to replenish the fire and see how the cooking was coming on, and when he went to put more water in the kettle, he found that to his disappointment the most of the meat was gone. I was rolled up in my blanket under his wagon and awoke when he came to the fire and saw him stand and look around as if to fasten the crime on the right party if possible, but soon he came to me, and in a whisper said: "Did you see anyone around the fire after we went to bed?" I assured him I did not, and then he told me someone had taken his meat. "Do you think," said he, "that anyone is so near out of food as to be starving? I know the meat is poor, and whoever took it must be nearly starving." After a whispered conversation we went to bed, but we both rose at daylight and, as we sat by the fire, kept watch of those who got up and came around. We thought we knew the right man, but were not sure, and could not imagine what might happen if stealing grub should begin and continue. It is a sort of unwritten law that in parties such as ours, he who steals provisions forfeits his life. We knew we must keep watch and if the offense was repeated the guilty one might be compelled to suffer. Bennett watched closely and for a few days I kept closely with the wagons for fear there might be trouble. It was really the most critical point in our experience. After three or four days all hope of detecting the criminal had passed, and all danger was over out of any difficulty.

One night we had a fair camp, as we were close to the base of the snow butte, and found a hole of clear or what seemed to be living water. There were a few minnows in it not much more than an inch long. This was among a big pile of rocks, and around these the oxen found some grass.

There now appeared to be a pass away to the south as a sort of outlet to the great plain which lay to the north of us, but immediately west and across the desert waste, extending to the foot of a low black range of mountains, through which there seemed to be no pass, the distant snowy peak lay still farther on, with Martin's Pass over it still a long way off, though we had been steering toward it for a month. Now as we were compelled to go west, this impassable barrier was in our way, and if no pass could be found in it we would be compelled to go south and make no progress in a westerly direction.

Our trail was now descending to the bottom of what seemed to be the narrowest part of the plain, the same one the Jayhawkers had started across, further north, ten days before. When we reached the lowest part of this valley we came to a running stream, and, as dead grass could be seen in the bed where the water ran very slowly, I concluded it only had water in it after hard rains in the mountains, perhaps a hundred miles to the north. This water was not pure; it had a bitter taste, and no doubt in dry weather was a rank poison. Those who partook of it were affected about as if they had taken a big dose of salts.

A short distance above this we found the trail of the Jayhawkers going west, and thus we knew they had got safely across the great plain and then turned southward. I hurried along their trail for several miles and looked the country over with field glass, becoming fully satisfied we should find no water till we reached the summit of the next range, and then fearing the party had not taken the precaution to bring along some water I went back to them and found they had none. I told them they would not see a drop for the next forty miles, and they unloaded the lightest wagon and drove back with everything they had which would hold water, to get a good supply.

I turned back again on the Jayhawker's road, and followed it so rapidly that well toward night I was pretty near the summit, where a pass through this rocky range had been found and on this mountain not a tree, a shrub, or spear of grass could be found—desolation beyond conception. I carried my gun along every day, but for the want of a chance to kill any game a single load would remain in my gun for a month. Very seldom a rabbit could be seen, but not a bird of any kind, not even a hawk, buzzard, or crow made their appearance here.

When near the steep part of the mountain, I found a dead ox the Jayhawkers had left; as no camp could be made here for lack of water and grass, the meat could not be saved. I found the body of the animal badly shrunken, but in condition, as far as putrefaction was concerned, as perfect as when alive. A big gash had been cut in the ham clear to the bone and the sun had dried the flesh in this. I was so awful hungry that I took my sheath knife and cut a big steak which I devoured as I walked along, without cooking or salt. Some may say they would starve before eating such meat, but if they have ever experienced hunger till it begins to draw down the life itself, they will find the impulse of self-preservation something not to be controlled by mere reason. It is an instinct that takes possession of one in spite of himself.

I went down a narrow, dark cañon, high on both sides and per-pendicular, and quite so in many places. In one of the perpendicular portions it seemed to be a variegated clay formation, and a little water seeped down its face. Here the Indians had made a clay bowl and fastened it to the wall so that it would collect and retain about a quart of water, and I had a good drink of water, the first one since leaving the running stream. Near here I stayed all night, for fear of Indians who I firmly believe would have taken my scalp had a good opportunity offered. I slept without a fire, and my supply of meat just obtained drove hunger away.

In the morning I started down the cañon, which descended rapidly and had a bed of sharp, volcanic, broken rock. I could some-times see an Indian track, and kept a sharp lookout at every turn, for fear of revenge on account of the store of squashes which had been taken. I felt I was in constant danger, but could do nothing else but go on and keep eyes open, trusting to circumstances to get out of any sudden emergency that might arise.

As I recollect, this was Christmas Day, and about dusk I came upon the camp of one man with his wife and family, the Rev. J. W. Brier, Mrs. Brier and two sons. I inquired for others of his party and he told me they were somewhere ahead. When I arrived at his camp I found the reverend gentleman very coolly delivering a lecture to his boys on education. It seemed very strange to me to hear a sol-emn discourse on the benefits of early education when, it seemed to me, starvation was staring us all in the face, and the barren desola-tion all around gave small promise of the need of any education higher than the natural impulses of nature. None of us knew exactly where we were, nor when the journey would be ended, nor when substantial relief would come. Provisions were wasting away, and some had been reduced to the last alternative of subsisting on the oxen alone. I slept by the fire that night without a blanket, as I had done on many nights before, and after they hitched up and drove on in the morning I searched the camp carefully, finding some bacon rinds they had thrown away. As I chewed these and could taste the rich grease they contained, I thought they were the sweetest morsels I ever tasted.

Here on the north side of the cañon were some rolling hills and some small weak springs, the water of which when gathered to-gether made a small stream which ran a few yards down the cañon before it lost itself in the rocks and sand. On the side there stood what seemed to be one-half of a butte, with the perpendicular face toward the cañon. Away on the summit of the butte I saw an Indian, so far away he looked no taller than my finger, and when he went out of sight I knew pretty well he was the very fellow who grew the squashes. I thought it might be he, at any rate.

I now turned back to meet the teams and found them seven or eight miles up the cañon, and although it was a downgrade the oxen were barely able to walk slowly with their loads which were light, as wagons were almost empty except the women and children. When night came on it seemed to be cloudy and we could hear the cries of the wild geese passing east. We regarded this as a very good sign, and no doubt Owen's Lake, which we expected to pass on this route, was not very far off. Around in those small hills and damp places was some coarse grass and other growths, but those who had gone before devoured the best, so our oxen had a hard time to get anything to eat.

Next morning I shouldered my gun and followed down the cañon keeping the wagon road, and when half a mile down, at the sink of the sickly stream, I killed a wild goose. This had undoubtedly been attracted here the night before by the light of our camp fire. When I got near the lower end of the cañon, there was a cliff on the north or right-hand side which was perpendicular or perhaps a little overhanging, and at the base a cave which had the appearance of being continuously occupied by Indians. As I went on down I saw a very strange looking track upon the ground. There were hand- and footprints, as if a human being had crawled upon all fours. As this track reached the valley where the sand had been clean swept by the wind, the tracks became more plain, and the sand had been blown into small hills not over three or four feet high. I followed the track till it led to the top of one of these small hills where a small well-like hole had been dug, and in this excavation was a kind of Indian mummy curled up like a dog. He was not dead, for I could see him move as he breathed, but his skin looked very much like the surface of a well-dried venison ham. I should think by his looks he must be 200 or 300 years old, indeed he might be Adam's brother and not look any older then he did. He was evidently crippled. A climate which would preserve for many days or weeks the carcass of an ox so that an eatable round steak could be cut from it, might perhaps preserve a live man for a longer period than would be believed.

I took a good long look at the wild creature and during all the time he never moved a muscle, though he must have known someone was in the well looking down at him. He was probably practicing on one of the directions for a successful political career, looking wise and saying nothing. At any rate he was not going to let his talk get him into any trouble. He probably had a friend around some-where who supplied his wants. I now left him and went farther out into the lowest part of the valley. I could look to the north for fifty miles and it seemed to rise gradually in that direction. To the south the view was equally extended, and down that way a lake could be seen. The valley was here quite narrow, and the lofty snowcapped peak we had tried so hard to reach for the past two months now stood before me. Its east side was almost perpendicular and seemed to reach the sky, and the snow was drifting over it, while here the day sun was shining uncomfortably hot. I believe this mountain was really miles from its base to its summit, and that nothing could climb it on the eastern side except a bird, and the only bird I had seen for two months was the goose I shot. I looked every day for some sort of game but had not seen any.

As I reached the lower part of the valley I walked over what seemed to be boulders of various sizes, and as I stepped from one to another the tops were covered with dirt and they grew larger as I went along. I could see behind them and they looked clear like ice, but on closer inspection proved to be immense blocks of rock salt while the water which stood at their bases was the strongest brine. After this discovery I took my way back to the road made by the Jayhawkers and found it quite level, but sandy. Following this I came to a camp fire soon after dark at which E. Doty and mess were camped. As I was better acquainted I camped with them. They said the water there was brackish and I soon found out the same thing for myself. It was a poor camp—no grass, poor water and scattering, bitter sagebrush for food for the cattle. It would not do to wait long here, and so they hurried on.

I inquired of them about Martin's Pass, as they were now quite near it, and they said it was no pass at all, only the mountain was a little lower than the one holding the snow. No wagon could get over it, and the party had made up their minds to go on foot, and were actually burning their wagons as fuel with which to dry the meat of some of the oxen which they had killed. They selected those which were weakest and least likely to stand the journey, and by drying it the food was much concentrated. They were to divide the provi-sions equally and it was agreed thereafter every one must look out for himself and not expect any help from anyone. If he used up his own provisions, he had no right to expect anyone else to divide with him. Rice, tea, and coffee were measured out by the spoonful and the small amount of flour and bacon which remained was divided out as evenly as possible. Everything was to be left behind but blankets and provisions, for the men were too weak to carry heavy packs and the oxen could not be relied on as beasts of burden and it was thought best not to load them so as to needlessly break them down.

When these fellows started out they were full of spirit, and the frolic and fun along the Platte River was something worth laughing at, but now they were very melancholy and talked in the lowest kind of low spirits. One fellow said he knew this was the Creator's dumping place where he had left the worthless dregs after making a world, and the devil had scraped these together a little. Another said this must be the very place where Lot's wife was turned into a pillar of salt, and the pillar been broken up and spread around the country. He said if a man was to die he would never decay on account of the salt. Thus the talk went on, and it seemed as if there were not bad words enough in the language to properly express their contempt and bad opinions of such a country as this. They treated me to some of their meat, a little better than mine, and before daylight in the morning I was headed back on the trail to report the bad news I had learned of the Jayhawkers.

About noon I met two of our camp companions with packs on their backs following the wagon trail, and we stopped and had a short talk. They were oldish men perhaps 50 years old, one a Mr. Fish of Indiana and another named Gould. They said they could perhaps do as well on foot as to follow the slow ox teams, but when I told them what those ahead of them were doing, and how they must go, they did not seem to be entirely satisfied, as what they had on their backs would need to be replenished, and no such chance could be expected. They had an idea that the end of the journey was not as far off as I predicted. Mr. Fish had a long, nicely made whiplash wound around his waist, and when I asked him why he carried such a useless thing, which he could not eat, he said perhaps he could trade it off for something to eat. After we had set on a sand hill and talked for awhile, we rose and shook each other by the hand, and bade each other good-bye with quivering lips. There was with me a sort of expression I could not repel that I should never see the middle-aged men again.

As my road was now out and away from the mountains, and level, I had no fear of being surprised by enemies, so walked on with eyes downcast, thinking over the situation and wondering what would be the final outcome. If I were alone, with no one to expect me to help them, I would be out before any other man, but with women and children in the party, to go and leave them would be to pile everlasting infamy on my head. The thought almost made me crazy, but I thought it would be better to stay and die with them, bravely struggling to escape than to forsake them in their weakness.

It was almost night before I reached our camp, and sitting around our little fire I told in the most easy way I could the unfavorable news of the party in advance. They seemed to look to me as a guide and adviser, I presume because I took much pains to inform myself on every point and my judgment was accepted with very little opposing opinion, they moved as I thought best. During my absence from camp for the two days the Indians had shot arrows into three of our oxen, and one still had an arrow in his side forward of the hip, which was a dangerous place. To be sure and save him for ourselves we killed him. Some were a little afraid to eat the meat, thinking perhaps the arrow might be poisoned, but I agreed that they wanted meat themselves and would not do that. I told them if they got a shot themselves it would be very likely to be a poisoned arrow and they must take the most instant measures to cut it out before it went into the blood. So we ventured to dry the meat and take it with us.

Now I said to the whole camp, "You can see how you have displeased the red men, taking their little squashes, and when we get into a place that suits them for that purpose, they may meet us with a superior force and massacre us, not only for revenge but to get our oxen and clothing." I told them we must ever be on guard against a surprise, as the chances were greatly against us.

We pulled the arrows out of the other oxen, and they seemed to sustain no great injury from the wounds. This little faint stream where we camped has since been named as Furnace Creek and is still known as such. It was named in 1862 by some prospectors who built what was called an air furnace on a small scale to reduce some ore found nearby, which they supposed to contain silver, but I believe it turned out to be lead and too far from transportations to be available.

Bennett and Arcane now concluded not to wait for me to go ahead and explore out a way for them to follow, as I had done for a long time, but to go ahead as it was evidently the best way to turn south and make our own road, and find the water and passes all for ourselves. So they hitched up and rolled down the cañon and out into the valley and then turned due south. We had not gone long on this course before we saw that we must cross the valley and get over to the west side. To do this we must cross through some water, and for fear the ground might be miry, I went to a sand hill nearby and got a mesquite stick about three feet long with which to sound out our way. I rolled up my pants, pulled off my moccasins and waded in, having the teams stand still till I could find out whether it was safe for them to follow or not by ascertaining the depth of the water and the character of the bottom.

The water was very clear and the bottom seemed uneven, there being some deep holes. Striking my stick on the bottom it seemed solid as a rock, and breaking off a small projecting point I found it to be solid rock salt. As the teams rolled along they scarcely roiled the water. It looked to me as if the whole valley which might be a hundred miles long might have been a solid bed of rock salt. Before we reached this water there were many solid blocks of salt lying around covered with a little dirt on the top.

The second night we found a good spring of fresh water coming out from the bottom of the snow peak almost over our heads. The small flow from it spread out over the sand and sank in a very short distance, and there was some quite good grass growing around.

This was a temporary relief, but brought us face to face with stranger difficulties and a more hopeless outlook. There was no possible way to cross this high, steep range of mountains anywhere to the north, and the Jayhawkers had abandoned their wagons and burned them and we could no longer follow on the trail they made. It seemed that there was no other alternative but for us to keep along the edge of the mountain to the south and search for another pass. Some who had read Fremont's travels said that the range immediately west of us must be the one he described, on the west side of which was a beautiful country, of rich soil and having plenty of cattle and horses, and containing some settlers, but on the east all was barren, dry, rocky, sandy desert as far as could be seen. We knew this eastern side answered well the description and believed that this was really the range described, or at least it was close by.

We had to look over the matter very carefully and consider all the conditions and circumstances of the case. We could see the mountains were lower to the south, but they held no snow and seemed only barren rocks piled up in lofty peaks, and as we looked it seemed the most godforsaken country in the world.

We had been in the region long enough to know the higher mountains contained most water, and that the valleys had bad water or none at all, so that while the lower altitudes to the south gave some promise of easier crossing it gave us no promise of water or grass, without which we must certainly perish. In a certain sense we were lost. The clear nights and days furnished us with the means of telling the points of compass as the sun rose and set, but not a sign of life in nature's wide domain had been seen for a month or more. A vest pocketful of powder and shot would last a good hunter till he starved to death, for there was not a living thing to shoot, great or small.

We talked over our present position pretty freely, and every one was asked to speak his unbiased mind, for we knew not who might be right or who might be wrong, and someone might make a suggestion of the utmost value. We all felt pretty much down-hearted. Our civilized provisions were getting so scarce that all must be saved for the women and children, and the men must get along some way on ox meat alone. It was decided not a scrap of anything that would sustain life must go to waste. The blood, hide, and intestines were all prepared in some way for food. This meeting lasted till late at night. If some of them had lost their minds I should not have been surprised, for hunger swallows all other feelings. A man in a starving condition is a savage. He may be as bloodshed and selfish as a wild beast, as docile and gentle as a lamb, or as wild and crazy as a terrified animal, devoid of affection, reason, or thought of justice. We were none of us as bad as this, and yet there was a strange look in the eyes of some of us sometimes, as I saw by looking round, and as others no doubt realized, for I saw them making mysterious glances even in my direction.

Morning came and all were silent. The dim prospect of the future seemed to check every tongue. When one left a water hole he went away as if in doubt whether he would ever enjoy the pleasure of another drop. Every camp was sad beyond description, and no one can guide the pen to make it tell the tale as it seemed to us. When our morning meal of soup and meat was finished, Bennett's two teamsters and the two of Arcane's concluded their chances of life were better if they could take some provisions and strike out on foot, and so they were given what they could carry, and they arranged their packs and bade us a sorrowful good-bye, hoping to meet again on the Pacific Coast. There were genuine tears shed at the parting and I believe neither party ever expected to see each other in this life again.

Bennett's two men were named Silas Helmer and S. S. or C. C. Abbott, but I have forgotten the names of Arcane's men. Mr. Abbott was from New York, a harness maker by trade, and he took his circular cutting knife with him, saying it was light to carry and the weapon he should need. One of them had a gun. They took the trail taken by the Jayhawkers. All the provisions they could carry besides their blankets could not last them to exceed 10 days, and I well knew they could hardly get off the desert in that time. Mr. Abbott was a man I loved fondly. He was good company in camp, and happy and sociable. He had shown no despondency at any time until the night of the last meeting and the morning of the parting. His chances seemed to me to be much poorer than my own, but I hardly think he realized it. When in bed I could not keep my thoughts back from the old home I had left, where good water and a bountiful spread were always ready at the proper hour. I know I dreamed of taking a draft of cool, sweet water from a full pitcher and then woke up with my mouth and throat as dry as dust. The good home I left behind was a favorite theme about the camp fire, and many a one told of the dream pictures, natural as life, that came to him of the happy Eastern home with comfort and happiness surrounding it, even if wealth was lacking. The home of the poorest man on earth was preferable to this place. Wealth was of no value here. A hoard of twenty-dollar gold pieces could now stand before us the whole day long with no temptation to touch a single coin, for its very weight would drag us nearer death. We could purchase nothing with it and we would have cared no more for it as a thing of value than we did the desert sands. We would have given much more for some of the snow which we could see drifting over the peak of the great snow mountains over our heads like a dusty cloud.

Deeming it best to spare the strength as much as possible, I threw away everything I could, retaining only my glass, some ammunition, sheath knife and tin cup. No unnecessary burden could be put on any man or beast, lest he lie down under it, never to rise again. Life and strength were sought to be husbanded in every possible way.

Leaving this camp where the water was appreciated we went over a road for perhaps 8 miles and came to the mouth of a rocky cañon leading up west to the summit of the range. This cañon was too rough for wagons to pass over. Out in the valley near its mouth was a mound about four feet high and in the top of this a little well that held about a pailful of water that was quite strong of sulphur. When stirred it would look quite black. About the mouth of the well was a wire grass that seemed to prevent it caving in. It seems the drifting sand had slowly built this little mound about the little well of water in a curious way. We spent the night here and kept a man at the well all night to keep the water dipped out as fast as it flowed, in order to get enough for ourselves and cattle. The oxen drank this water better than they did the brackish water of the former camp. The plain was thinly scattered with sagebrush, and up near the base of the mountain some greasewood grew in little bunches like currant bushes.

The men with wagons decided they would take this cañon and follow it up to try to get over the range, and not wait for me to go ahead and explore, as they said it took too much time and the provisions, consisting now of only ox meat, were getting more precarious every day. To help them all I could and if possible to be forewarned a little of danger, I shouldered my gun and pushed on ahead as fast as I could. The bottom was a sharp, broken rock, which would be very hard for the feet of the oxen, although we had rawhide moccasins for them for some time, and this was the kind of footgear I wore myself. I walked on as rapidly as I could, and after a time came to where the cañon spread out into a kind of basin enclosed on all sides but the entrance with a wall of high, steep rock, possible to ascend on foot but which would apparently bar the further progress of the wagons, and I turned back utterly disappointed. I got on an elevation where I could look over the country east and south, and it looked as if there was not a drop of water in its whole extent, and there was no snow on the dark mountains that stretched away to the southward and it seemed to me as if difficulties beset me on every hand.

I hurried back down the cañon, but it was nearly dark before I met the wagons. By a mishap I fell and broke the stock of my gun, over which I was very sorry, for it was an excellent one, the best I ever owned. I carried it in two pieces to the camp and told them the way was barred, at which they could hardly endure their disappointment. They turned in the morning, as the cattle had nothing to eat here and no water, and not much of any food since leaving the spring; they looked terribly bad, and the rough road coming up had nearly finished them. They were yoked up and the wagons turned about for the return. They went better downhill, but it was not long before one of Bennett's oxen lay down and could not be persuaded to rise again. This was no place to tarry in the hot sun, so the ox was killed and the carcass distributed among the wagons. So little draft was required that the remaining oxen took the wagon down. When within two or three miles of the water hole one of Arcane's oxen also failed and lay down, so they turned him out and when he had rested a little he came on again for a while, but soon lay down again. Arcane took a bucket of water back from camp, and after drinking it and resting awhile the ox was driven down to the spring.

This night we had another meeting to decide upon our course and determine what to do. At this meeting no one was wiser than another, for no one had explored the country and knew what to expect. The questions that now arose were: "How long can we endure this work in this situation?" "How long will our oxen be able to endure the great hardship on the small nourishment they receive?" "How long can we provide ourselves with food?"

We had a few small pieces of dry bread. This was kept for the children, giving them a little now and then. Our only food was in the flesh of the oxen, and when they failed to carry themselves along we must begin to starve. It began to look as if the chances of leaving our bones to bleach upon the desert were the most prominent ones.

One thing was certain—we must move somewhere at once. If we stay here we can live as long as the oxen do and no longer, and if we go on it is uncertain where to go to get a better place. We had guns and ammunition to be sure, but of late we had seen no living creature in this desert wild. Finally Mr. Bennett spoke and said:

"Now I will make you a proposition. I propose that we select two of our youngest, strongest men and ask them to take some food and go ahead on foot to try to seek a settlement and food, and we will go back to the good spring we have just left and wait for their return. It will surely not take them more than ten days for the trip, and when they get back we shall know all about the road and its character and how long it will take us to travel it. They can secure some other kind of food that will make us feel better, and when the oxen have rested a little at the spring we can get out with our wagons and animals and be safe. I think this is the best and safest way. Now what do you all say?"

After a little discussion all seemed to agree that this was the best, and now it remained to find the men to go. No one offered to accept the position of advance messengers. Finally Mr. Bennett said he knew one man well enough to know that he would come back if he lived, and he was sure he would push his way through. "I will take Lewis (myself) if he will consent to go." I consented, though I knew it was a hazardous journey, exposed to all sorts of things—Indians, climate, and probable lack of water—but I thought I could do it and would not refuse. John Rogers, a large, strong Tennessee man, was then chosen as the other one and he consented also.

Now preparations began. Mr. Arcane killed the ox which had so nearly failed, and all the men went to drying and preparing meat. Others made us some new moccasins out of rawhide, and the women made us each a knapsack.

Our meat was closely packed, and one can form an idea how poor our cattle were from the fact that John and I actually packed seven-eights of all the flesh of an ox into our knapsacks and carried it away. They put in a couple of spoonfulls of rice and about as much tea. This seemed like robbery to the children, but the good women said that in case of sickness even that little bit might save our lives. I wore no coat or vest, but took half of a light blanket, while Rogers wore a thin summer coat and took no blanket. We each had a small cup and a small camp kettle holding a quart. Bennett had me take his seven-shooter rifle, and Rogers had a good double-barreled shotgun. We each had a sheath knife, and our hats were small-brimmed, drab affairs fitting close to the head and not very conspicuous to an enemy as we might rise up from behind a hill into possible views. We tried on our packs and fitted the straps a little so they would carry easy. They collected all the money there was in camp and gave it to us. Mr. Arcane had about $30 and others threw in small amounts from forty cents upward. We received all sorts of advice. Capt. Culverwell was an old seafaring man and was going to tell us how to find our way back, but Mr. Bennett told the captain that he had known Lewis as a hunter for many years, and that if he went over a place in the daytime he could find his way back at night every time. Others cautioned us about the Indians and told us how to manage. Others told us not to get caught in deep snow which we might find on the mountains.

This advice we received in all the kindness in which it was given, and then we bade them all good-bye. Some turned away, too much affected to approach us, and others shook our hands with deep feeling, grasping them firmly and heartily hoping we would be successful and be able to pilot them out of this dreary place into a better land. Everyone felt that a little food to make a change from the poor dried meat would be acceptable. Mr. and Mrs. Bennett and J. B. Arcane and wife were the last to remain when the others had turned away. They had most faith in the plan and felt deeply. Mrs. Bennett was the last, and she asked God to bless us and bring some food to her starving children.

We were so much affected that we could not speak, and silently turned away and took our course again up the cañon we had descended the night before. After a while we looked back and when they saw us turn around, all the hats and bonnets waved us a final parting.

Those left in the camp were Asabel Bennett and Sarah his wife, with three children, George, Melissa, and Martha; J. B. Arcane and wife with son Charles. The youngest children were not more than two years old. There were also the two Earhart brothers, and a grown son, Capt. Culverwell, and some others I cannot recall; eleven grown people in all, besides a Mr. Wade, his wife and three children, who did not mingle with our party but usually camped a little distance off, followed our trail but seemed to shun company. We soon passed round a bend of the cañon and then walked on in silence. We both of us meditated some over the homes of our fathers, but took new courage in view of the importance of our mission and passed on as fast as we could.

By night we were far up the mountain, near the perpendicular rough peak, and far above us on a slope we could see some bunches of grass and sagebrush. We went to this and found some small water holes. No water ran from them they were so small. Here we stayed all night. It did not seem very far to the snowy peak to the north of us. Just where we were seemed the lowest pass, for to the south were higher peaks, and the rocks looked as if they were too steep to be got over.

Through this gap came a cold breeze, and we had to look round to get a sheltered place in which to sleep. We lay down close together, spoon fashion, and made the little blanket do as cover for the both of us. In the morning we filled our canteens, which we had made by binding two powder cans together with strips of cloth, and started for the summit nearby. From this was the grandest sight we ever beheld. Looking east we could see the country we had been crawling over since November 4th. "Just look at the cursed country we have come over!" said Rogers as he pointed over it. To the north was the biggest mountain we ever saw, peaks on peaks and towering far above our heads, and covered with snow which was apparently everlasting.

This mountain seemed to have very few trees on it, and in extent as it reached away to the north seemed interminable. South was a nearly level plain, and to the west I thought I could dimly see a range of mountain that held a little snow upon their summits, but on the main range to the south there was none. It seemed to me the dim snowy mountains must be as far as 200 miles away, but of course I could not judge accurately. After looking at this grand but worthless landscape long enough to take in its principal features, we asked each other what we supposed the people we left behind would think to see mountains so far ahead. We knew that they had an idea that the coast range was not very far ahead, but we saw at once to go over all these mountains and return within the limits of fifteen days, which had been agreed upon between us, would probably be impossible, but we must try as best we could, so down the rocky steep we clambered and hurried on our way. In places the way was so steep that we had to help each other down, and the hard work made us perspire freely so that the water was a prime necessity. In one place near here we found a little water and filled our canteens, besides drinking a good present supply. There were two low, black rocky ranges directly ahead of us which we must cross.

When partway down the mountain a valley or depression opened up in that direction up which it seemed as if we could look a hundred miles. Nearby and a short distance north was a lake of water, and when we reached the valley we crossed a clear stream of water flowing slowly toward the lake. Being in need of water, we rushed eagerly to it and prepared to take a big drink, but the tempting fluid was as salt as brine and made our thirst all the more intolerable. Nothing grew on the bank of this stream and the bed was of hard clay, which glistened in the sun.

We now began the ascent of the next ridge, keeping a westernly course, and walked as fast as we could up the rough mountainside. We crossed the head of a cañon near the summit about dark, and here we found a trail which from indications we knew to be that of the Jayhawkers, who had evidently been forced to the southward of the course they intended to take. They had camped here and had dug holes in the sand in search of water, but had found none. We stayed all night here and dug around in some other places in the bottom of the cañon, in the hope to have better luck than they did, but we got no water anywhere.

We seemed almost perishing for want of water; the hard exercise made us perspire so freely. In the morning we started on, and near the summit we came to the dead body of Mr. Fish, laying in the hot sun, as there was no material near here with which his friends could cover the remains. This Mr. Fish was the man who left camp some two weeks before in company with another and who carried the long whiplash wound about his body in hope he could somewhere be able to trade it for bread. No doubt in this very place where he breathed his last, his bones still lie.

As we came in sight of the next valley, we could see a lake of water some distance south of our western course. We had followed the Jayhawkers' trail thus far, but as we found no water in small holes in the rocks as we were likely to do when we were the first to pass, we decided to take a new route in the hope to find a little water in this way, for we had no hope of finding it in any other. This valley we now crossed seemed to come to an end about ten miles to the north of us. To the south it widened out, enclosing the lake spoken of. This valley was very sandy and hard to walk over. When about halfway across we saw some ox tracks leading toward the lake, and in the hope we might find the water drinkable we turned off at right angles to our course and went that way also. Long before we reached the water of the lake, the bottom became a thin, slimy mud which was very hard on our moccasins. When we reached the water we found it to be of a wine color and so strongly alkaline as to feel slippery to the touch and under our feet. This side trip had cost us much exertion and made us feel more thirsty than ever.

We turned now west again, making for a cañon, up which we passed in the hope we should at some turn find a little basin of rainwater in some rock. We traveled in it miles and miles, and our mouths became so dry we had to put a bullet or a small smooth stone in and chew it and turn it around with the tongue to induce a flow of saliva. If we saw a spear of green grass on the north side of a rock, it was quickly pulled and eaten to obtain the little moisture it contained.

Thus we traveled along for hours, never speaking, for we found it much better for our thirst to keep our mouths closed as much as possible and prevent the evaporation. The dry air of that region took up water as a sponge does. We passed the summit of this ridge without finding any water, and on our way down the western side we came to a flat place where there was an Indian hut made of small brush. We now thought there surely must be some water near and we began a thorough search. The great snow mountain did not seem far off, but to the south and southwest a level or inclined plain extended for a long distance. Our thirst began to be something terrible to endure, and in the warm weather and hard walking we had secured only two drinks since leaving camp.

We were so sure that there must be water near here that we laid our knapsacks down by the little hut and looked around in every possible place we could think of. Soon it got dark and then we made a little fire as a guide and looked again. Soon the moon arose and helped us some, and we shouted frequently to each other so as not to get lost.

We were so nearly worn out that we tried to eat a little meat, but after chewing a long time, the mouth would not moisten it enough so we could swallow, and we had to reject it. It seemed as if we were going to die with plenty of food in our hand, because we could not eat it.

We tried to sleep but could not, but after a little rest we noticed a bright star two hours above the horizon, and from the course of the moon we saw the star must be pretty truly west of us. We talked a little, and the burden of it was a fear that we could not endure the terrible thirst a while longer. The thought of the women and children waiting for our return made us feel more desperate than if we were the only ones concerned. We thought we could fight to the death over a water hole if we could only secure a little of the precious fluid. No one who hasn't ever felt the extreme of thirst can

The Forty-Niners

imagine the distress, the despair which it brings. I can find no words, no way to express it so others can understand.

The moon gave us so much light that we decided we would start on our course and get as far as we could before the hot sun came out, and so we went on slowly and carefully in the partial darkness, the only hope left to us being that our strength would hold out till we could get to the shining snow on the great mountain before us. We reached the foot of the range we were descending about sunrise. There was here a wide wash from the snow mountain, down which some water had sometime run after a big storm, and had divided into little rivulets only reaching out a little way before they had sunk into the sand.

We had no idea we could now find any water till we at least got very near the snow, and as the best way to reach it we turned up the wash, although the course was nearly to the north. The course was up a gentle grade and seemed quite sandy and not easy to travel. It looked as if there was an all-day walk before us, and it was quite a question if we could live long enough to make the distance. There were quite strong indications that the water had run here not so very long ago, and we could trace the course of the little streams round among little sandy islands. A little stunted brush grew here but it was so brittle that the stems would break as easy as an icicle.

In order to not miss a possible bit of water we separated and agreed upon a general course, and that if either one found water he should fire his gun as a signal. After about a mile or so had been gone over I heard Rogers' gun and went in his direction. He had found a little ice that had frozen under the clear sky. It was not thicker than window glass. After putting a piece in our mouths we gathered all we could and put it into the little quart camp kettle to melt. We gathered just a kettle full, besides what we ate as we were gathering, and kindled a little fire and melted it.

I can but think how providential it was that we started in the night for in an hour after the sun had risen that little sheet of ice would have melted and the water sank into the sand. Having quenched our thirst we could now eat, and found that we were nearly starved also. In making this meal we used up all our little store of water, but we felt refreshed and our lives renewed so that we had better courage to go on.

We now took our course west again taking a beeline for a bluff that lay a little to the south of the big snow mountain. On and on we walked till the dark shadow of the great mountain in the setting sun was thrown about us, and still we did not seem more than half way to the bluff before us. All the way had been hill and very tiresome walking. There was considerable small brush scattered about here and there over this steeply inclined plain.

We were still several miles from the base of the largest of the mountains and we could now see that it extended west for many miles. The buttes to the south were low, black, and barren, and to the west as far as we could see there were no mountains with any snow. As the sun got further down we could see a small smoke curling up near the base of the mountain, and we thought it must be some signal made by the Indians, as we had often seen them signal in that way, but we stopped and talked the matter over, and as we were yet a long way from the bluff which had been our objective point, we concluded we would investigate the smoke signal a little closer. So we set off toward it in the dusk and darkness and when within about a mile we found we were in a track that had been somewhat beaten. Feeling with my fingers I was quite sure I could distinguish ox tracks, and then was quite sure that we had overtaken the Jayhawkers, or at least were on their trail. And then I thought perhaps they had fallen among the Indians, who now might be feasting on their oxen, and it became necessary to use great caution in approaching the little smoke.

We took a circuitous route and soon saw that the persons were on a little bench above us and we kept very cautious and quiet, listening for any sounds that might tell us who they were. If they were Indians we should probably hear some of their dogs, but we heard none, and kept creeping closer and closer, till we were within fifty yards without hearing a sound to give us any idea of who they were.

We decided to get our guns at full cock and then hail the camp, feeling that we had a little the advantage of position. We hailed and were answered in English. "Don't shoot," said we, and they assured us they had no idea of such a thing, and asked us to come in. We found here, to our surprise, Ed Doty, Tom Shannon, L. D. Stevens, and others whom I do not recollect, the real Jayhawkers. They gave us some fresh meat for supper, and near the camp were some water holes that answered well for camp purposes. Here an ox had given out and they had stopped long enough to dry the meat, while the others had gone on a day ahead.

Coming around the mountain from the north was quite a well-defined trail leading to the west and they said they were satisfied someone lived at the end of it, and they were going to follow it if it lead to Mexico or anywhere else. They said that Mr. Brier and his family were still on behind, and alone. Every one must look out for himself here, and we could not do much for another in any way.

[After leaving these stragglers and overtaking the rest of the Jayhawkers, Manly
and Rogers made their way along the margins of the Mojave Desert and over
Soledad Pass, arriving at the Rancho San Francisquito on January 26, 1850.
There they quickly provisioned themselves for the return to rescue those left
behind in Death Valley. Their hard-driven journey back, which only a brave
little mule among their pack animals survived, brought them to the summit of the
Panamints fearing they were too late.]

We made the summit about noon, and from here we could see
the place where we found a water hole and camped the first night
after we left the wagons. Down the steep cañon we turned, the same
one in which we had turned back with the wagons, and over the
sharp broken pieces of volcanic rock that formed our only footing
we hobbled along with sore and tender feet. We had to watch for
the smoothest place for every step, and then moved only with the
greatest difficulty. The Indians could have caught us easily if they
had been around, for we must keep our eyes on the ground constantly and stop if we looked up and around. But we at last got down
and camped on the same spot where we had set out twenty-five days
before to seek the settlements. Here was the same little water hole in
the sand plain, and the same strong sulphur water which we had to
drink the day we left. The mule was turned loose dragging the same
piece of rawhide she had attached to her when we purchased her,
and she ranged and searched faithfully for food, finding little except
the very scattering bunches of sagebrush. She was industrious and
walked around rapidly, picking here and there, but at dark came into
camp and lay down close to us to sleep.

There was no sign that anyone had been here during our absence, and if the people had gone to hunt a way out, they must either have followed the Jayhawker's trail or some other one. We were
much afraid that they might have fallen victims to the Indians. Remaining in camp so long, it was quite likely they had been discovered by them and it was quite likely they had been murdered for the
sake of the oxen and camp equipage. It might be that we should find
the hostiles waiting for us when we reached the appointed camping
place, and it was small show for two against a party. Our mule and
her load would be a great capture for them. We talked a great deal
and said a great many things at that camp fire, for we knew we were
in great danger and we had many doubts about the safety of our
people, that would soon be decided, and whether for joy or sorrow
we could not tell.

From this place, as we walked along, we had a wagon road to

follow in soft sand, but not a sign of a human footstep could we see as we marched toward this, the camp of the last hope. We had the greatest fears the people had given up our return and started out for themselves, and that we should follow on, only to find them dead or dying. My pen fails me as I try to tell the feelings and thoughts of this trying hour. I can never hope to do so, but if the reader can place himself in my place, his imagination cannot form a picture that shall go beyond reality.

We were some seven or eight miles along the road when I stopped to fix my moccasin while Rogers went slowly along. The little mule went on ahead of both of us, searching all around for little bunches of dry grass, but always came back to the trail again and gave us no trouble. When I had started up again, I saw Rogers ahead leaning on his gun and waiting for me, apparently looking at something on the ground. As I came near enough to speak I asked what he had found and he said, "Here is Capt. Culverwell, dead." He did not look much like a dead man. He lay upon his back with arms extended wide, and his little canteen made of two powder flasks lying by his side. This looked indeed as if some of our saddest forebodings were coming true. How many more bodies should we find? Or should we find the camp deserted and never a trace of the former occupants?

We marched toward camp like two Indians, silent and alert, looking out for dead bodies and live Indians, for really we more expected to find the camp devastated by those rascals than to find that it still contained our friends. To the east we could plainly see what seemed to be a large salt lake with a bed that looked as if of the finest, whitest sand, but really a wonder of salt crystal. We put the dreary steps steadily one forward of another, the little mule the only unconcerned one of the party, ever looking for an odd blade of grass, dried in the hot dry wind but yet retaining nourishment which she preferred.

About noon we came in sight of the wagons, still a long way off, but in the clear air we could make them out and tell what they were without being able to see anything more. Half a mile was the distance between us and the camp before we could see very plainly, as they were in a little depression. We could see the covers had been taken off, and this was an ominous sort of circumstance to us, for we feared the depredations of the Indians in retaliation for the capture of their squashes. They had shot our oxen before we left and they have slain them this time and the people too.

We surely left seven wagons. Now we could see only four and

nowhere the sign of an ox. They must have gone ahead with a small train, and left these four standing after dismantling them.

No signs of life were anywhere about, and the thought of our hard struggles between life and death, to go out and return with the fruitless results that now seemed apparent was almost more than human heart could bear. When should we know their fate? When should we find their remains, and how learn of their sad history if we ourselves should live to get back again to settlements and life? If ever two men were troubled, Rogers and I surely passed through the furnace.

We kept as low and as much out of sight as possible, trusting very much to the little mule that was ahead, for we felt sure she would detect danger in the air sooner than we, and we watched her closely to see how she acted. She slowly walked along looking out for food, and we followed a little way behind, but still no decisive sign to settle the awful suspense in which we lived and suffered. We became more and more convinced that they had taken the trail of the Jayhawkers and we had missed them on the road, or they had perished before reaching the place where we turned from their trail.

One hundred yards now to the wagons and still no sign of life, no positive sign of death, though we looked carefully for both. We fear that perhaps there are Indians in ambush, and with nervous, irregular breathing we counsel what to do. Finally Rogers suggested that he had two charges in his shotgun and I seven in the Colt's rifle, and that I fire one of mine and await results before we ventured any nearer, and if there are any of the red devils there we can kill some of them before they get to us. And now, both closely watching the wagons, I fired the shot. Still as death and not a move for a moment, and then as if by magic a man came out from under a wagon and stood up looking all around, for he did not see us. Then he threw up his arms high over his head and shouted, "The boys have come!" "The boys have come!" Then other bare heads appeared, and Mr. Bennett and wife and Mr. Arcane came toward us as fast as ever they could. The great suspense was over and our hearts were first in our mouths, and then the blood all went away and left us almost fainting as we stood and tried to step. Some were safe, perhaps all of those nearest us, and the dark shadow of death that had hovered over us and cast what seemed a pall upon every thought and action was lifted and fell away, a heavy oppression gone. Bennett and Arcane caught us in their arms and embraced us with all their strength, and Mrs. Bennett when she came fell down on her knees and clung to me like a maniac in the great emotion that came to her, and not a word was spoken. If they had been strong enough they would have carried us to camp upon their shoulders. As it was they stopped two or three times and turned as if to speak, but there was too much feeling for words; convulsive weeping would choke the voice.

All were a little calmer soon, and Bennett soon found voice to say: "I know you have found someplace, for you have a mule," and Mrs. Bennett through her tears looked staringly at us, as she could hardly believe our coming back was a reality, and then exclaimed: "Good boys! O, you have saved us all! God bless you forever! Such boys should never die!" It was some time before they could talk without weeping. Hope almost died within them, and now when the first bright ray came it almost turned reason from its throne. A brighter happier look came to them than we had seen, and then they plied us with questions, the first of which was: "Where were you?"

We told them it must be 250 miles yet to any part of California where we could live. Then came the question: "Can we take our wagons?" "You will have to walk," was our answer, for no wagons could go over that unbroken road that we had traveled. As rapidly and carefully as we could we told them of our journey, and the long distance between the water holes; that we had lost no time and yet had been twenty-six days on the road; that for a long distance the country was about as dry and desolate as the region we had crossed east of this camp. We told them of the scarcity of grass, and all the reasons that had kept us so long away from them.

We inquired after the others whom we had left in camp when we went away, and we were told all they knew about them. Hardly were we gone before they began to talk about the state of affairs which existed. They said that as they had nothing to live on but their oxen it would be certain death to wait here and eat them up, and that it would be much better to move on a little every day and get nearer and nearer the goal before the food failed. Bennett told them they would know surely about the way when the boys returned, and knowing the road would know how to manage and what to expect and work for, and could get out successfully. But the general opinion of all but Mr. Bennett and Mr. Arcane and their families was, as expressed by one of them: "If those boys ever get out of this cussed hole, they are d——d fools if they ever come back to help anybody."

Some did not stay more than a week after we were gone, but took their oxen and blankets and started on. They could not be content to stay idly in camp with nothing to occupy their minds or bodies. They could see that an ox when killed would feed them only a few days, and that they could not live long on them, and it stood them in hand to get nearer the western shore, as the less distance the more hope while the meat lasted. Bennett implored them to stay, as he was sure we would come back, and if the most of them deserted him he would be exposed to the danger of the Indians, with no hope of a successful resistance against them.

But the most seemed to think that to stay was to die, and it would be better to die trying to escape than to set idly down to perish. These men seemed to think their first duty was to save themselves, and, if fortunate, help others afterward, so they packed their oxen and left in separate parties, the last some two weeks before. They said that Capt. Culverwell went with the last party. I afterward learned that he could not keep up with them, and turned to go back to the wagons again and perished, stretched out upon the sand as we saw him, dying all alone, with no one to transmit his last words to family or friends. Not a morsel to eat, and the little canteen by his side empty. A sad and lonely death indeed!

There was no end to the questions about the road we had to answer, for this was uppermost on their minds, and we tried to tell them and show them how we must get along on our return. We told them of the great snow mountains we had seen all to the north of our road, and how deep the snow appeared to be, and how far west it extended. We told them of the black and desolate ranges and buttes to the south, and of the great dry plains in the same direction. We told them of the Jayhawkers' trail; of Fish's dead body; of the salt lake and slippery alkali water to which we walked, only to turn away in disappointment; of the little sheets of ice which saved our lives; of Doty's camp and what we knew of those gone before; of the discouraged ones who gave us their names to send back to friends; of the hawk and crow diet; of my lameness; of the final coming out into a beautiful valley in the midst of fat cattle and green meadows, and the trouble to get the help arranged on account of not knowing the language to tell the people what we needed. They were deeply impressed that my lameness had been a blessing in disguise, or we would have gone on to the coast and consumed more time than we did in walking slowly to favor the crippled knee. Our sad adventures and loss of the horses in returning was sorrowfully told and we spoke of the provisions we had been able to bring on the little mule which had clambered over the rocks like a cat; that we had a little flour and beans and some good dried meat with fat on it which we hoped would help to eke out the poorer fare and get them through at last. They were so full of compliments that we really began to think we had been brought into the world on purpose to assist someone, and the one who could forecast all things had directed us and all our ways so that we should save those people and bring them to a better part of God's footstool, where plenty might be enjoyed and the sorrows of the desert forgotten. It was midnight before we could get them all satisfied with their knowledge of our experience.

It was quite a treat to us to sleep again between good blankets arranged by a womans' hand, and it was much better resting than the curled up, cramped position we had slept in while away, with only the poor protection of the half blanket for both of us, in nights that were pretty chilly.

We had plenty of water here, and there being no fear of the mule going astray we turned her loose. As the party had seen no Indians during our absence, we did not concern ourselves much about them. At breakfast we cautioned them about eating too much bread, remembering our own experience in that way.

They said they had about given up our coming back a week before, and had set about getting ready to try to move on themselves. Bennett said he was satisfied that they never could have got through alone after what we had told them of the route and its dangers. He said he knew it now, that not one of them would have lived if they had undertaken the journey alone without knowledge of the way.

They had taken off the covers of the wagons to make them into harnesses for the oxen, so they could be used as pack animals. The strong cloth had been cut into narrow strips and well made into breast straps and breeching, for the cattle were so poor and their hide so loose it was almost impossible to keep anything on their backs. They had emptied the feathers out of the beds to get the cloth to use, and had tried to do everything that seemed best to do to get along without wagons. The oxen came up for water, and the mule with them. They looked better than when we left, but were still poor. They had rested for some time and might feel able to go along willingly for a few days at least. I was handy with the needle, and helped them to complete the harness for the oxen, while Bennett and John went to the lake to get a supply of salt to take along, a most necessary article with our fresh meat. I looked around a little at our surroundings, and could see the snow still drifting over the peak of the snowy mountain as we had seen it farther east, where we were ourselves under the burning sun. This was now pretty near February first, or midwinter. The eastern side of this great mountain was too steep to be ascended, and no sign of a tree could be seen on the whole eastern slope. The range of mountains on the east side of this narrow valley were nearly all the volcanic, barren in the extreme, and the roughest of all the mountains we had ever seen. I had now

The Forty-Niners

looked pretty thoroughly, and found it to be pretty nearly a hundred miles long, and this was the only camp I had seen where water could be had.

When Mrs. Bennett was ready to show me what to do on the cloth harness, we took a seat under the wagon, the only shady place, and began work. The great mountain I have spoken of as the snow mountain has since been known as Telescope Peak, reported to be 11,000 feet high. It is in the range running north and south and has no other peak so high. Mrs. Bennett questioned me closely about the trip, and particularly if I had left anything out which I did not want her to know. She said she saw her chance to ride was very slim, and she spoke particularly of the children, and that it was impossible for them to walk. She said little Martha had been very sick since we had been gone, and that for many days they had expected her to die. They had no medicine to relieve her and the best they could do was to select the best of the ox meat and make a little soup of it and feed her. They had watched her carefully for many days and nights, expecting they would have to part with her any time and bury her little body in the sands. Sometimes it seemed as if her breath would stop, but they had never failed in their attentions, and were at last rewarded by seeing her improve slowly, and even to relish a little food, so that if no relapse set in they had hopes to bring her through. They brought the little one and showed her to me, and she seemed so different from what she was when we went away. Then she could run about camp, climb out and in the wagons and move about so spry that she reminded one of a quail. Now she was strangely misshapen. Her limbs had lost all the flesh and seemed nothing but skin and bones, while her body had grown corpulent and distended, and her face had a starved, pinched, and suffering look, with no healthy color in it.

She told me of their sufferings while we were gone, and said she often dreamed she saw us suffering fearfully for water and lack of food, and could only picture to herself as their own fate that they must leave the children by the trail side dead, and one by one drop out themselves in the same way. She said she dreamed often of her old home where bread was plenty, and then to awake to find her husband and children starving was a severe trial indeed, and the contrast terrible. She was anxious to get me to express an opinion as to whether I thought we could get the oxen down the falls where we had so much trouble.

I talked to her as encouragingly as I could, but she did not cheer up much and sobbed and wept over her work most all the time. It was not possible to encourage her much, the outlook seemed so dark.

Mrs. Arcane sat under another wagon and said nothing, but she probably heard all we had to say, and did not look as if her hopes were any brighter. Bennett and Rogers soon returned with a supply of salt and said the whole shore of the lake was a winrow of it that could be shoveled up in enormous quantities.

We now in a counsel of the whole talked over the matter and the way which seemed most promising. If we went by the Jay-hawkers' trail, there was a week of solid travel to get over the range and back south again as far as a point directly opposite our camp, and this had taken us only three days to come over as we had come. The only obstacle in the way was the falls, and when we explained that there was some sand at the bottom of them, Bennett said he thought we could get them over without killing them, and that, as we knew exactly where the water was, this was the best trail to take. Arcane was quite of the same opinion, the saving of a week of hard and tiresome travel being in each case the deciding reason. They then explained to me what they had decided on doing if we had not come back. They had selected two oxen for the women to ride, one to carry water, and one to carry the four children. There were no saddles, but blankets enough to make a soft seat, and they proposed to put a band or belt around the animals for them to hold on by, and the blankets would be retained in place by breast and breeching straps which we had made. They had found out that it was very difficult to keep a load of any kind upon an ox, and had devised all this harness to meet the trouble.

Bennett had one old bridle ox called Old Crump, which had been selected to carry the children because he was slow and steady. How in the world do you expect it to keep the children on? said I. "Well," said Bennett, with a sort of comical air, about the first relief from the sad line of thought that had possessed us all, "we have taken two strong hickory shirts, turned the sleeves inside, sewed up the necks, then sewed the two shirts together by the tail, and when these are placed on the ox they will make two pockets for the young-est children, and we think the two others will be able to cling to his back with the help of a band around the body of the ox to which they can cling to with their hands." Now, if Old Crump went steady and did not kick up and scatter things, he thought this plan would operate first rate. Now, as to the mule, they proposed as we knew how to pack the animal, that we should use her to pack our provi-sions so they would go safe.

From a piece of hide yet remaining, John and I made ourselves some new moccasins, and were all ready to try the trip over our old trail for now, the third time, and the last, we hoped.

The Forty-Niners

Mrs. Bennett and Mrs. Arcane had taken our advice, and in cooking had not put too much of the flour or beans in the soup for the children, and they had gotten along nicely and even began to smile a little with satisfaction after a full meal. They got along better than John and I did when we got hold of the first nutritions after our arrival on the other side.

We must leave everything here we can get along without. No clothing except that on our backs. Only a camp kettle in which to make soup, a tin cup for each one, and some knives and spoons which each happen to have. Each one had some sort of a canteen for water, which we must fill up at every opportunity, and we decided to carry a shovel along so we might bury the body of Capt. Culverwell and shovel up a pile of sand at the falls to enable us to get the oxen over. Every ox had a cloth halter on his head so he might be led, or tied up at night when we had a dry camp and they would most assuredly wander off if not secured. Old Crump was chosen to lead the train, and Rogers was to lead him. We had made an extra halter for this old fellow, and quite a long strip of bed ticking sewed into a strap to lead him by.

This packing business was a new idea, and a hard matter to get anything firmly fixed on their backs. We had made shoulder straps, hip straps, breast straps, and breeching as the correct idea for a harness. The only way we could fasten the band around the animals was for one to get on each side and pull it as tight as possible then tie a knot, as we had no buckles or ring in our harness.

The loads of the oxen consisted of blankets and bedding and a small, light tent of their sheeting about four by six feet in size. We rose early and worked hard till about the middle of the forenoon getting all things ready. They had been in a state of masterly inactivity so long in this one camp that they were anxious to leave it now forever. Only in progress was there hope, and this was our last and only chance. We must succeed or perish. We loaded the animals from the wagons, and some of the oxen seemed quite afraid at this new way of carrying loads. Old Crump was pretty steady, and so was the one with the two water kegs, one on each side, but the other oxen did not seem to think they needed any blankets on these warm days.

Mrs. Arcane was from a city, and had fondly conveyed thus far some articles of finery, of considerable value and much prized. She could not be persuaded to leave them here to deck the red man's wife and have her go flirting over the mountains with, and as they had little weight she concluded she would wear them and this perhaps would preserve them. So she got out her best hat and trimmed it up with extra ribbon, leaving some with quite long ends to stream out behind. Arcane brought up his ox, Old Brigham, for he had been purchased at Salt Lake and named in honor of the great Mormon Saint.

Mrs. Arcane also dressed her little boy Charlie up in his best suit of clothes, for she thought they might as well wear them out as to throw them away. She made one think of a fairy in gay and flying apparel. In the same way all selected their best and most serviceable garments, for it was not considered prudent to carry any load, and poor clothes were good enough to leave for Indians. We set it down as a principle that we must save ourselves all we could, for it would be a close contested struggle with us and death, at the very best, and we wanted to get all the advantage for ourselves we could. As we were making the preparations the women grew more hopeful, as it seemed as if something was really going to be accomplished.

Bennett and Arcane were emphatic in their belief and expressions that we would succeed. "I know it—Don't you Sally?" said Bennett very cheerfully, but after all Mrs. Bennett could not answer quite as positively, but said, "I hope so." Mrs. Bennett's maiden name was Sarah Dilley, which I mention here as I may otherwise forget it afterward. She realized that hers was no easy place to ride, that they would have hard fare at best, and that it must be nearly or quite a month before they could reach a fertile spot on which to place her feet. One could easily see that the future looked quite a little dark to her, on account of her children, as a mother naturally would.

High overhead was the sun, and very warm indeed on that day in the forepart of February 1850, when the two children were put on Old Crump to see if he would let them ride. The two small children were placed in the pockets on each side, face outward, and they could stand or sit as they should choose. George and Melissa were placed on top and given hold of the strap that was to steady them in their place. I now led up Mrs. Bennett's ox, and Mr. Bennett helped his wife to mount the animal, on whose back as soft a seat as possible had been constructed. Mrs. Arcane in her ribbons was now helped to her seat on the back of Old Brigham and she carefully adjusted herself to position and arranged her dress and ornaments to suit, then took hold of the strap that served to hold on by, as there were no bridles on these two.

Rogers led the march with his ox; Bennett and I started the others along, and Arcane followed with Old Crump and the children. Bennett and Arcane took off their hats and bade the old camp good-bye. The whole procession moved, and we were once more going toward our journey's end, we hoped. The road was sandy and soft, the grade practically level, and everything went well for about four miles, when the pack on one of the oxen near the lead got loose and turned over to one side, which he no sooner saw thus out of position than he tried to get away from it by moving sidewise. Not getting clear of the objectionable load in this way, he tried to kick it off, and thus really got his foot in it, making matters worse instead of better. Then he began a regular waltz, and bawled at the top of his voice in terror. Rogers tried to catch him, but his own animal was so frisky that he could not hold him and do much else, and the spirit of fear soon began to be communicated to the others and soon the whole train seemed to be taken crazy.

They would jump up high and then come down, sticking their forefeet as far as possible into the sand, after which, with elevated tails and terrible plunges, would kick and thrash and run till the packs came off, when they stopped, apparently quite satisfied. Mrs. Bennett slipped off her ox as quick as she could, grabbed her baby from the pocket on Old Crump, and shouting to Melissa and George to jump, got her family into safe position in pretty short order. Arcane took his Charley from the other pocket and laid him on the ground, while he devoted his own attention to the animals. Mrs. Arcane's ox followed suit and waltzed around in the sand, bawled at every turn, fully as bad as any of the others, but Mrs. Arcane proved to be a good rider and hard to unseat, clinging desperately to her strap as she was tossed up and down and whirled about at a rate enough to make anyone dizzy. Her many fine ribbons flew out behind like the streamers from a masthead, and the many fancy fixin's she had donned fluttered in the air in gayest mockery. Eventually she was thrown, however, but without the least injury to herself, but somewhat disordered in raiment. When I saw Bennett, he was standing half bent over, laughing in almost hysterical convulsion at the entirely impromptu circus which had so suddenly performed an act not on the program. Arcane was much pleased and laughed heartily when he saw no one was hurt. We did not think the cattle had so much life and so little sense as to waste their energies so uselessly. The little mule stepped out to one side and looked on in amazement, without disarranging any article of her load.

Mrs. Bennett, carrying her baby and walking around to keep out of the way, got very much exhausted and sat down on the sand, her face as red as if the blood were about to burst through the skin, and perspiring freely. We carried a blanket and spread down for her while we gathered in the scattered baggage. Then the oxen were got together again, and submitted to being loaded up again as quietly as if nothing had happened. Myself and the women had to mend the harness considerably, and Arcane and his ox went back for some water, while Rogers and Bennett took the shovel and went ahead about a mile to cover up the body of Capt. Culverwell, for some of the party feared the cattle might be terrified at seeing it. All this took so much time that we had to make a camp of it right here.

We put the camp kettle on two stones, built a fire, put in some beans and dried meat cut very fine, which cooked till Arcane came with more water, which was added, and thickened with a little of the unbolted flour, making a pretty good and nutritious soup which we all enjoyed. We had to secure the animals, for there was neither grass nor water for them, and we thought they might not be in so good spirits another day.

We had little trouble in packing up again in the morning, and concluded to take a nearer route to the summit, so as to more quickly reach the water holes where Rogers and I camped on our first trip over the country. This would be a hard, rocky road on its course leading up a small rocky cañon, hard on the feet of the oxen, so they had to be constantly urged on, as they seemed very tender footed. They showed no disposition to go on a spree again and so far as keeping the loads on, behaved very well indeed. The women did not attempt to ride, but followed on close after Old Crump and the children, who required almost constant attention, for in their cramped position they made many cries and complaints. To think of it, two children cramped up in narrow pockets in which they could not turn around, jolted and pitched around over the rough road, made them objects of great suffering to themselves and anxiety and labor on the part of the mothers.

Mrs. Bennett said she would carry her baby if she could, but her own body was so heavy for her strength that she could not do it. Bennett, Rogers and myself hurried the oxen all we could, so that we could reach the water and let Bennett go back with some to meet the rest and refresh them for the end of the day's march, and he could take poor little Martha from the pocket and carry her in his arms, which would be a great relief to her. Arcane also took his child when he met them, throwing away his double-barrel gun, saying: "I have no use for you."

When the women reached camp we had blankets already spread down for them, on which they cast themselves, so tired as to be nearly dead. They were so tired and discouraged they were ready to die, for they felt they could not endure many days like this.

We told them this was the first day and they were not used to exercise, therefore more easily tired than after they became a little used to it. We told them not to be discouraged, for we knew every

The Forty-Niners

water hole and all the road over which we would pilot them safely. They would not consent to try riding again, after their circus experience, and Mrs. Arcane said her limbs ached so much she did not think she could even go on the next day. They had climbed over the rocks all day, and were lame and sore, and truly thought they could not endure such another day. The trail had been more like stairs than a road in its steep ascent, and our camp was at a narrow pass in the range. The sky was clear and cloudless, as it had been for so long, for thus far upon this route no rain had fallen, and only once a little snow that came to us like manna in the desert. For many days we had been obliged to go without water, both we and our cattle, and over the route we had come we had not seen any signs of a white man's presence older than our own. I have no doubt we were the first to cross the valley in this location, a visible sinkhole in the desert.

The women did not recover sufficient energy to remove their clothing, but slept as they were, and sat up and looked around with uncombed hair in the morning, perfect pictures of dejection. We let them rest as long as we could, for their swollen eyes and stiffened joints told how sadly unprepared they were to go forward at once. The sun came out early and made it comfortable, while a cool and tonic breeze came down from the great snow mountain, the very thing to brace them up after a thorough rest.

The slope to the east was soon met by a high ridge and between this and the main mountain was a gentle slope scattered over with sagebrush and a few little stools of bunchgrass here and there between. This gave our oxen a little food, and by dipping out the water from the holes and letting them fill up again we managed to get water for camp use and to give the animals nearly all they wanted.

While waiting for the women, Bennett and Arcane wanted to go out and get a good view of the great snowy mountain I had told them so much about. The best point of view was near our camp, perhaps three or four hundred yards away, and I went with them. This place where we now stood was lower than the mountains either north or south, but was difficult to climb and gave a good view in almost every direction, and there, on the backbone of the ridge, we had a grand outlook, but some parts of it brought back doleful recollections. They said they had traveled in sight of that mountain for months and seen many strange formations, but never one like this, as developed from this point. It looked to be seventy-five miles to its base, and to the north and west there was a succession of snowy peaks that seemed to have no end. Bennett and Arcane said they never before supposed America contained mountains so grand, with peaks that so nearly seemed to pierce the sky. Nothing except a bird could ever cross such steep ranges as that one.

West and south it seemed level, and low, dark, and barren buttes rose from the plain, but never high enough to carry snow, even at this season of the year. I pointed out to them the route we were to follow, noting the prominent points, and it could be traced for fully one hundred and twenty-five miles from the point on which we stood. This plain, with its barren ranges and buttes is now known as the Mojave Desert. This part of the view they seemed to study over as if to fix every point and water hole upon their memory. We turned to go to camp, but no one looked back on the country we had come over since we first made out the distant snow peak, now so near us, on November 4th, 1849. The only butte in this direction that carried snow was the one where we captured the Indian and where the squashes were found.

The range next east of us across the low valley was barren to look upon as a naked, single rock. There were peaks of various heights and colors, yellow, blue, fiery red, and nearly black. It looked as if it might sometime have been the center of a mammoth furnace. I believe this range is known as the Coffin's Mountains. It would be difficult to find earth enough in the whole of it to cover a coffin.

Just as we were ready to leave and return to camp, we took off our hats and then, overlooking the scene of so much trial, suffering and death, spoke the thought uppermost, saying: "Good-bye Death Valley!" then faced away and made our steps toward camp. Ever after this, in speaking of this long and narrow valley over which we had crossed into its nearly central part, and on the edge of which the lone camp was made for so many days, it was called Death Valley.

Many accounts have been given to the world as to the origin of the name and by whom it was thus designated, but ours were the first visible footsteps, and we the party which named it the saddest and most dreadful name that came to us first from its memories.

[They all finally reached the settlements and safety on March 7, 1850, the last of the argonauts to escape from the "jaws of Hell." The other stragglers, who had followed Manly into the valley, got out on their own with their wagons over Wingate Pass before he and Rogers returned.]

Lost Ledges

*T*HE FEW BITS OF GOLD AND SILVER
ore that the forty-niners carried out of the Death Valley country fired the
imaginations of nearly all who saw them. And they became the lodestones
that drew men back again and again to search for the lost ledges from which
they had come—the fabulous Gunsight silver and Goller's gold. No one ever
found the elusive ledges, however, for they had grown richer and more elusive
with every telling until they surpassed all finding. Yet a couple of lost-ledge
hunters—Alvord and Breyfogle—did find more gold, but they lost that, too,
magnifying even more the valley's imagined riches. The Lost Breyfogle soon
became one of the best-known and most sought-after ledges in the West, and
"Breyfogling" became synonymous with lost mine hunting. Some of the
mystery, excitement, and frustration of these quests is
captured in the stories that follow.

Adventurer J. Ross Browne first laid the already thoroughly tangled tales of Death Valley's lost ledges before the nation in 1869 in his popular classic Adventures in the Apache Country, A Tour Through Arizona and Sonora with Notes on the Silver Regions of Nevada.

THE LOST LEDGE

by John Ross Browne

THERE IS A CLASS of men peculiar to our new mineral territories to whom the world has not yet done justice. In truth they are but little known individually, though in the aggregate they have accomplished wonderful things. I speak of those vagrant spirits commonly called "prospectors," who never make anything for themselves, but are always on the move to make fortunes for other people. Regular miners, traders, and speculators belong to an entirely different genus. They come in after the way has been opened; but with them the spirit of adventure is not a controlling power. They are no more to be compared with the genuine "prospector" than the motley crowd of merchants and artisans who flocked over to the New World in the tracks of the great Columbus are to be named in the same day with that renowned discoverer.

The prospector is a man of imagination. He is a poet—though not generally aware of the fact. Ragged and unshaved, he owns millions, yet seldom has two dimes to jingle in his pocket—for his wealth lies in the undeveloped wilds. The spirit of unrest burns in his blood. He scorns work, but will endure any amount of hardship in his endless search for "rich leads." There is no desert too barren, no tribe of Indians too hostile, no climate too rigorous for his researches. From the rugged cañons of the Toyabe he roams to the arid wastes of the Great Basin. Hunger, thirst, chilling snows, and scorching sands seem to give him new life and inspiration. It matters nothing that he discovers "a good thing"—a nest of ledges, worth say a million apiece—this is well enough, but he wants something better; and after a day or two spent in "locating his claims" he is off again—nobody knows where—often with scarcely provision enough to last him back to the settlements. He travels on muleback when he happens to own a mule; on foot when he must; with company when any offers; without when there is none; any way to be driving ahead, discovering new regions and locating claims. He locates so many claims that he forgets where his possessions are located. If he discovered a ledge of pure silver six feet thick, he would die in a week if he had to work it on his own account. His industry runs in another direction. Variety is the spice of his existence, the motive-power of his life.

By no means do I intend to depreciate the services of this class of men. They have done more to open up our vast interior territories to settlement and civilization than all the scientific expeditions ever sent across the Rocky Mountains. The indomitable courage, the powers of endurance, the spirit of enterprise, the self-reliance, and the fertility of resource exhibited by this class of men, under circumstances of extraordinary difficulty, have no parallel in the annals of daring adventure. Where is there a desert so barren or a mountain so rugged that it is not traversed or explored by the irrepressible Prospector? In the wild declivities of the South Pass, in the desolate wastes of Colorado and Utah, in the alkali plains and sage deserts and rugged mountain ranges of Nevada, you find him with his pick and shovel—ever hopeful, ever on the strike for "a new lead." He is the most sanguine of men—the most persistent of explorers. Neither disappointment nor the vicissitudes of climate can check the ardor of his enthusiasm. As privation is his lot in this world, it is to be hoped he will strike "a better lead" in the next.

Early in the summer of 1852 a train of sixty wagons left the Mountain Meadows for San Bernardino. The party consisted chiefly of Mormons, but among them were some Gentiles who availed themselves of the protection afforded by the train against the attacks of hostile Indians. The road taken was that known as the old Spanish trail between Salt Lake and San Bernardino. It was the intention of the emigrants to cut off a bend in the road running by Las Vegas Springs, which approaches within thirty or forty miles of the Rio Colorado and considerably increases the distance. At the Armagosa a difference of opinion arose as to the proper direction to be pursued—some being in favor of striking straight across the desert, while others, who knew the terrible sufferings likely to be encountered from want of water in those arid wastes, thought it more prudent to keep within range of the river. As usual in such cases, the discussion ended in a quarrel. Fifty-one of the wagons started down the Armagosa, determined to gain the old road again and follow the beaten track. The remaining nine crossed the range of mountains between the Armagosa and Death Valley.

On reaching Furnace Creek another dispute arose. The weary wanderers were in the midst of a wilderness, with nothing in sight but barren mountains and desolate plains save the wretched little water hole at which they were camped. Seven of the wagons finally started to explore Death Valley for an outlet to the northwest. The other two struck out to the southwest; but were soon lost in the rugged declivities of the mountains bordering on Panamint Valley. On their route they discovered the skeletons of three men at a point called Poison Springs—the waters of which are supposed to cause death. The bones of cattle and of various wild animals were found scattered about in the vicinity. From the train that went down the Armagosa there was a further division of three men, named Farley, Cadwallader and Towne, who, tired of the slow rate of progress and the constant dissensions that prevailed, determined to strike out for themselves. Providing themselves with some jerked beef and such other articles of subsistence as they could carry on their backs, they left the wagons, taking a route a little north of west. For several days they wandered about in the wilderness, suffering greatly from thirst and heat. At Daylight Springs they found water. Thence they crossed Death Valley and ascended the range of mountains lying between that desolate region and the Valley of Panamint, at a point called Folly's Pass. In the course of their wanderings they saw many wonders in the way of mineral ledges, but were unable to examine them carefully owing to their sufferings from thirst and the necessity of reaching some spring or water hole while they had strength. At one place, supposed to be in the foothills of the Panamint range, they discovered a silver ledge of such extraordinary richness that, in the language of one of the party, the "virgin silver glittered in the sun." Weary as they were, and precious as their time was, they stopped long enough to break off a few masses of the ore and locate a claim. The ledge cropped up boldly out of the earth, showing a well-defined vein of four or five feet in thickness, and so rich that the virgin ore was visible all over it.

After great hardships and terrible suffering from thirst, the three men found water at a place called the "Last Chance Springs," where they camped for several days. While resting there, the two wagons that separated from the nine at Furnace Creek came in with the small party accompanying them. They had been many times lost; their stock was nearly broken down with fatigue and thirst, and they were now seeking to get on some known trail that would lead them to California. A Methodist minister named King, with his wife, occupied one of these wagons. The three men, Farley, Cadwallader and Towne, told King of the wonderful discovery they had made, and showed him the ore they had obtained from the ledge. King knew but little of mining practically, but he was an intelligent man and saw no reason to doubt the representations made to him. Provisions were getting short, however, and there was a long journey before them. It was not possible to go back to the ledge and make any further examination of it without a strong chance of perishing in the attempt. The party then joined together and pursued their way in a southwesterly direction till they struck the San Bernardino road and entered California. King and his wife had relatives in the Santa Clara Valley, and settled there. Accounts given by them of the great silver ledge attracted considerable attention, though not so much, probably, as would have been the case after the discovery of the Washoe mines. The people of California were not prepared to attach any great importance to discoveries of silver while their attention was so fully occupied in the development of the gold mines. The Kings had with them a specimen of the ore presented to them by the discoverers, which of course tended to authenticate their statement; but they were not skilled in getting up speculations, and consequently the matter soon died out so far as they were concerned.

Farley, Cadwallader, and Towne separated on their arrival at San Bernardino. Cadwallader went on a prospecting expedition to Sonora. Farley and Towne roved about the southern country for some time, finally stopping at Los Angeles. While there they talked freely about their great silver ledge near Death Valley. The attention of some practical gentlemen in Los Angeles was attracted by the specimens of ore which these two men carried with them. A company was organized and capital paid in to make the necessary tests and fit out an expedition to work the ledge. Some of the ore was taken to San Francisco by a member of the company and assayed. The yield surpassed their most extravagant anticipations—being 85 percent of silver. Such a yield from croppings, taken at random from the surface by travelers hurrying along on a journey of life or death, was well calculated to inspire confidence in the richness of the ledge. Provisions and mining implements were purchased and a party fitted out, under the guidance of Farley, to find this wonderful deposit and work it. On the approach to Folly's Pass, Farley got into a quarrel with a member of the party named Wilson, in the course of which Wilson shot him dead. There was no hope of finding the ledge after this unfortunate event, without the aid of one of the remaining discoverers.

Not knowing what else to do, and none being willing to stay behind upon an uncertainty, the members of the expedition returned to Los Angeles, where they procured the services of Towne as a guide. Another start was made, and all went on successfully till they reached Owen's Lake, on the eastern side of the Sierra Nevada Mountains. There Towne was taken with a fever and died. It seemed as if fate were against the enterprise. Compelled once more to return to Los Angeles, the company next set to work to find Cadwallader, the only surviving member of the party by whom the ledge was discovered, and who knew of its location. Without his guidance the whole enterprise must prove a failure. A reliable agent was sent down into Sonora to search for him and make him such propositions as would secure his services. The search was successful, insofar as Cadwallader was found; but he was in such a condition from habits of intemperance into which he had fallen that it was almost impossible to get him sober. When he became sober enough to listen to any proposition understandingly, he died.

All attempts to find the ledge having thus failed through a strange fatality attending the discoverers, the company was compelled to abandon the enterprise. Other parties, however, undertook to find it from the general descriptions given of the locality. Three years after the death of Cadwallader a new company was formed under the leadership of a Lieutenant Bailey, who professed to be well acquainted with the country. This gentleman had explored Death Valley and the Panamint, and even claimed to have discovered the "Lost Ledge." He brought with him to San Francisco some extraordinarily rich ore, and had no difficulty in procuring from capitalists a large amount of money for the purpose of developing the ledge. Some say he collected as much as $70,000. He refused to sell any portion of the original ledge, but got up subscriptions on a continuation or extension, which was rich enough to satisfy the sagacious men of San Francisco. A party was fitted out with wagons, provisions, implements, etc., and started from Los Angeles. Bailey was to overtake them in a few days at some point near Owen's Lake, and conduct them to that wonderful deposit of virgin silver which was to make them all rich. The expedition reached the point designated, and halted according to agreement. Days passed, and weeks passed, and months passed. No Bailey came. I tell the story as I heard it. If that gentleman be among the living, he will greatly oblige his San Francisco friends by accounting for his absence. The party left at Owen's Lake are under the impression that there would be no difficulty whatever in finding the "Lost Ledge" if they could only find the lost Bailey.

But if anybody supposes such a mining population as we have on the Pacific Coast can be disheartened by disaster and failure, he greatly mistakes the character of our people. No sooner was the Reese River country opened up to settlement and enterprise than prospecting parties started out in every direction to find new ledges. My old friend, Dave Buel, having located all the claims he wanted in the neighborhood of Austin, became inspired with the grand idea of discovering a new route to the Colorado River. Such at least was the ostensible object of the famous expedition made by him in the winter of 1865. But I strongly suspect the "Lost Ledge" formed a prominent feature in the enterprise. Buel had obtained some valuable information respecting its supposed locality from one of the men who had accompanied the train of wagons in 1852. He had carefully studied the whole subject, and thought he could "spot the treasure." Certainly if any man living could do it, Buel could. Of gigantic frame, great powers of endurance, unerring sagacity, and indomitable perseverance, he was well fitted by nature for such an enterprise.

The history of that memorable expedition remains yet to be written. The party consisted of six—all chosen spirits—hardy and sanguine. They left Austin on muleback—they came back on foot. Of their sufferings from thirst in the burning wastes of Death Valley; the loss of all their animals save one little pack mule; the dreary days they spent in "prospecting" for the ledge while death stared them in the face; their escapes from roving bands of hostile Indians, and miraculous preservation from starvation, I cannot now give a detailed account. Gaunt and haggard, blackened by the sun, ragged and footsore, they returned to Austin after an absence of two months. Buel lost thirty-five pounds of flesh, but he gained a large amount of experience concerning lost ledges generally. He thinks he was on the right track and could have found the identical ledge discovered by Farley, Cadwallader, and Towne had the provisions held out. The indications were wonderfully encouraging—mineral everywhere, nothing but mineral, not even a blade of grass or a drop of water. At one time the party lived for three days on a little streak of snow which they found under a shelving rock. Buel considers it a fine country for horned frogs. From the skeletons of men and broken wagons that he encountered near some of the water holes, he is disposed to think that there may be better routes to the Colorado.

Inspired by the disasters of the Buel expedition, which were deemed rather encouraging in a mineral point of view, another company was formed during the past summer, of which a Mr. Breyfogle was a prominent member. I knew Breyfogle in former years. He was tax collector of Alameda County, California, and seemed to be a man of good sense, much respected by the community. During the Washoe excitement he departed for that region and was engaged for several years in mining speculations. Like many others, he had ups and downs of fortune. It was during a downturn that he became infatuated with the idea of discovering the "Lost Ledge." The failure of all attempts hitherto made he attributed to want of perseverance,

Lost Ledges

and he announced it as his determination "to find the ledge or die." That was the only spirit that would lead to its discovery. He would "come back a rich man or leave his bones in Death Valley." Everybody said that was the way to talk, but nobody knew how much in earnest was Breyfogle.

Some five or six enterprising spirits united their resources and started with this irrepressible prospector, full of glorious visions of the Lost Ledge. They traveled to the southward, following the Toyabe range till they struck into the dreary desert of Death Valley. There they wandered for many days, probing the foothills of the Panamint range. They crossed and recrossed Buel's trail; they camped at the Poison Springs and saw the skeletons of dead men; they went through Folly's Pass and ranged through the Panamint Valley. North, south, east, and west they traversed the country, till their mules broke down and their provisions fell short. Breyfogle urged them to continue the search. "Stick to it, boys, and we'll find it yet," he would say. "Never give up while there's a ghost of a chance." But they were all ghosts by that time, and were rapidly becoming skeletons. Their only hope of saving their lives was to strike for the nearest mining camp—San Antonio—which was distant over a hundred miles. Breyfogle had been getting more and more excited for several days. He begged his companions to try it a little longer—only two days, even a day—as Columbus did in the days of yore. But here was certain death, or so, at least, it appeared; for what could they do without food in this fearful desert, remote from any point where they could obtain human aid, and already so weak that they could scarcely drag their limbs over the heavy sand? Breyfogle's eyes were bloodshot and had a wild and haggard expression. When it was announced to him that it was the determination of the party to abandon the search, he said: "Then I will continue it alone. I have sworn to find the Lost Ledge or leave my bones here, and I intend to do it."

His comrades entreated him not to stay behind—they had scarcely provision enough to last them to San Antonio and could not spare him more than two days' supply at the furthest. What if he found the ledge? The discovery would be of no use to him or anybody else, for he would be sure to die. These arguments fell without effect upon the excited brain of the visionary. Too weak and weary to take him by force, Breyfogle's comrades reluctantly bade him good-bye and left him to his fate. With great difficulty they reached San Antonio. There they recruited till they were able to pursue their journey homeward to Austin. In the meantime, Breyfogle wandered about searching the deserts and the mountains for the Lost Ledge. When his provisions gave out he lived on frogs and lizards, but became very weak. It is probable his reason had been affected for some time. How long he wandered in this crazy condition would be difficult to say without a more accurate knowledge of dates. While thus helpless, a party of two or three Indians who had been watching him for several days, came upon him suddenly, beat him with their clubs, robbed him of his clothes, and ended by scalping him. One might think this rigorous course of treatment would have put an end to the poor wanderer, but such was not the case. Two days after the attack upon him by the Indians, a wagon train, on the way from Los Angeles to Salt Lake City picked him up and carried him to the City of the Saints. The injury to his scalp seemed to restore his faculties. He gave a graphic narrative of his adventures from the time his companions left him. At Austin it was reported that he was dead; but he turned up at Salt Lake City a few weeks after, as much alive as ever and still determined to find the Lost Ledge. My visit to Salt Lake was shortly after his arrival. Hearing that he was there, I was about to hunt him up when an attack of mountain fever laid me on my back, so that I lost the chance of seeing him before his departure on a little side expedition to Idaho and Montana.

BREYFOGLE'S

Nevada mining promoter Standish Rood took a few knocks at the myth of riches in this sometimes fanciful tale of a maddening search for elusive gold with the enigmatic and irascible Charles Breyfogle. It was published in Whittaker's Milwaukee Monthly in August and September of 1872. In the Paiutes' defense it should be said that they did not scalp Breyfogle, but rather clubbed his already bald, and sun-blistered head in the act of stealing his outsized shoes. They also didn't shoot him in the knee with an arrow; that happened at the hands of the Hualapai on a later trip across the Colorado River.

LOST LEDGE
by Standish Rood

IN THE FALL OF 1866, quite an excitement was created in southeastern Nevada by the representations of an individual named Breyfogle, who professed to have discovered during the summer of 1862 a fabulously rich gold mine in the vicinity of Death Valley. (This notable valley lies in the western part of the state of Nevada.) The discovery was made by Breyfogle and two companions who were lost in that region for a number of days; his partners were murdered by the Indians, and he, in making his escape came across a gold mine, a specimen from which he picked up and put in his pocket.

It may be remarked that it was somewhat singular that a man under those circumstances should have waited to examine any mineral-bearing quartz, much less to have retained a specimen of it, when he knew the Indians were in hot pursuit of him. But as he had the specimen with him and we had no good reason to doubt his word, the stampede was effected, and fourteen men agreed to place themselves under the guidance of Breyfogle to search for the famous, "Lost Ledge." As this was the sixth excursion that had been organized and carried out by this indefatigable mountaineer and prospector, with no benefits or discoveries resulting from any of them, it can be inferred that the party did not feel any too sanguine in regard to the discoveries of any remarkable deposits of gold. It was thought, however, that other discoveries might be made, so that the trip, in the event of not being successful in Death Valley, would, on the whole, be a successful one. Hiko, the county seat of Lincoln County, Nevada, was appointed as the rendezvous.

On the fifteenth day of September, 1866, a party of fourteen hardy, resolute miners met at Hiko to complete the arrangements for the journey which was to commence on the morrow. With the exception of two men, the party consisted of veterans in the line of prospecting and mining; men who were used to hardships, who would undertake almost any journey, no matter how hazardous or perilous, if prospects for gold, silver, or an Indian skirmish were good at the end of it.

We may as well speak at the outset of some of the peculiarities of our guide, Breyfogle, or as he was more familiarly called, "Old Brey"; he was a stout, hale-appearing man, evidently capable of enduring greater hardships than some of the younger members of the party. He was extremely taciturn, hardly ever spoke unless he was addressed, and then only answered in gruff monosyllables. His head was perfectly bald, not from the effects of early piety but from the results of a scalping which he had undergone at the hands of the Death Valley Indians on his first memorable trip to their country; this operation had not tended to make him the most amiable person in the world. It was thought, on the contrary, that it was what made him so gloomy and irritable. I apprehend that such an operation would not tend to soften the asperities of any of our lives. His one redeeming quality was that he was temperate in his habits. He had been working hard all summer to obtain means to make this trip. The crowning point of his ambition, the whole aim of his life, was centered upon this one object, the rediscovery of his "Lost Ledge." All his earnings for the last six years have been expended in unsuccessful trips to the region of Death Valley; he only working long enough for a "prospecting stake," when, inducing a few others to join him, he goes off in search of his "*ignus fatus*"; he is as sanguine and visionary as a child, and avers that he will never give up the search as long as he retains his health and vigor and the pecuniary means to prosecute it.

It is sad to see a man of his age wearing the few remaining years of his life out in wandering about the desert valleys and desolate mountains of this godforsaken, sterile country, mounted on an old Piute pony, following a still poorer one ladened with all his worldly goods, consisting of a chunk of old bacon, a sack of flour, a battered iron coffee pot and a greasy frying pan, lying out nights with no shelter, exposed to the inclemency of the weather and constantly looking out for and fearing attack from predatory bands of hostile Indians.

Yet as it is his way of enjoying life, what need have we to pity his lot in this world.

On the morning of the sixteenth of September, 1866, our arrangements had all been completed, and at nine o'clock we were mounted, our pack mules were wheeled into line, and bidding farewell to the village of Hiko and the fertile valley of Pah Ranagat, we turned our faces westward toward the desolate regions of the Great American Desert. Our caravan, as it left the valley, presented quite an imposing appearance: fourteen men, well mounted on fat, sleek-looking ponies, driving before them seven frisky, obstinate Spanish

Lost Ledges

mules that were packed with our provisions and blankets, formed quite an array. I venture to say that the outfit would have created an excitement had they appeared in any of our eastern cities. Each man was armed with a brace of Colt's six-shooters, a bowie knife, and a Henry rifle. We were prepared for any contingency that might arise from the bands of hostile Indians who occupy the country between Pah Ranagat and Death Valley. Our pack mules acted that morning as if each one of them was infested with seven devils; they would not have been mules had they done otherwise; they seemed bound to go in every direction but the right one; they were fresh and plum full of meanness and activity, and evidently did not wish to leave the rich pasturelands of Pah Ranagat Valley. Finding that we could not drive them, we secured five of them, to try what effect leading and the moral suasion of a stick would have on them. It kept two men busy to each mule, one behind with a sharp stick, another in front tugging at a rope attached to the mule's nose. Curses, loud and deep, were levelled at those mules that morning, and many were the threats that were made that we would be even with the obstinate brutes before the journey was over. If there is anything in the world that will make a man forget his country and his religion, it is his first experience with a Spanish mule; they can grand discount the meanest American mule that was ever raised. It is almost impossible to drive them for the first two or three days; it would require a regiment of cavalry to keep half a dozen of them in the road. When you attempt to lead them, they have a pleasant way of trying to nip a piece of flesh out of your leg. When that amusement ceases to be a source of pleasure to them, they try their teeth on your horse's flank; a person has to be continually on the lookout to keep his seat in the saddle.

After various delays on the road, adjusting packs and chasing mules, we are last arrived at Logan Springs in the middle of the afternoon. This is a small mining town situated on the eastern slope of the Pah Ranagat range of mountains; it contains a population of about forty able-bodied miners, one saloon keeper, one Jew, the district recorder, and a washerwoman with two children.

I have seen towns more flourishing than Logan. We remained at this place during the night, securing quarters for our animals in a large corral and giving them a generous feed of hay and barley.

It may be about this time appropriate to speak of the different characters that composed our expedition:

Frank Roberts, a genuine New England Yankee born on the sunny banks of "Cape Cod," was the self-constituted leader of the party. He talked a great deal and had numberless suggestions to make, which nobody heeded. He was a small, active, wiry, red-headed chap; did as much work around the camp as any two men in it; he was a favorite because of his industry. By the way, he was the only man in the party who owned a dog. Frank's partner was a Cornishman by the name of Joe Williams, a good deal better miner than prospector. Joe was as quiet as his partner was noisy.

The next in order came Harry Hendricks, a young Missourian of rebel proclivities, having served in "Pap Price's" army during the rebellion. He was long, lean, and lank; his clothes hung about him loosely, giving him a dirty, slouchy appearance; he was lazy and shiftless. Harry was the only "tender-footed American" in the party, this being his first prospecting trip. He had for blanket roommate an Englishman by the name of John Tours, the quietest man in the outfit! He smoked more tobacco and talked less than any man I ever saw. He was under the complete control of Harry; in camp he did the work of both.

Our best-dressed man, and the most particular one, was S. R. Ware; he hailed from Boston, Mass., but had been in the mountains ten years, quite long enough to have all the rough edges of Puritanism rubbed off. He was good looking, companionable, and witty, just the man to pick out for a prospecting trip. Ware's "bunky" was a Kanuck Irishman rejoicing in the name of Dan McGraw. Dan was not an exception to his countrymen, but loved his whiskey well and was not averse to having a fight every hour in the day. He was a good, jolly companion.

Our educated man was Charles Denton; he was a graduate of Williams College, but his learning was not appreciated in this country, the boys not considering that he outranked any of them. He was the most slovenly man in the outfit; he would occasionally rinse the loose dirt from his hands, but was never known to wash his face on the trip. The "New West" had demoralized him, as it has done many a better man. His partner was a Virginian, a red-hot rebel by the name of Frank Pitt; he professed to have been a member of the "Black Horse Cavalry"; as he was a good deal of a yarner, his stories were taken with a great many grains of allowance. He was the largest man in the party, weighing two hundred pounds and standing six feet four inches in his brogans. He boasted of his valor like other barking dogs we read of, and turned out to be the veriest coward in the country.

The best miner and prospector in the party was Bill Huxton, a native of Ohio, a quiet and unobtrusive man; but before the journey was over, he showed his hand as the bravest man among us, was always found ready to volunteer for any enterprise, however hazardous, provided it was to benefit the party; in miner's parlance, he was a thoroughbred. His partner was a hardy young fellow by the name of Dave Cobb; he hailed from the young state of Minnesota. Dave was a good companion and was always ready to do his duty without grumbling.

We had a wit, an ex-wit of the Nevada Legislature: an honest fellow he was, by the name of Tom Lane; he was a blacksmith by trade, and said to have been a very good one; it is to be hoped that he was; we never discovered that he was good for anything else. The ruination of Tom was his election to the Legislature of Nevada about four years before; his brain never recovered from the shock. They ruined a good mechanic in trying to make an assemblyman. In point of cleanliness he ranked next to Denton; neither of them were allowed to do any cooking or to handle any provisions, except what they consumed themselves.

Tom's chum was an ex-Methodist preacher by the name of Charles Kean; if he was as good a preacher as he was a prospector, he should have remained in the ministry; he was very energetic, and as industrious as a bee, and proved a most desirable addition to our party; but what little piety he had left was effectually cleaned out before we returned. He made as grammatical a curser as I ever listened to.

Breyfogle and the humble subscriber made up the tail end of our caravan. As we have spoken of our guide, we will try and resume the subject and commence our journey.

By the way, I must not forget to give a passing remark to Frank's dog; he was a long-bodied, short-legged, homely, yellow dog, rejoicing in the name of Bummer; he was the most serious looking dog I ever saw, "a melancholy dog, the saddest of his kind"; withal "Bummer" was a good watchdog, he evinced a decided antipathy towards Indians, and would not let one come near the camp if he had his way.

At eight o'clock on the morning of the 17th of September, we bade adieu to the little mining town of Logan. As we filed over the mountain range, one mile west of the town, we made a more presentable appearance than we did the day before. The mules were all led—we had wisely given up the idea of trying to drive them at the outset—our experience of the day before having been quite sufficient.

After crossing the Pah Ranagat Range, we entered on a large, barren valley not dignified with a name, the soil dry and sandy; the only vegetation that seemed to luxuriate was the everlasting sagebrush and a gigantic species of cactus called Josiahs. We crossed the valley in a westerly direction and camped for noon at the base of the Timpeute mountain. This giant mountain stands alone in the middle of the valley, an oasis in the desert, one of the prominent landmarks of the country. It is of a beautiful conical shape, and covered with the green foliage of the Pingon pine nearly to its summit; it lifts its head to an altitude of ten thousand feet above the level of the sea. Around its base are numerous fine springs of pure cold water, which give moisture to the bench lands of the mountain, thus affording good grazing ground for stock.

Around most of these springs are to be seen numbers of old "Wakeups," or wigwams, that have been formerly built and used by the Indians. This mountain is a harvest field for the Indians in the fall. A thick forest of Pingon pines covers the mountain. This tree bears a nut which forms one of the chief articles of food for the Indians. They are enclosed in a conical burr about one inch in diameter at the thickest part and about four inches in length; each burr contains from thirty to fifty nuts about the size of a white bean. They are very palatable and are eagerly sought after by the white people in this country.

We continued in a westerly course across the valley and encamped for the night at Indian Springs, twelve miles west of Timpeute mountain.

The water was warm and brackish, the grass very poor, and there was very little of it. Most of our animals had to be secured with lariats; if let loose, they would leave us and return to Pah Ranagat valley. The country through which we passed that day was sterile, barren, and uninteresting. Some romantic young lady or young gent just newly fledged from college might call it romantic, picturesque, beautiful, &c.; the subscriber fails to see it. Our party was divided into three messes. As our larder only consisted of bacon, flour, coffee, and tea, it did not take much knowledge of the fine arts to cook it. The only vegetables we had consisted of a bushel of onions; they were taken along as an *anti-scorbutic*—I think that's what they call it. It is well known by miners that onions eaten raw are a great promoter of good health on a prospecting tour.

At six in the morning we were up and on the road. We left our cheerless camping ground without regret; did not even wait for morning prayers by Charley. The morning was bright and beautiful; if the country had been as charming as the weather, we would be tempted to try to be romantic; but who could be this in a wilderness of sagebrush and cactus. After leaving the springs, our course lay to the southwest; we had no trail to follow, but scattered along over the desert, following in the wake of our veteran guide. We ate our lunch at noon, encamped in the middle of the desert, without water.

It would be useless and uninteresting to give the details of every day's march across this sterile country, where every valley looks like the one that you have just left, and every mountain range is a counterpart of its neighbor in all the general outlines. There are even no hostile Indians here to occasion a little excitement, to help drive away the blues and relieve the monotony. It would require a more romantic nature than ours to find anything very enticing or beautiful in the Great American Desert.

The valleys here are not capable of ever being cultivated, owing to the utter absence of water for irrigating purposes. The only plant that seems to thrive is the different species of cactus; they grow luxuriantly, and produce some of the most beautiful waxlike blossoms that were ever allowed to "waste their sweetness on the desert air."

These regions are not blessed with a respectable shower half a dozen times a year; consequently, it does not seem strange that anything should refuse to grow.

We did not arrive at our camping place this evening until nearly dark, having traveled forty miles since morning without water. We camped at Ash Spring; there were three stunted white oak trees near the pool that looked as if they were ashamed of being found in such a region. We deplored their lonely and desolate fate. The grass round the spring was not very luxuriant or plentiful. What there was of it was dry but nutritious. We gave our animals in charge of a couple of Indians, who volunteered to guard them all night for an old shirt and one pint of flour, and they were brought into camp next day looking as if they had fared well.

The most difficult job that we had in the morning was arranging the packs on our mules, as they of necessity grew lighter every day, and had to be arranged differently every morning. About the middle of the forenoon we crossed a low range of mountains and entered the Amagosh Valley. There was nothing material to distinguish it from the one we had just left. It appeared to be about thirty miles wide; its length we could not determine or even guess at, as we entered only about twenty-five miles above the Amagosh River. At this point we made a detour to the south to visit the abandoned gold mines of the Amagosh mountains. At five o'clock we reached the Amagosh Springs, or head of the Amagosh River—called a river in this country, although not over twenty feet in width, and running but ten miles down the valley, where it sinks into the sand.

We were visited at our camp by at least fifty dirty, squalid, Digger Indians; they had the appearance of having maintained a protracted fast. They clamored loudly for biscuit and tobacco, offering to trade for the same a few dressed antelope skins. The boys felt generous this evening, and knowing that flour stirred into boiling water went a good ways and was very filling for the price, we made them two camp kettles full of hasty pudding. They went at the mixture with a gusto that was delightful to see; it was devoured in even less time than it took to make it.

We had to trust our animals to the tender mercies of the Indians. It was far safer to give them in their charge than to show that we doubted their honesty by herding them ourselves. It is seldom that an Indian will betray his trust when anything is put under his charge. They are more proud of their honor than many a white man.

We had an abundance of fuel at our camp. Cords of wood ready cut lay scattered all around. There was also a deserted log cabin, but the interior was so dirty and suggestive of fleas that we preferred the clean banks of the spring.

The next morning we visited the gold mines; they are located about five miles from the spring and at the base of the highest peak of the Amagosh range. These mines were discovered in 1856 by a party of prospectors from Southern California. The first specimens that were found were very rich; the indications were favorable that immense wealth was to be obtained. Great excitement was created in Southern California by the discovery, but the location was kept a secret until a company was formed in Los Angeles, Cal., and money raised to develop the mine and to erect reduction works. A large company of miners, with a twelve months' supply of provisions, were sent out from Los Angeles under the auspices of a stock company. The Amagosh gold fields bade fair to become famous. After a few tons of ore had been extracted, the vein gave out, while underneath was found a caprock of grey granite. After trying in vain for six months to pierce the rock and find the vein again, the company abandoned the mine and employed the men to prospect in the vicinity. The miners had lived here for a year without the least trouble from the Indians. They felt themselves perfectly secure, not even taking their rifles or revolvers with them when they went out alone in the mountains, but leaving them scattered around their cabins unloaded, rusty and useless.

The Indians noting their carelessness, being allowed to visit the cabins and doing as they pleased, quietly made arrangements to murder the whole population. In August 1859 they attacked the settlement and massacred the whole outfit, with the exception of one man who managed to escape to the mountains.

They burnt the quartz mill, the storehouses, and the cabins. The only building left was the one near the spring. No effort has ever been made since that time to open or prospect the country in the vicinity. The mines have been visited by numbers of prospectors since, more with a view to gratifying their curiosity in regard to the place than to prospecting for gold. The formation of the mountain in which the veins are located is a dark grey granite; the matrix of the gold-bearing quartz is a white crystallized quartz, stratified with veins of feldspar. All the gold that has ever been found to pay here has been discovered in pockets. A true fissure vein bearing gold quartz in paying quantities remains yet to be discovered in Amagosh.

The principal mine has been so thoroughly worked out that we could not even obtain a specimen as large as a hickory nut.

After working hard all day climbing the mountains, exploring old shafts and tunnels, we returned to camp by dark, tired and disgusted with the mines of Amagosh and ashamed that our curiosity should lead us so far out of our way to visit them.

The Indians had taken good care of our stock; their well-filled hides gave token that they had improved the time. The Indians appeared very friendly to us, and evidently regretted our departure. They were probably the same treacherous wretches who had murdered the unarmed miners eight years ago. We watched them closely, and were prepared for any demonstrations that they might choose to make. We would have liked an excuse to have revenged the deaths of the unfortunate miners who perished here. They saw that we were all armed with the "Henry Rifle"—the "magic gun," they call it—and think a white man can fire it all day without loading.

We now proceeded in a northwesterly direction up the Amagosh Valley, continued along the western side of the valley about fifteen miles. (We had to guess at the distances as we had no trail or road to go by.) We then passed a high range of mountains (name unknown) and entered a small circular valley surrounded by high mountains, traveled across the valley a distance of fifteen or twenty miles, and camped at some sulphur springs situated at the mouth of a high, precipitous canyon. This canyon, with the exception of the pass through which we entered the valley, was evidently the only outlet. Our horses had to drink the warm mineral water, although they did not relish it. Provided the water in this country is not too strong of alkali, it is always acceptable, and warm sulphur water is not so unpalatable as warm water without that ingredient.

The grass around the springs was fair, but not nearly so good and nutritious as that we had left at the Amagosh.

To relieve the monotony, we had a small quarrel this evening between our Cape Cod Yankee, Frank Roberts, and our rebel Missourian, Henry Hendricks. The little row commenced at supper; it began in an argument about politics; before we were aware that they were in earnest, their six-shooters were drawn and shots exchanged. Frank was unharmed, while his bullet cut away a piece of Harry's ear; it so astonished and alarmed the Missourian that he incontinently dropped his six-shooter and fled up the canyon at an alarming pace, howling at every jump. We were well aware from his pace that he could not be mortally wounded, so no one took the trouble to go after him. We concluded that a little solitude would be good for what ailed him. The affair was a laughable one; no one was sorry that it happened, as we hoped it would have a good effect on him and cure him of boasting. Frank took it very coolly, and went on with his supper as though nothing had happened. In about an hour Harry made his appearance; he was in rather a dilapidated condition, looked pale and tired. One of the boys asked him if he had been up the canyon selecting a site for a graveyard where he could bury his dead. His prestige for valor was gone; he was the butt of the camp; insults and ridicule were heaped upon him, and he dared not resent anything. If he had dared to return to Pah Ranagat alone, he would have left the party.

We broke camp this morning at daylight; pursued our journey in a northwesterly course. The canyon through which we passed was not quite ten miles in length. It was very narrow, tortuous, and rocky; in some places there was hardly room enough to allow our pack mules to pass in single file. We named it "Arrow Canyon"; huge masses of gray metamorphic limestone bounded the canyon on both sides, towering up to a height of at least two thousand feet above our heads; huge masses of rock seemed almost detached and ready to fall upon us. The scenery was grand, gloomy, and picturesque. The sun's rays could never penetrate to the depths of this place; it was always in shadow—a good place for a misanthrope to dwell.

We emerged from the canyon into a large, beautiful valley. We call it beautiful, as it presented, some twenty miles distant, charming green meadowlands; several groves of trees could also be seen, a sight quite unusual in this country. Our guide informed us that this was "Ash Meadows." After traversing about twenty-five miles of sand and gravel, covered with a heavy growth of sagebrush and cactus, we arrived at the springs.

We were not surprised to find the water warm; it would astonish us to find cold water in this region of thermal springs. The water was pure and sweet, but a little too warm to be pleasant. About two hundred ash trees were scattered about the meadows, giving to the place a cheerful and homelike aspect. There were numerous springs all around us; some of them were quite large, forming little streams that flowed down through the meadows. The banks of the streams and springs were fringed with a luxuriant growth of tulu, a species of flag, the root of which furnishes one of the chief articles of food for the Indians.

Before we had removed the packs from our wearied mules, Indians were to be seen coming from all directions towards our camp. The grass being thick and heavy, we picketed our animals. We were in a strange land, surrounded by bands of hostile Indians. We came to the conclusion that we would exercise more prudence hereafter in regard to our horses. Before we had fairly got settled and finished our supper, we were surrounded by over one hundred and fifty of the vilest looking Indians that were ever seen; they were all partially naked, and some of them entirely so; all of them were armed with bows, with their quivers full of flint-pointed arrows. There were perhaps half a dozen old rifles in the band, but there was not much danger to be apprehended from them. Rifles in the hands of these Indians are generally useless, as they can obtain no percussion caps, and they have not genius enough to make a flintlock. They sometimes fire them off by applying a lighted brand to the touchhole; this mode of firing a rifle interferes somewhat with the aim. As we did not have provisions enough to feed the whole band, we concluded to treat them all alike and give them nothing. They kept up a most incessant jabbering; they wanted food; they were the most importunate beggars we had ever met. When they found they could get nothing out of us in that way, they changed their base and demanded pay for the water and fuel that we were using, and for the grass which our horses were eating.

On our refusal to comply with their demands they waxed exceedingly wroth; they tried to bluff us, but we would not scare. Bill Huxton became so enraged at them that he picked up a club and made a foray on them; he knocked three of them down before they could recover from their astonishment. The balance of them took to their heels, and ran off about five hundred yards, where they set up a terrible howling, pulling their bow strings and making warlike demonstrations. We secured the three Indians that Huxton had knocked down, keeping them as hostages for the safety of our horses and their general good behavior. Tonight we appointed men to stand guard, for the first time on the trip, partly for the purpose of watching our captives. We bound them with the ropes that we used on our pack animals. The Indians camped about a quarter of a mile from us.

Little camp fires could be seen glistening like torches through the darkness. The howling of the wolves, and the occasional whooping of our savage neighbors, could be heard all night. The Indians were evidently holding a war council. Signal fires were seen in all directions, gleaming like stars from the tops and sides of mountains. These fires are built to give the warning that something extraordinary has happened, and are intended to call the clans together. We were up in the morning before daylight, our traps were packed, and we were on the march before sunrise. After we were ready to move we released our captives; their imprisonment was a benefit to them, as they thereby secured two square meals and would have willingly undergone the infliction again at the same price.

This morning we had another evidence of the stupidity of our guide. We supposed Death Valley lay in an almost westerly direction from Ash Meadows, but he insisted that it lay over fifty miles to the north. We had no alternative but to follow him. About five miles from our camp, we came upon some old wagon tracks that were just discernible; they were the outlines of the old Bennet trail, and were made by a party of emigrants in the fall of 1856. The party had started across the plains late in the season, and left the northern route at Salt Lake City through fear of being snowed in on the mountain ranges between that city and Sacramento, Cal. From Cedar City, three hundred miles south of Salt Lake City, they started in a due westerly course across an unknown country, under the guidance of a Mormon named Bennet.

They proceeded as far as Death Valley, where they all perished, with the exception of the guide (Bennet), a young girl, and an ox on which the girl rode. One hundred and thirty men, women, and children perished in the desert that borders on Death Valley. This circumstance gave the valley its singular name. At the lower end of Ash Meadows, we came upon the iron work of several wagons, old broken camp kettles, &c., relics of that unfortunate party. When we left the old emigrant camp, our guide made us ascend a high mountain to the north of Ash Meadows; there were plenty of lower and better passes than this, but he seemed to have a fancy for wishing us to climb all the high mountains that lay anywhere near our route. The prospect that met our gaze from the top of this mountain was anything but encouraging for grass and water. If romantic scenery were what we were seeking, we had it unfolded for us here in all its primitive splendor and beauty; an immense, dreary, barren looking desert lay spread out at our feet, with not a single tree or spot of green verdure to relieve the monotony; in the distance, range after range of mountains appeared, as regular as the swells upon the ocean. Over a hundred miles to the west, the snowy crests of the Sierra Nevadas lifted up their heads, making a beautiful background to our panorama.

As we descended the mountain into the desert, we submitted to another one of the vagaries of our luny old guide. He now led us in a northeastern direction toward a high mound, that appeared to be about twenty miles distant; he declared that he had once camped at the foot of this mound and found an abundance of water and grass. The weather was very hot; the refraction of the sun's rays upon the sands of the valley made the heat more intense. Believing that we would find water at the mound, we were not saving of that in our canteens, and there was not more than a gallon left in the outfit when we arrived at our supposed camping ground. Not a drop of water was to be found near the mound, nor any indications that there had ever been any there. "Old Brey" was astonished, while we were disappointed and mad; had it not been for his gray hairs and the faint hopes we had of finding the "Lost Ledge," we would have been tempted to have started a graveyard near this mound. Our horses had traveled at least twenty-five miles since leaving the last spring at Ash Meadows, over a red-hot desert without grass or water, and the indications were that we would not be able to give them any for the next twenty-four hours, as there was not a spear of grass at Brey's Mound.

We concluded to turn and take a due westerly course across the valley, towards a low range of mountains that bounded the valley on the west. The men had not suffered for water, as they had had sufficient for their wants during the day. The little that we had left was put into a keg for morning's use, provided we found none during the night. About two o'clock in the morning we arrived at the base of the mountain and camped, not caring to seek for water in the dark. We picketed our animals and laid down, determined to obtain a little rest before daylight. In the morning we sought for water but found none, everything was dry as a bone; there were no dry beds of what had once been creeks, even, to gladden our eyes. Our horses looked melancholy, and would not touch the dry mountain grass.

After eating a lunch, washing it down with a little of the water we still had, we packed our animals and proceeded across the range. The valley on the west side of the range presented no better prospect for water than the one we had just left. About fifteen miles to the north appeared another mound, looking so much like the one that we had left yesterday that it would be taken for its twin sister.

Brey insisted that this was the right mound, and that we should immediately make for it; we declined making any more experiments by going twenty miles out of our way without knowing we should find water. Our guide was overruled, so we continued on our course due west. The valley did not look over fifteen miles wide; we were in hopes that the next range would be well supplied with water. The sun shone bright and warm; we wished in vain for clouds to hide his burning face.

Great columns of sand appeared all over the valley, formed by whirlwinds; some of them rose to a height of at least five hundred feet; they had the appearance of water spouts upon the ocean—we only wished they had been formed of water instead of sand. At noon we arrived at the mountain; we were about as dry as the animals, but no water appeared; we could almost believe that the range was the one that we had left in the morning.

Our dog "Bummer" had given up the ghost. Poor dog! He was sincerely mourned, although we left him on the desert a prey to the wolves.

We camped at the base of the mountain some two hours, in order to rest our animals. We had to secure them with ropes, as they would have left us in short order in search of water. We did not cook any dinner; there was not a man in the outfit that felt hungry—all felt cross and thirsty. We thought of the Bennet party and their horrible fate in this same region ten years ago, and we were just having a foretaste ourselves of what their sufferings must have been. This country was evidently never intended to be of any use to man. Sagebrush even refuses to grow, and is displaced by a thorny species of greasewood. The cactus seems to luxuriate here, as we see hundreds of different varieties every day, their beautiful blossoms being the only objects of interest in this desolate region.

Brey assured us that we would find water before sundown; he knew of a spring in the next range of mountains. His assurances did not make us feel any happier. We had arrived at the conclusion that he had forgotten all that he ever knew about the country. We proposed to follow our own course.

Proceeding on our journey, we passed through a canyon about three miles in length, emerging into another valley as like unto the one we had just left as two peas. No signs of water were visible; the weather was intensely hot; most of the party were now suffering the pangs of thirst; our tongues clove to the roofs of our mouths; our throats were dry and parched. We would gladly have given all our interests in the mining districts of Nevada for the sight of a spring of good, cool water. Our horses staggered like drunken men; it was evident that if we did not obtain water before midnight, some or all of the party would have to pursue their journey on foot.

We arrived at the western side of the valley about five o'clock, no signs of water; we pushed on and crossed the range. From the top of the divide, we saw some green verdure some six miles distant to the north. The sight of it made our hearts leap for joy; everybody acted on his own hook; the only thing now in view was to reach that green spot as soon as possible.

The horses seemed to understand that there was water near at hand, and it put "life and mettle in their heels." There was scarcely a word spoken during that ride of six miles; in fact, most of our party were suffering so from thirst that they could hardly articulate. When within half a mile of the spring our animals scented the water, and in spite of their weakness and wearied limbs, they broke into a gallop. Upon reaching the spot indicated, we found a beautiful little stream about three feet in width. The horses could with difficulty be checked from drinking too much; we were obliged to tie them to some giant specimens of the greasewood that grew near the creek. Hendricks and Tom Lane acted more foolishly than the dumb brutes; in spite of our protests, they drank their fill; as the result, they both fainted, and it was with great difficulty that Hendricks could be restored to consciousness. The others drank moderately, waiting for a cup of hot coffee to quench their thirst. After we had been in camp about two hours, we turned our animals loose, satisfied that they would not leave us this night.

There being no signs of Indians around the camp, we concluded, as we were very tired, to omit standing guard. It was ten o'clock before we turned in, and we were soon in a sound slumber; nor did we awake until the sun was high in the heavens. Our horses were found to be all right; they had not wandered half a mile during the night. We concluded to remain here for the day, to recruit them and ourselves. About half a mile below where we camped, we found some more relics of the unfortunate Bennet party, consisting principally of the iron work of their wagons. Some forty miles to the southwest could be seen a lofty, barren-looking range of mountains, which our guide informed us was the range constituting the eastern boundary of Death Valley. Nothing worth recording transpired in camp today. The boys were engaged in fixing up the packs and in repairing their saddles and old clothes.

We had not yet fully recovered our amiability, our recollections of the two preceding days not being of the most pleasant description. We were not visited by any Indians during the day, and had no idea that they were massing their bands to give us a warm reception before we left their country. The banks of the creek near where it takes its rise are covered with the ruins of old Indian wake-ups, made of tulu, that had not been used this season.

Another night of refreshing sleep found us in the morning fully recruited and ready to pursue our journey. Our horses had not grown fat to any alarming extent during their thirty-six hours rest, but they were willing and able to do a good day's work. Our pack mules had had the vim and obstinacy taken out of them during the last three days; they had become attached to the horses, and could not be driven away.

A mule is a much better animal on a prospecting expedition than a horse; they can stand more fatigue in a warm country, and they are not so liable to wander off during the night. An old mare with a bell attached to her neck will keep a large herd of mules together when all other means fail. They will follow the "bell-mare" through anything, over anything, or anywhere.

Our course this morning was to the southwest; at noon we reached the western side of the valley and camped at the base of a low range of mountains. There were several small springs here, but the water was warm and brackish. Our animals did not relish it, but were obliged to drink it for want of better; they had not forgotten their late experience, and thought a belly full of poor water better than none. We remained at this camp but an hour, when we packed up and proceeded on our journey. Crossing the divide, we entered a valley much larger than any we had seen since leaving Ash Meadows. Some twenty miles to the north we could see large meadows of green grass or tulus; volumes of steam rising from the midst of the green verdure indicated hot springs in that vicinity. We had no curiosity to visit them. Where we crossed the valley there was no indication of water or grass; cactus and greasewood had taken possession of the soil. At five o'clock we reached the banks of Furnace Creek, a small stream about five feet wide, the only stream that is known to empty its waters into Death Valley. The water was quite warm, and had a strong taste of sulphur, but it was wet and we were thankful for that in this region. The grass in the vicinity was very good, much better than we expected to find.

Our horses were turned loose, two of our men standing guard. We had now reached the end of our journey, and were supposed to be in the vicinity of the famous "Lost Ledge." We were to make the camp on Furnace Creek our headquarters. Two men were to take charge of the camp, while the balance were to prospect in the surrounding mountains.

It was remarked as we rode up to Furnace Creek that night that the indications in the surrounding mountains were anything but flattering for the existence of the precious metals. As far as we could judge, the country rock was composed principally of metamorphic limestone, a formation that rarely carries with it any of the precious metals.

The first thing in the morning was to visit the far-famed Death Valley. Furnace Creek takes its rise in an isolated mountain some five miles north of Death Valley, it runs across a small flat about one mile in diameter (where we camped), and then enters a high, precipitous canyon, down which it flows into Death Valley.

We followed this canyon up to the danger of our lives. It was very narrow, not being over thirty feet in width at its widest part; the sides of it were rough and rugged, towering to a height of at least four thousand feet above our heads. The bed of the canyon was so steep that the water of the little creek was lashed into a sheet of white foam or spray passing over it. The scenery through this immense fissure in the mountain baffles description. It was too grand, too sublime, too terrible for me to attempt its description. It was almost as dark as night in the cavern; we had to grope our way through it, over rocks and precipices; although it was nearly midday, we could plainly see the stars shining through the little ribbon of light above us. It took us three hours to make the descent into the valley. As we emerged from the canyon into the daylight and into the valley, everyone was struck dumb with astonishment and wonder at the scene of grandeur and desolation that met our eyes.

The desert valleys that we had passed through in our journey were vales of beauty and productiveness compared to this. The air was hot, stifling and oppressive. There was not a sign of anything to be seen growing, even the moisture-shunning cactus refusing to luxuriate here.

The bosom of the valley was seamed with a thousand cracks. The earth was thrown up in little hard cakes, giving it the appearance of a river in the spring, choked up with broken ice. The valley seemed to be about twenty-five miles wide and sixty or seventy miles in length. The mountains that surrounded it appeared to be of an immense height; the valley was so low, five hundred feet below the sea level. There is not a valley east of the Sierra Nevadas and west of the Rocky Mountains, with this exception, that is not at least one thousand feet above the sea level; the valley of Salt Lake is four thousand feet above the level of the sea.

It has been generally supposed that the members of the Bennet expedition perished in this valley, but this is not the fact; it was on the eastern side of this range of mountains. No white man would ever attempt to cross this valley. The Bennet party probably saw it from the top of the mountains, but it is not probable that any of them were ever in it.

It was about three o'clock when we started to return; as we ascended the canyon, it was even more dark and gloomy than before. The ascent was terribly tedious; we clambered over rocks at the peril of life and limb. The air was so hot and stifling that we could not walk over twenty yards at a time without stopping to rest. We had not proceeded over halfway up the canyon when we were surrounded by almost total darkness and had to feel and grope our way along as best we might; it was terrible to hear the expression of the boys as they met with unseen obstacles.

The canyon echoed with oaths; everything in the country was cursed, including themselves for being led into such a region. We would not advance over two rods through the darkness when a voice would be heard in front telling us to go back; some insurmountable obstacle had been met and we would have to try the other side of our narrow pass. Every little while some rock would become detached and come thundering down the canyon; we would instinctively hug the walls to let it pass. We did not feel desirous of trying to stop it as an experiment.

We did not reach our camp until midnight, and were utterly tired out and used up, and yet we had traveled only about seven miles during the day. If there are any doubts in regard to these statements, I wish to remark that the route down Furnace Creek Canyon is still open to anyone who wishes to undertake the journey. The boys who had been out with our guide prospecting for the "Lost Ledge" had not met with any success, had not discovered anything that indicated even a trace of either gold or silver. We were afraid that "Old Brey's" memory was not improved when he underwent the scalping process.

The water of Furnace Creek was made very palatable by filling our canteens the night before, allowing the water to remain in them all night; in the morning it was cool and refreshing. With the exception of a slight sulphurous taste, it was good, pure water.

The nights were quite cool, requiring us to sleep under a heavy pair of blankets. The second morning we left two men in charge of the camp, the rest of us going out on a prospecting expedition.

"Old Brey" knew that the Ledge could not be over ten miles from the camp, but he could not tell the direction; this gave us a wide field in which to exercise our prospecting talents. Our faith in the guide was daily growing weaker; he was as taciturn as any Indian, and we began to believe that he was silent because he did not wish to expose his ignorance, and had come to the conclusion that he was either a fool or insane.

Six of the party, under the lead of Huxton, proceeded in a northerly direction; the rest put themselves under the guidance of Brey, feeling friendly towards the old man. I joined his party for the day; we took a southeasterly course towards half a dozen isolated mountains that were bunched together in the valley, about eight miles distant.

We found these mountains rocky and barren of vegetation. The formation was metamorphic limestone, a formation in which silver is sometimes found, but there never have been any true fissure veins discovered in it. Where silver has been discovered in limestone formations, as in the case of White Pine, Hot Creek, and Belmont, it has always been in "pockets," or "chimneys" as they are called in mining parlance. Huge outcropping of gray bastard quartz broke through the limestone formation; we found, upon examination, that they contained no mineral beyond a small trace of iron. We prospected about thirty of these ledges with the same result, and traveled over the little bunch of mountains all day without finding the "Lost Ledge," or anything else worth recording.

We returned to camp about sundown, and found that the other party had just arrived. They had met with no better success, nor even as good, as they had not even found a bastard quartz ledge. Twenty or thirty Indians had visited our camp during our absence; they had offered no violence, and had behaved very gentlemanly for Digger Indians.

After comparing notes of the day's work and laying out a programme for the morrow, we retired to our blankets to dream of golden ledges encased in walls of virgin silver. The third morning we concluded to go in one party. Leaving four men in charge of the camp, we bent our steps towards the range of mountains that border Death Valley on the east, and entered the mountains about six miles south of camp. We found the formation to be the same as that of the day before. Gigantic ledges of gray and red bastard quartz loomed up on all sides. The general direction of these barren ledges was northeast and southwest.

We prospected in vain until the middle of the afternoon, when we returned towards the camp, almost satisfied that no mineral existed in this vicinity. We came to the sage conclusion that our guide was a liar, and we politely told him so; had he been a younger man, we would have been tempted to have hung him; as it was, we thought him old and insane and not worth the trouble.

In the evening we held a consultation; the majority voted to remain here three days longer. The fourth morning, Hendricks and his English partner caught their horses and pack mule and expressed their determination to leave at once for Pah Ranagat Valley; they had had a sufficiency of this sort of thing. We did not try to detain them, as they were both of them disagreeable companions—one an obstinate, bull-headed Englishman; the other a cowardly, blatant rebel. We bade them "so long" with no regrets. Neither of them knew anything about the country, and in all probability they would either lose themselves on the desert or fall at the hands of hostile bands of Indians. It is unnecessary to follow the details of our daily trips from our camp on Furnace Creek to the surrounding mountains.

We remained here a week longer, during which time we prospected as thoroughly as possible the country for a circuit of twenty miles around. We were not rewarded in our search by even finding a trace of either gold or silver.

The last day of our prospecting we discovered the last camp that was made by the unfortunate pilgrims who were led into this country by Bennet. The iron work of the wagons, pieces of broken camp utensils, and the bleached bones of human skeletons lay scattered around the desert. They had perished from thirst when within one mile of a beautiful spring.

A monument of stone five feet high had been erected here by Gov. Blaisdell's party, who had traveled through this country one year ago. Three men of his party died from thirst about twenty miles from this place. The whole party would have perished from thirst and hunger had they not met a company of prospectors about seventy miles east of here. The trip of the chief executive of the state of Nevada was one that will be long remembered in this country.

One week from the time of the departure of Hendricks and his partner we left the cheerless vicinity of Death Valley to take up our homeward march towards Pah Ranagat Valley. We were perfectly satisfied that no valuable gold or silver mine lay hidden in the recesses of the mountains that surround Death Valley, although our guide was still sanguine that he would yet live to discover it. We were perfectly willing to leave the search after the golden apples of Death Valley to the next batch of fools who would venture into the country under the leadership of old Breyfogle. In spite of our guide's remonstrances, we concluded to take an almost easterly course on our homeward trip.

Our animals were not what they call "fat" in the States, but they were in good traveling order and able to stand almost any degree of fatigue. The first day after leaving Furnace Creek we traveled about forty miles, crossing two ranges of mountains. We camped on a small creek, not large enough to be dignified with a name, and found the grass very poor. We observed a number of signal fires on the mountains during the night, and were aware that it betokened danger, so we put ourselves in fighting condition. The valley which we were to cross today looked to be about thirty miles in width. We reached the eastern side about four o'clock, and encamped on the banks of a large creek at the mouth of an immense canyon. We had been in camp about thirty minutes when we were alarmed by the cry of Indians; as we heard the alarm, a volley of arrows were received, one of them taking effect in Breyfogle's knee. While four of the party hastened to secure the stock, the balance of us recovered our presence of mind sufficiently to pour a volley into the wretches from our Henry's rifles, killing five of them. The rest beat a hasty retreat; they fired clouds of arrows, but they fell far short of us. They did not even succeed in stealing a single animal; the only injury they inflicted upon us was the wounding of Breyfogle. He remarked "that it was just his d——d luck; if there had been one hundred men in the party, he would have been selected as the victim."

We were now in a dilemma; it was unsafe to remain at our camp. We could not proceed through the canyon, as that would give the Indians an opportunity to kill us all without exposing themselves. We moved our camp about half a mile below the mouth of the canyon, picketed our horses, and placed a guard of four men around them.

Breyfogle's wound was not considered dangerous, but it was very painful; the old man stood it without a murmur, but took a terrible oath against the lives of the whole Indian fraternity, whether friendly or otherwise. There was no disturbance during the night. We had no fears of their attacking us again so long as we remained in an open place, as they had had sufficient evidence of the efficiency of our rifles in the death of five of their number not to want to repeat the attack.

In the morning we proceeded down the valley about six miles in search of a pass over the range; we had no desire to try the experiment of riding through the canyon. We made a litter for Breyfogle, and slung it between two mules so that he rode along very comfortably.

We passed over a small mountain some seven miles south of the canyon, into the next valley. No Indians were seen during the day, nor any fresh traces of them.

We were very cautious, and approached ravines and clusters of greasewood bushes very carefully, to avoid being ambushed. Breyfogle was quite comfortable during the day, and uttered no complaints. We traveled some forty miles, and camped at a spring in the valley about three miles west of a high range of mountains. The grass about the spring was very good, and our horses fared luxuriantly at the end of a picket rope. We stood guard during the night, as we feared that they would try to stampede our stock.

In the morning our animals were packed, and we started, as we hoped, on our last day's drive. We had already traveled over one hundred miles since leaving Death Valley, so that we could not possibly be any great distance from Pah Ranagat. As we crossed a high range of mountains to the east of the valley, we saw in the distance the round snowy summit of Timpeute mountain. It was hailed with joy by every member of the party, I imagine with the same sensation that is felt by the mariner who has been out of sight of land for months. This was the only landmark we had seen since we left that could be called an acquaintance. We almost worshipped his hoary old head as he stood in his gigantic proportions against the eastern sky.

We calculated the distance to the mountain to be about twenty-five miles; our bearings had been correct from the time of leaving Death Valley. Pah Ranagat lay almost due east from this point. We arrived at Timpeute Mountain at dusk, and camped at our old place. A few Indians visited the camp in the early part of the evening, but fled incontinently as "Old Brey," lifting himself up on his elbow, sent a leaden messenger into the band from his revolver; he was satisfied, as he killed one unfortunate wretch who was made to suffer for the crimes of others. Breyfogle was blamed for his rash act, but we did not deem it necessary to get up a quarrel on account of a dead Indian. Owing to this little episode, we were again obliged to picket our horses and stand guard.

In the morning we were up bright and early, and taking nothing but a cup of strong coffee, started for the valley of Pah Ranagat, distant only ten miles. Arrived at Logan Springs at nine o'clock, tired and satisfied with the trip.

Hendricks and his man had not yet arrived; it was easy to guess at their fate. They had undoubtedly been murdered by the same band of Indians who attacked us. Our party now separated; the animals were turned out to graze in the Valley; the men returned to their labor in the mines, to try in that way to make up for the loss of time and money incurred by their trip in search of the Lost Ledge.

Even forty-niner hero William Lewis Manly was lured back into Death Valley again by the promise of lost ledges, as he reveals in this story of the ill-fated Alvord's lost gold, published in the San Jose Pioneer *in May and June of 1895.*

CHARLES ALVORD
by William Lewis Manly

IN 1860 I was requested by my old friend and mining companion Wm. M. Stockton to come to his place near the Mission San Gabriel, in Los Angeles county, and assist him and Mr. Alvord to relocate a rich find Alvord had found in the Death Valley country.

Some enterprising men had fitted out an expedition to go and prospect what had been for years reported to be rich in precious metals, including the wonderful "Gunsight Lead," found out there in Death Valley by the lost emigrants in 1849.

It was now known that the Valley could be entered by wagon from the south, so a good mule team and a load of provisions furnished by a party of five or six men went on a prospecting tour to the supposed rich mines.

With this party went Charles Alvord. He had been educated in a New York college; was ambitious, industrious and energetic; was a thorough horticulturist; and to be able to purchase lands for the purpose of engaging in that business, resolved to go after the "stuff" to that inhospitable region. He was well read in mineralogy, and was familiar with the works of wise men on the subject of the earth's formation. Though perhaps 60 years old, his mind was clear on any subject. In conversation he was easily understood, and could entertain most listeners. He was the foremost man in the prospecting enterprise, and his friends placed all confidence in his ability and honesty. He was a medium-sized man, and quite bald. He enjoyed excellent health, and could endure as much foot work as any man of his age. I am not capable of saying enough of Charles Alvord's good qualities.

Another of the party was Asabel Bennett, who stayed with J. B. Arcane and their wives and families in this barren place in 1849. He was an uneducated man, but was honest, and used to hardships. I think the others were Mormons. One name that I remember was that of John Shipe.

When this party got well out on the desert, they found it too hot to travel in daytime, so they had to work along early and late, lay under their wagons in the middle of the day, and pour water on themselves and wet their clothes in order to keep cool enough to live. They made their camp well up on the south end of the mountain west of Death Valley, where the air was cooler and some holes of water were found and some grass among the sagebrush for the mules.

Mr. Alvord now fixed up a little bundle of grub, took his small pick and shotgun and started off to hunt his fortune. In this big barren mountain he was gone nearly two weeks, and they had about given up his return, supposing the Indians had picked his bones; but he returned and brought many specimens, some that looked extremely well and were supposed to be rich in silver. All the others had been indolent, were in camp every night, but had discovered two veins of bright mineral near camp and believed it to be nearly pure silver. To prove its value, Bennett proposed to go to a high point and build an air furnace such as we used to make in the lead mines in Wisconsin to sharpen our picks. He believed that in this way they could melt the ore, if it was lead. When this was well tried and the ore would not melt, they were all jubilant, and believed they had enough to make the whole company rich.

It would be folly to search any further, so as soon as Mr. Alvord came in they hitched up and went back to Los Angeles, and lost no time in sending their bright shining ore to San Francisco for assay (by Isaac Hartman, a lawyer). When it returned the certificate showed a predominate of lead, and as it was situated where there was no timber nor much water for a hundred miles, it was pronounced worthless—so their mining venture was a failure.

When Mr. Hartman went to San Francisco, Mr. Alvord gave him a specimen that he had not shown to anyone, and told him to keep the result a secret, which Hartman did until his return, when he showed Alvord the assay. Alvord told his best friends, including Bennett and Stockton, what he had found. Mr. Hartman reported that the assayer said that a vein of such ore was only found in one other place in the world, and it was called Nice, and that Alvord's specimens would sell for a fabulous price. On my arrival I was shown the specimens; they were nearly as dark as stone-coal, and speckled with gold.

It seemed that such a good thing could not be kept a secret, and it got out somehow. Several objectionable members of the company insisted that Alvord go and show them the rich ledge, and he was persuaded to return with them. They again fitted out, taking a small set of blacksmith's tools in addition to the usual supplies. They camped as before, and Alvord went in search of the mine. He returned in a few days and stated that he could not find the place; the snow was lower down on the mountain, and the country appeared very different from what it did at his former visit. He had hunted faithfully and could not find the place, but would try again if they would stay during his absence. The vicious Mormons in the company were much incensed because of his failure. The grub was getting low, and they could not stay much longer and have enough on their return trip. The recalcitrants, with Porter Rockwell's sense of justice, proposed to hang Alvord for not finding the mine. Alvord tried to reason with them, showing that his taking off would do them no good, and that no one else would be benefited thereby. "Leave me here, if you think it for your best interest to do so," said Alvord. After a day or two of threatening talk, they concluded to go and "leave the old son-of-a-gun to starve to death," as they said he deserved. They hustled around in anger, and soon had the mules hitched to the wagon and all the best grub loaded in. They swore big oaths as they drove off, no one except Bennett saying good-bye. Alvord was now left alone, and how long his scanty store of provisions would last and what course to pursue bothered him. It was a ten-days' tramp, most of the way over a desert waste, to get out; his provisions scanty; little game in the country. It was a dismal outlook for Alvord.

I will now go back to Los Angeles, where I met Bennett on his return. The others of the party had stopped at San Bernardino. Stockton, Bennett and myself talked the matter over and decided that Alvord must be rescued. If we neglected him, no one would lift a finger in his behalf. We invited Caesar Twitchell to accompany us (Bennett and myself). He was interested in a store at the Mission, and sold out on purpose to take the trip. We took five mules, for riding and packing. In order to go unobserved, we took a back way, by the Mission of San Fernando, and went up the stream where Newhall is now, and took the trail that we came over from Death Valley in 1849. I may say here that the Alvord find created much excitement in Los Angeles at the time, and the Alvord lead is hunted for to this day.

When I concluded that it was my duty to go once again to Death Valley, to save and relieve as good a man as ever lived from starvation, it seemed that I was born for the unwelcome task of rescuing the unfortunate of that terrible Valley. But this man must be saved. We would follow on our '49 trail. I went with Stockton to interview Goller, who with his comrade, another German, came by way of Death Valley in 1849. They could not speak English, and did not become acquainted with others in the train; they traveled together, camped together and slept in the same bed, and were only known as "The Two Dutchmen." After the wagons were all left behind, these two men still kept together as company for each other. When they got through, they told through an interpreter of what they found on the trail—that one day while out hunting for water, one sat down on a rock to rest and his companion called out, "See what I have found." The other asked if it was water, and the answer was, "No, it is gold." Quickly came the answer: "I want no gold now; I want water and bread, that gold will not buy in this dry place. I would not pick up gold here—let us go on and see if we can find water, or we will soon die." Goller, when he got through, started a wagonshop in Los Angeles, and his companion established a clothing store at the Mission San Luis Rey and was soon after killed. Goller carried on his wagon and blacksmith business and was well liked. After a while, a party was fitted out to go with Goller and locate the spot where the gold was found; but upon their arrival in the country he could not discover the place; neither rock, ravine nor mountain was familiar. Wandering about in search of the location for several days without success, the party abandoned the search and returned home. Not long afterward he piloted a second expedition that went to look for the gold they had seen on the trail. They took a different route and came out into a similar looking country. But all was strange; not a mark of any kind could he recognize. He felt lost and bewildered. Discouraged and disappointed, he again returned home, regretting that his friends had placed so much confidence in his story of the finding of gold in that awful country. I asked Goller what trail he came in on in 1849, and he did not know, nor did he know the name of any person he met out there. When I suggested that the find might have been only mica, of which there is plenty and as bright and yellow as gold, he said, "I know how gold looks; I was in the gold mines in Germany; I know I am not mistaken, and if my then partner was now alive he could go right to it." Goller seemed to be without "locality" in his head, and all my inquiries did me no good.

We had camped near the summit. I was the only hunter in the camp and had the only gun; Twitchell was no hunter, and Bennett had partially lost his eyesight and laid his gun away—the one he used to be proud of in 1849. The next day we camped over on the east slope of the Coast Range, at the same water holes we camped at in 1849. Our early troubles and trials now began to come back to me, and I could see quite clearly all that took place on this barren, lonely trail. I thought how foolish I was to go over this trail again. But Alvord's starving condition drove my fears away. I took a field

Lost Ledges

glass and went out on a prominent point of the mountain where I could sweep the country for 150 miles east and south, and it looked as desolate, black, and barren as it did in '49. I sat here perhaps half an hour, and looked the country over and over again, and thought I could see the mountain near Death Valley and could follow with the eye our old trail.

I went back to camp almost sick. Everything that took place on that route, when starvation and death claimed more than a dozen of our party, came to my mind. Strange sensations passed through my brain, my limbs lost their strength, and there was an indifference to my surroundings. When I expressed a doubt as to the expediency of my proceeding with the search, my companions said: "You used to be brave and fearless; why do you weaken so? Spunk up!—don't talk about backing out now." They did not realize how sad and gloomy the remembrance of the time when women, children and strong men were dying in our midst of starvation. But I resolved to throw off the spell and make a supreme effort to discover our lost friend Alvord.

We saddled up and started. Nearly two days before us without a hill, water or grass. The second night we camped in the place we called the Willow Corral. We searched the range faithfully for our second consideration—Goller's lead. First of all, it was our purpose to find the abandoned Alvord, and then to look for mineral. No traces of gold could be found.

As we passed across the level plain before us, we saw the rotten brush we fixed around our camp for a windbreak in 1849. We followed our early trail to the place (now called Providence Spring), where the rocks we fixed up to put our camp-kettle on still stood as we left them, in two rows, with a place for the fire between.

As I had been in the gold mines for several years, I believed I could tell a gold-bearing country. As I had seen nothing that looked to be gold-bearing, we did not search much for the Goller mine, but made up our minds he was mistaken.

The next night we camped at the same falls in a canyon where we pulled our oxen down over a ten-foot fall in '49. Here the Alvord party had pulled rock off the mountain and made a mule trail over the falls. We camped at the water, just above.

In the twilight of that evening, when all was calm and still, we were startled by the sound of footsteps, and turning to look, saw before us what appeared to be the form of our friend Alvord! Was it a mirage, a delusion, or was it reality? We were soon assured that Alvord was found, or rather, that he had found us, for he had seen a mule track and followed it to our camp. The meeting was a joyful

Charles Alvord

one, as he had escaped death by starvation, and our anxiety for his safety was at an end.

Alvord had about exhausted his grub sack and, being eight or ten days' travel from anyplace where he could expect relief, must have soon perished. He was now safe in our company, free from the Mormon ghouls who had left him to starve in the desert because he had failed to discover the gold they coveted, and would be returned to home and friends.

At this place, an Indian came into our camp, followed by his mahala with a basket on her back containing all their earthly possessions. The red man was armed with his bow and arrows, and in the belt about his waist were five or six wood rats, which they skinned, roasted and ate without further separation—nothing was lost.

In the morning we decided to move camp, and get away from Indians who, in my experience, could not be refused grub and kept at peace.

It was now winter, and prospecting on the high peaks difficult, with but little chance of discovering minerals in the valley, and we saddled up and moved on to escape Indians and locate in a safer place. Alvord could make himself understood in the Digger jargon, and assured Mr. Lo in his own language that we were going home, as everything in his country was no good.

We were now comparatively happy, with the rescue of our friend, a supply of provisions, and trusty mules to take us out of the country. Alvord had a narrow escape, as he had not a mouthful of bread and only a few spoonfuls of coffee left when he came to our camp. His prospect was almost hopeless, and if not relieved very soon, his bones, liks those of the '49ers, would shortly have been bleaching in the fiery sun. We were greatly overjoyed on account of the deliverance from the terrible fate that seemed awaiting him.

When we left camp at Providence Springs, they told me to take the lead and try to follow our old '49 trail. As the valley was seven or eight miles wide and very sandy, no sign of it could be seen; the wind had moved the sand and made all smooth, and no sign of our trail was found. But I followed in the most favorable and likely places that we would naturally have traveled, and when we came onto the summit of the range before us, where all the surface was bare rocks, we could see Mr. Fish's bones scattered around among the rocks. This man died here for the want of food and water in 1849.

My feelings as we passed down the mountain cannot be described. As our mules were picking their way among the rocks, all our trials and troubles getting along here years before came to mind.

When we got to the Valley, we had to go some distance south to get around a sluggish stream that ran north into a salt lake. On either side of the stream was a smooth clay bed, where we drove our oxen in '49. Nothing lighter than an ox or mule would make a track in this salt and alkali formation, and here we could plainly see our ox tracks that were made twelve years before.

We now went in a northerly direction some ten or fifteen miles. In a lonely, dark canyon, we found water, some willows, and sage-brush for wood. Here we pitched our little tent, and Bennett and Twitchell took all the mules and started on the trail we came, to go out and get supplies and return as soon as they thought would be necessary before our grub would be exhausted.

I was to do the hunting and Alvord was to prospect. In my wan-derings I occasionally killed a hare. One day, in a deep canyon, I killed three red-tailed henhawks and dressed them, and found them very fat, and as good as any chicken when mixed with lean hare, and all was relished. One night a heavy rain set in, and it loosened many rocks that thundered down the mountainside, one as big as a nail-keg coming within a foot of our tent when we were asleep. We bounded to our feet, supposing that another might follow. It was as narrow an escape as some that were made at the battle of Bull Run, thought we.

We remained here the length of time that was agreed upon for their return, and no one came. We concluded to go and meet them, as they were to come back the way we came out. We baked all of our flour into two small cakes and each took one; wrote a note and left it in the tent telling them when they came that we were nearly starved out and could stay no longer, and would go by Walker's Pass. We took our little knapsacks and started south to strike the trail, which we did the first day. We then turned west, and camped over the sum-mit in an elevated valley. Here we stayed the second night. The wind at this high altitude was cold and disagreeable. Alvord had a boil come on his knee, and walked with much difficulty, so we laid over on his account one day. I went among the low hills, in a wind-break and sunny place, and killed two hare, which gave us grub enough to last to Walker's Pass.

We started early in the morning, but Alvord was very lame and we had a 30-mile tramp to the next water. We sat down to rest by some big rocks, and Alvord says, "Show me where the water is, and then you go ahead, and when you get there make a smoke so I can go straight to you. I may not get there today, but I may travel all night." I fixed my gun on the rocks and sighted it as near as I could to the objective point. When he looked over the gun, he said: "Yes,

I see that barren peak away beyond; it is in exact range; you go on, and I will try to make my way as straight and short as possible; if I should not get there by morning, come back and bring me some water. I know I shall be very thirsty."

With these instructions and agreements, I shouldered my pack and took a beeline for the designated spot. I kept my course on a gradual inclined plane all day; never stopped to rest. The brush that grew on this plain was from four inches to a foot high—I never turned out for one. I reached the place about dark, near the base of the Sierra Nevadas, and went to work gathering sagebrush to make the agreed signal smoke for Alvord's guidance. After filling up with water and grub, I kept up a smoke and blaze until after midnight, when I brushed away the coals and laid down to sleep on the ground I had warmed. The first thing I knew after I laid down—it must have been near morning—Alvord stumbled over me.

On account of his lameness we were obliged to lay by another day. I hunted faithfully, but killed only one hare. Our bread was now reduced to one large biscuit, and more grub must soon be found. Alvord was not able to go to the next water, about eight miles ahead, and we stayed here two nights. The third morning, five or six men came along on mules and horses, going to Visalia. They were acquaintances of Alvord; had found him two months before in the Death Valley country and had camped together. They had also been out to locate a piece of Alvord's reported discovery. They were his friends, and were willing to walk and let him ride. They gave us bread and meat, and we went through Walker's Pass to Kern River, where we stayed all night with a new settler.

A Dr. George of Visalia, and a man named Jackson (a Mormon) were with the party we met, and of whom I shall again speak in this narrative.

From here we pushed on over Greenhorn Mountain, and came out near Tule River, where I found one of my old Moore's Flat, Nevada County, friends—Jim Tyler. As soon as he found out where I had been, he said, "'Spose you're broke." I said, "Yes, flat down." He pulled out three twenties and handed them to me. This was a happy find, and when we reached Visalia we got on the overland stage for San Jose, where we arrived in due time via Pacheco Pass and Gilroy.

Some years afterwards, we learned that the party we sent for supplies became snowed in and nearly perished, and, believing that we would starve or go out of the valley before they could reach us, had failed to return.

It had been agreed that we would go back to Death Valley in the spring, as early as we could get over the Greenhorn Mountain. . . . In

Lost Ledges

March, 1861, Alvord and I secured the services of Dick Hickman (a Moore's Flat acquaintance) to drive our team, and starting with a good pair of mules hitched to a strong spring wagon, with the proper supply of bacon, flour, sugar, coffee, etc., we took our way by Gilroy and Pacheco Pass to Visalia, and so on over Greenhorn Mountain.

The Visalia people, after the discovery of the Coso mines, came to believe that the "Gunsight lead" and the "Alvord find" would soon be located, and they built a wagon road over the roughest part of Greenhorn Mountain, to draw the mine hunters their way and make a market for their products. The road was a rough one, but we had a reliable team, and arrived safely in Kernville, a mining town at the forks of Kern River. Here we crossed the river and went up a valley several miles long, through Walker's Pass, and followed around the base of the Sierra Nevada mountains in a northerly direction to Owen's Little Lake, where we turned east and drove toward the Coso mines, lately discovered and reported to be good. We expected to store some of our supplies when the road got too rough. We soon left our wagon and load, with Alvord to guard them, while Hickman and myself went to look out a way to the mining camp— some five or six miles before us. When we got there, a friend loaned us three or four pack mules to bring in our stuff.

On our way back to Coso we passed a lone butte; all around its base was quite a windrow of what appeared to be broken blue or green glass—this was Bottle Glass Mountain. Further east we came on top of the ridge, and here a small volume of sulphurous smoke came out of a hole in the ground, and all around it was thickly coated with sulphur. I was a little afraid to go too near, for fear I might break through and go to "that undiscovered country" before I was quite ready. As this descended east, it and some other small points came together and formed a main canyon; at this spot was one of the hottest springs I ever saw; all around there the surface was as smooth as a plastered wall—no living thing grew upon it. One pond, twenty or more feet square, was deep and clear as crystal, and more than a thousand jets of steam came through the water, making a hissing noise that could be heard a hundred yards away, and the water was as hot as steam could make it—the best place to wash dishes I ever saw.

As we walked around over this clean, white floor, we looked into some big cauldron-shaped holes; as the floor was hot, we stretched our necks and gazed down and down, and could see a single rolling, boiling pot of green, red and blue liquid continuously in motion, like a big pot of dirty-looking stuff. Further up the ravine was a larger pond, resembling an excavation for a house, and in the middle the water seemed to be agitated. The man I stayed with on Kern River told me he came there on his mule and rode around to see the boiling pots and his mule broke through the crust formed there; but Mr. Mule took his foot out awful quick. The red mud took the hair and hoof off his mule's leg, and the hoof never grew on again.

This was a good place to camp for a warm bed, but the water was unfit to drink; some who hunted for the coolest and drank it were affected like one who has taken strychnine. We passed on, and reached Crystal Springs, and our journey by wagon was ended. We now put our provisions in a large tent belonging to the Rough and Ready Company, who had come here from San Francisco to prospect a claim by that name.

Mr. Alvord thought he would be able to obtain some mining information of those passing this point daily, as some good specimens were shown that had been found in the vicinity. He stayed to make discoveries, and I returned to the wagon with Hickman, who rolled away for San Jose. I returned to Coso.

A few days after, we got news that the War of the Rebellion had broken out and that South Carolina had seceded and Sumpter been fired upon. Southern sympathizers were plentiful, and several left promptly for the front. Pistol practice was brisk, the shooters were jubilant and declared that they would soon have a new government of their own, as "one Southern man was good for three or four Yanks," etc. Things were hot for a time.

We prospected here until near the first of July. I bought a donkey and was making preparations to cross the valley east and into the mountain near Death Valley, in search of "Alvord's find." He said: "I want you to go with me and try to find that vein, as whether we discover it or not, they will believe you—but never me."

We told some friends where we were going. They said: "You are making a mistake; you will, at this time of the year, have to cross the Valley in the night; you can never endure the midday sun; no water for 40 miles; besides you should not go alone—some were killed there last year by the Indians, and a party is safer." Indians do not like to have the top of that mountain, where there are pingone pines, taken possession of by white men. They consider the pinaries especially theirs—as it is from those trees that they procure the pine nuts for food.

Many of the prospectors believed that Alvord would locate his mine, and that if they were with him it would be to their advantage, and they told us that if we would go up on the Sierras where it was

124   Lost Ledges

cool and there were fish and game, and remain there until several of them should visit Visalia for supplies and return, that they would accompany us on our trip. We concluded to wait for them, and went onto the mount on the 4th of July—to the head of the south fork of Kern River. Here was a beautiful, clear stream running through a wide valley, hundreds of springs feeding the river, timber, grass and water abundant, trout, grouse, woodchucks, deer, and bear. I killed one fine buck and two small grizzlies. What a contrast between this place and the country a few miles to the east, where we come to a desert hot as purgatory, dry as powder, and almost worthless to mankind.

We remained on the mountain about two weeks, in sight of perpetual snow. As our acquaintances did not return as agreed, we loaded our donkey and started for Kernville, thinking perhaps they had come back that way. We went over to the north fork and followed it down. Hunted on a trail two days—plenty of "signs" but no bear. We camped near Caldwell's, a short distance above the little town. Our friends had not come that way. We were welcome to share the house of Mr. Caldwell, who was a miner and run an *arrastra* by water. We were warned not to attempt to go upon the desert in the summertime, that it was the hottest place on earth, that the air became so arid that men died through lack of moisture in the atmosphere, although supplied with water, and that a man without water could not live an hour.

Finding that it would be perilous to proceed further, I resolved to return home. Alvord, the donkey and myself crossed the mountain via Wagg's ranch, to Lyn Valley, to meet the Visalia stage. I gave Alvord the donkey and what money I had after paying my fare to Visalia, where I borrowed of the Agent of the Overland Stage Co. to pay my way to San Francisco. At Stockton I left my moccasins made of the skins of the bears I had killed, got a pair of cheap shoes, and took deck passage for San Francisco—sleeping on the heads of some barrels. Arriving in the city, I borrowed fifty dollars of my friend T. Barker and sent money to pay that I had borrowed at Visalia.

Soon after I reached home, I received a letter from Mr. Caldwell dated at Kernville, saying that Mr. Jackson had persuaded Alvord to go with him and prospect for coal on the west side of Kern Lake, where Jackson said he had been and found bituminous springs. Caldwell expressed anxiety for the safety of Alvord, stating that he had been down the river, where he saw a man in possession of Alvord's gun, and when asked where he got it, said that he had bought it of Jackson. The gun was one easily recognized, as it was of a kind seldom seen, with long barrels and silver ornaments on the wood—a double-barrelled shotgun. A few days later Caldwell had been down the river and seen Alvord's donkey. Inquiring where the donkey was obtained, the possessor said he bought him of Jackson, and that he thought things looked very crooked. The suspicions of those living in the vicinity were aroused. Jackson's camp was visited, but neither Alvord nor Jackson could be found. They watched and waited for their return, but they never came. Jackson's mule was gone, but otherwise the place did not seem to be abandoned. There was a delay; officers were three or four days distant, and it was thought best to await his return, then try him on the spot, and hang him if deemed guilty of murder. But Jackson did not appear. He was afterwards heard of in Shasta County, and was supposed to have gone to Salt Lake, as he was of the Mormon persuasion. Alvord was never again seen alive by his friends.

The news of Alvord's supposed murder caused much interest to be taken in an effort to investigate the circumstances and a party, including his friend Dr. George, saddled their horses and left Visalia for Alvord and Jackson's camp with a view to make a thorough investigation and discover if possible the fate of Alvord. During their search they found near the camp a human skeleton, stripped of every particle of flesh by birds and wild animals. The Doctor examined the head and found there had been a murder committed. The top of the head had been pierced with a charge of buckshot, and this was probably done while the murdered man was in bed and asleep. Dr. George also found a pocketknife nearby, which he recognized as one that belonged to Alvord. The particulars of the search and finding of the evidence named was related to me by Dr. George, who declared that he believed that Alvord was murdered by Jackson. Of the motive which would lead to a murder as indicated, there were various conclusions. It might have been done solely for the purpose of plunder, or it might have been the result of a misunderstanding. At any rate it was certain that Jackson had in his possession Alvord's property, which he disposed of and then disappeared.

Alvord was a man about 60 years of age, healthy, vigorous and strong in body and mind, a college-educated man, a linguist, liberty-loving, companionable, and a true friend. He was a genuine Pioneer.

SEARCHING FOR

*By the latter part of the nineteenth century, when veteran prospector Milo
Page began his quest, the elusive ledges were thoroughly lost in myth. Yet
Page was rewarded in his search by the discovery of what he, at least,
believed was Goller's lost gold, as he tells in this reminiscence from the Sierra
Magazine of February 1909. Page actually made wages for a few years
working the high-grade ore in a little arrastra near Anvil Spring.*

THE LOST GOLLER
by Milo Page

WHEN SOFT WINDS sigh upon the Amargosa, and the mists begin to
gather over the spectral wastes of Death Valley, the sand devils
cease their play and Berg Hexen come out for their nightly orgies. It
is said, even to this day, that the disappointed ghost of old Anton
Breyfogle is taken in hand by these evil spirits and made to dance in
spritely celebration about Stump Springs. Be that as it may, I will
not here begin to account for all of the strange superstitions of prospectors, nor attempt to draw up a heavy artillery of cosmic philosophy to aid me in dispelling the illusions of lost mines. I too have
sipped of the Lethian waters of Stump Springs on a hot day, and
have gazed upon the weird mirages ever hovering over the dismal
desert that weaves its fantastic terrors about this land, but I have
never lost a mine once I had found it, nor have I stumbled from here
in a half-dazed condition upon nuggets of pure gold or ledges of
solid silver, in my wanderings through this land. Yet to Stump
Springs we trace the origin of three well-authenticated Lost Mines,
and no doubt if the exact history of all such were known, others
who quenched their thirst at Stump Springs have traced from here
their route to the will-o'-the-wisp mine, which they could never
relocate.

Old Anton Breyfogle was not the first to visit this isolated water
hole in the heart of the great Amargosa desert. In the spring of 1849
a party of eighty emigrants, many of them Mormons, making their
tortuous way across country en route to California, followed an uncertain route from Vegas springs westward, bearing a few points
to the north. They were a weary, hopeless caravan of desert wanderers, whose throats were parched with alkali dust and whose faith
in God and man had been severely shaken. Among them was John
Goller, a sturdy man of 34, who had joined the outfit at Independence, Missouri. From Salt Lake they had followed the old Mormon
road down the Rio Virgin, and then westward to the Muddy river,
from where they had come directly to Vegas springs. Their most
treasured possession was a map of California, on which were marked

the Sierra Nevada mountains and Walker Pass, for which they were making. They had no guide. Drifting sands had obliterated the road out from Vegas. I have been told by members of this party that in a short time they became thoroughly bewildered. The orders and advice of their leaders were not obeyed. About them was an endless, discouraging waste of pale green desert, dotted between its shifting sand dunes by sickly sagebrush and the more brilliant greasewood. Across their horizon, directly in front, lay a low range of mountains, black as burned basalt. They formed an uninviting prospect, with a grim skyline and bleak sides, but there was no better in sight. And furthermore, by sheer accident the wanderers had come upon a faint sort of a line marked upon the sand, which was recognized as an Indian trail, and its way by nightfall led them to Stump Springs, at the foot of the Tecopah range.

This same party of emigrants worked their way westward from these springs into the very heart of Death Valley where, leaderless and thoroughly bewildered, many of them perished a few weeks later at Emigrant Springs; but in tracing out the history of the Goller mine, we must follow a different route. Goller, it appears, became dissatisfied with the manner in which the party was being conducted, and thoroughly disgusted with the entire outfit. Unwilling, however, to brave the unknown terrors of this land entirely alone, he persuaded another man to join him, and with a fair supply of food and one canteenful of water for each, they left the rest of the party at Stump Springs and took a due westerly course. It was in August, when the nights are not cold, and the two men carried no blankets. Indian trails were their sole guide, but these proved good guides, leading them from one spring to another, so that at no time did Goller and his companion suffer from thirst. They were bearing as straight as possible towards Walker's Pass. They must have been good travelers too, for in about ten days they reached Elizabeth Lake, some forty miles southwest of the present town of Mojave, and falling in with another party, presumably Mexicans, they soon reached Los Angeles, where Goller established himself in business as a blacksmith and wheelwright.

Goller's companion went north, first to San Francisco, then to northern mines, where he made a small fortune, and in time returned to his old home in Maine. I became acquainted with Goller in 1861. He was then a man of 45, a jovial sort of a man too, as one frequently finds among his kind and profession, and I enjoyed visiting his shop, where he presided with sledge and tongs over anvil and forge. But our acquaintance, the result of our business dealings, remained always on a business footing, and strange as it now seems to me, I learned nothing from him about the lost mine of which he was the hero and discoverer. All this I learned in after years from a younger man, whose last name was Riley and whose first name I have either forgotten or have never known. Riley served an apprenticeship under Goller, and, as an apprentice will, when, no doubt, he should have been working, frequently overheard Goller confiding in some favorite patron the story of his lost mine. He was never overfree in these confidences when Riley was about, and from the many different versions of the story which Goller told, I doubt not that Riley's eavesdropping was little to his liking. And yet Riley was a pleasant sort of a fellow too, with whom I became very well acquainted during the years of '60 and '61 at Darwin, but if Goller mistrusted him and purposely permitted the apprentice to gather a confused idea of the lost mine story, he was entirely successful, for Riley was not only confused, but disbelieved the whole yarn. I met Riley again at Darwin in '76, and we talked about the Goller mine. He confessed then that in his opinion Goller was merely a shrewd speculator, who purposedly told a luring tale to prospectors in order that he might induce them to go into this dangerous country, where gold was believed to lie in great quantities, and if, perchance, one of these should find a mine, that he might share with the finder in its riches.

The fact remains, however, that Goller did possess two very rich and peculiar specimens of gold rock. One was red, like the gold from the Kern River section, and the other was yellow, like specimens from Holcomb Valley. And my faith in Goller's story was considerably strengthened by the fact that I had, myself, found three different classes of gold rock in Holcomb Valley, and all in the same gulch, which differed in color as well as in fineness.

Up to this time, however, I had thought little of the Goller mine, and had made no attempt either to verify his story or to locate the rich deposit of placer gold which he claimed to have discovered during that eventful trip from Stump Springs to Elizabeth Lake. But as years passed, more and more was to be heard about it. It became a topic of common conversation around camp fires, where miners and prospectors gathered, and as the story traveled, from camp to camp and from man to man, it grew as such stories always grow. I think at one time its fame and richness equalled that of the old Gunsight, while some variations became extremely absurd. I remember one man describing the Goller lost mine, and speaking of Goller as the leader of a large body of men with whom he traveled through this section and from whom he strayed, only to wander, in the manner of sailor Sinbad, into a deep valley which was literally covered with gold nuggets. These, so accurate was the description of this vivid tale, had crumbled from a great outcrop of gold quartz, and could this mysterious spot be relocated, a reward of tons upon tons of the precious stuff would fall to the lucky discoverer. Despite these exaggerated versions of the Goller mine, however, and Goller's frequently repeated story of his find, few men made the attempt to trace his route through the desert or take up the trail which he with his companion had traveled from Stump Springs to Elizabeth Lake. No doubt the reason for this was largely due to the vague descriptions which Goller gave of the land, and that indefiniteness about the whole affair which causes even the most hardy adventurer to pause before a trip into Death Valley.

I think, in fact, that the story of Goller's lost mine would in time have passed utterly into the realm of myths, but for one man in whom Goller confided, with a remarkable vividness of details and accuracy of descriptions about water holes, mesquite groves, willows, and other landmarks, outlining the whole route so clearly and simply that anyone familiar with this country could easily follow it. Accompanying this story of his wanderings and discovery of the mine, Goller gave this man, a Mr. John Taggert, a rancher living near Azusa near the San Gabriel River, a map drawn entirely from memory in the early fifties, only a few years after the events described took place.

I too had become acquainted with Taggert in 1859, but it was not until 1880 that he told me of his possessions relating to the Goller mine. We met accidentally at the Gilbert's ranch in Deep Springs Valley, some thirty miles east of the town of Bishop. Neither had heard of the other for many years, and we renewed our friendship, which had been only casual, into one of an intimate acquaintance. He then confided the fact that he possessed the map, and also that he had taken a number of trips into the region described by it, sometimes alone and sometimes with companions. Taggert was then a man of fifty. It was almost thirty years since he had received from Goller that incentive which was to keep him for so many years a veritable slave to this mysterious land of illusions, but now, too, his days of adventure had nearly passed. He had come to Deep Springs Valley for his health and, accompanied by his daughter, had no inclination to venture again into the heart of the Panamints where the Goller mine, according to his map, was located. And it was here that he finally gave me that authentic map and account of Goller's trip from Stump Springs, which subsequently enabled me to follow almost step by step, as it seemed, in the trail taken by Goller and his companion. Both the map and the story, as told by Goller and repeated by Taggert to me, I give here item for item and word for word, as nearly as my memory serves me. Thoroughly acquainted with all the ground covered by these early travelers, I saw vividly the whole route over which they passed, from the curious springs from which they started alone, to the lonely canyon in the Panamints where lay, no doubt to this very day, the rich ledges of Goller's dreams.

Having left the emigrants at Stump Springs, Goller and his companion walked westward, following an Indian trail which they knew would take them by the shortest possible route to the nearest water, in which they were not mistaken, for they soon came to a broad and very low valley in which lay a fine meadow. Large springs of good water bubbled from the ground. A forest of trees more than a mile in length and half a mile wide extended along the course of a creek of flowing water. They crossed the valley, continuing still in the westerly direction, and passed over a low range of mountains through a gap which led them down a very precipitous dry wash. This wash also opened upon a deep and large valley. A creek broke from the heat-blistered rocks at the foot of the wash, leading them onward for about a mile, when it suddenly again disappeared in the sand. This was Furness Creek, a name to be applied in after years, and this deep, broad valley into which they had come was that same silent, uncompromising place where death so soon would begin his heavy taking of toll.

Across Death Valley and still to the westward arose before them a high mountain, rough and precipitous. Yet the Indian trail which had brought them into the valley still held its true course onward, crossing the level floor of the valley from the creek to the base of the mountain in a somewhat southerly direction. It was only a few miles across the valley at this point, and neither Goller nor his companion appear to have experienced any difficulty in crossing. They followed their trail. First it led up a broad, sandy wash, but this soon narrowed to a deep gulch, coming finally to three mesas where springs and grass invited them to rest. One of these springs formed a small creek which fell over a considerable precipice. From these springs their trail led upwards and through a dense growth of mesquite trees, and above these the narrow canyon opened out into a small valley at the extreme north end of which nestled closely against a high mountain was a butte, colored in stripes, and one of these peculiarly tinted hills which are commonly known as "calico" in this desert country. Along the southern edge of the valley was a willow grove through which the trail led, and forking on the further side, one leading westward through a divide lying between two high peaks and the other turning abruptly toward the south and passing to the left of a high mountain. Goller and his companion disagreed here as to the best course to follow, the disagreement ending in a separation, Goller following the westerly trail, while his companion followed the one toward the south. Goller, after passing through the low divide, found himself in a deep canyon where he came upon a stream of running water, thickly wooded by clumps of mesquite and willows. The stream here was fully two feet wide and had its course directly through the midst of the trees, but it was a shallow little creek, not over four inches deep.

Tired and footsore, Goller here rested, taking off his boots and laving and bathing his inflamed feet. While so engaged he noticed a piece of brick-colored rock lying in the water, and from it, showing on all sides of its washed surface, the delicate particles of yellow metal. Yet Goller was not a mining man. He had never seen gold in its original state. Curious, however, and wondering if this was gold, he took up the piece of rock, examined it carefully, even to an adhesion of black substance which interested him quite as much as the yellow. The black substance was firmly attached, however, and an attempt to break it off with the knife resulted in a broken blade, which so disgusted Goller that he threw the piece of rock down, pulled on his boots, and stalked resolutely down the canyon. He walked until night overtook him, slept under a shelving of cemented rock, and the following morning made his way to three falls, the lower one so abrupt he was compelled to climb around the hillside to pass. This fall was at the extreme end or mouth of the canyon, and this he held to be by far the best landmark by which this particular canyon might be found. This canyon once located, Goller insisted the rest would be easy enough, and firmly believed, that no doubt a rich ledge of free gold rock could easily be found in the vicinity of the piece which he had taken from the stream and had again so foolishly thrown away.

After leaving the canyon his trail cut southward, and towards noon he came upon a broad alkali flat where, to his great surprise, he again met and joined his companion, who had arrived at the same flat by the other trail. Glad to get together again, they walked south. About three miles from the valley and upon a tableland they came to another spring, which was at the foot of another low range of mountains. They crossed this range, bearing always toward the southwest, and in passing on the western slope down a very rocky canyon, he picked up those specimens of gold ore which he later exhibited at his shop in Los Angeles. They crossed one more broad valley, and without another mishap came safely to Oak Creek and

Willow Springs, west of Mojave, from where the road to Elizabeth Lake was straight and easy. By following always Indian trails, they had come regularly to the various springs en route, but had missed their objective, Walker's Pass, by many miles.

With reference to the map outlined by Goller, I determined to make an effort to trace his course from Stump Springs to where he located the rich gold float in the creek wherein he bathed his feet, and I had no difficulty in marking upon Goller's map the following places, which received names after Goller had passed that way. In the order in which Goller discovered them, they must have been as follows: Stump Springs, Ash Meadows, Furnace Creek, Butte Valley, Goller Canyon, Lone Willow Spring, Garlock, Willow Springs and Elizabeth Lake. At Butte Valley, the two forks of the trail at which Goller and his companion separated are still in evidence, and on the south side of Goller's Canyon, I indicated the quartz mines, below which he no doubt found the rich float. The placer specimens which he found later on were in all probability from Garlock, where the location was shown on Goller's map as placer mines.

All this was made clear to me by Taggert's map and story. In 1878, while prospecting in the vicinity of Ash Meadows, I met a party of men who frankly admitted they were searching for the Lost Goller. They said they had traced out Goller's companion, finding him in Maine, and showed me both a letter from him and a rough sketch of a map which had marked upon it the route taken by the two men. This was before I met Taggert, and my interest in this alleged myth was not very great. In fact, so slight was my interest in the whole matter that I did not remember the name of Goller's companion, and very few of the details described in his letter, excepting that he did speak of having been separated from Goller for one night, of their meeting on the alkali flat the next day, and the fact that Goller made the discovery of the mine during the time they separated. He described the place where the trails forked, marking it plainly as south of the calico butte. This was identical with the facts given by Goller himself. The letter further advised the owners of it to search the small valley into which the western trail followed by Goller must take them. Even then I recognized the calico butte and the valley referred to, but despite the numerous questions which these men asked of me, I was reticent with information. Such knowledge as I possessed of this country had cost me many years of hard labor, and great privations to acquire, and if profit was to come therefrom, I proposed to enjoy this profit myself. I had become acquainted with calico butte as early as 1874 and 1877, and had, when I met this party, come from the section of the Panamints not over four months hence. We parted after some conversation, and to this day I have no knowledge as to what became of this party.

I cannot think, in my quest for lost mines, that I have ever had strong within me the hope of finding a great treasure for which many have searched hopelessly. And yet, there is a fascination in these quests among bewildering mountains and the mysterious deserts. In June, 1883, I was again in the Panamints and in the vicinity of the old town of Panamint. About thirty miles south of this town lies a little valley with the colored butte, and this valley in every respect answers the description given by Goller. On the west side of this valley, elevated on a tableland, is an old landmark now known as Anvil Spring, and near here some Mormon prospector as early as 1858 erected a crude furnace in which they smelted the ores found in a nearby mine.

Without really thinking much about Goller's discovery near here, I came by accident upon a spring some three miles south of Anvil Spring, and moving my camp to this place, I prospected on a ridge south of a deep canyon, and was rewarded by finding a rich but small vein of quartz, a pure white mixed with a dark red in color, and containing a large percentage of galena and silver ore, some pieces of this galena adhering to the quartz. Much of the red ore was highly impregnated with gold, the yellow particles showing plainly at a distance of ten or twelve feet, and where galena appeared the ore seemed richest. And my wonderment regarding the possibility of having discovered the long-lost Goller mine was made even greater by a clump of mesquite trees some 600 yards below this mine, but water there was none. And still the idea that I had found the Goller mine did not become positive in my mind until much later, when I had realized on my rich discovery, some of the ore going into thousands of dollars to the ton. Yet far down the canyon were the same falls; here was the calico butte, here were the two forks of the trail, the three springs, the clumps of mesquite and willows. Everything seemed almost identical as related to me by Taggert, excepting the flowing water. For miles up and down, the canyon was as dry as a bone. There was no rivulet breaking its way through the grove of trees in which a tired wanderer might bathe his feet. Only the grim canyon walls on both sides and the immutable peaks of the Panamints, and below, far below, the silent valley that held so many of the emigrants whom Goller and his companion had abandoned at Stump Springs.

Once, in my wanderings about these mountains I met an Indian. He came with his family from Elizabeth Lake. "Ben," he said, when I asked his name. He was not an old man, not over 40 perhaps, but he had been born in the Panamints and had gone away when a boy. He seemed to take great delight in visiting the scenes of his childhood, too, and only in one instance did he appear to have been disappointed. "Heap water here," he indicated the canyon, and would have had me believe a stream, three feet wide, six inches deep, had disappeared. Perhaps this was so. Who knows? Perhaps this was Goller's canyon? It may be. And the ledge which I found may have been his fabulous mine. If so, its fame was far more important than its existence. Who knows? A lost mine is never really found, for the gold ledge that is once lost must forever glitter in the minds of men.

Twenty-Mule Teams

THE REAL MINERAL WEALTH OF Death Valley was not in the lodes of silver and gold presumably hidden in the surrounding hills, but in the great borax bonanza, much of which lay exposed for all to see right under foot. The vast deposits on the floor of the valley were worked for only half a dozen years from 1882 to 1888. But the saga of the twenty-mule teams that hauled out that borax has become one of the best-known episodes of Death Valley's history. For in the years that followed, "Borax King" Francis Marion Smith sent the famous teams on tours throughout the Eastern states promoting sales of the washday miracle through the romance of Death Valley until "Twenty Mule Team Borax" became a household phrase. The romance of those early days has almost completely overshadowed the story of the later, much more productive borax mining on up Furnace Creek at Ryan.

SHE BURNS

John Randolph Spears, an adventuresome New York Sun *correspondent hired by "Borax" Smith, first told the romantic story of Aaron Winters's Death Valley borax discovery in his now classic little book* Illustrated Sketches of Death Valley and Other Borax Deserts of the Pacific Coast, *published in 1892.*

GREEN, ROSIE!
by John Randolph Spears

NOTWITHSTANDING the fact that prospecting parties, some of them composed of educated, practical men, lured by the story of the Gunsight lead, visited Death Valley frequently after the fatal journey of the emigrant party in 1850, it was not until about thirty years had passed that any substance of commercial value was found within the limits of the valley, and then it was a citizen of the country, a genuine white Arab of this great American desert, who made the discovery, and the subsequent discoveries in the Furnace Creek Cañon and the Amargosa were all made by men of the same class.

These citizens of the American desert are a remarkable class of frontiersmen in more respects than one, but in no respect more remarkable than in their choice of a homesite. Some of them have been there from twenty to thirty years—white men had been in Death Valley before the emigrant party that gave it its name perished there. Where they came from and why they went there are questions not to be answered. It is not polite in desert society to ask questions of that kind. This rule, one may say, is *de rigueur*. Society leaders there have been known to resent an infraction of desert social usages with a Winchester, but I apprehend that some of these men went there during the Civil War in an effort to escape the draft, some were deserters from the army, some went there because there were sheriffs with warrants in some other places, and some for the same reason that the old sailors drank whiskey—because they liked it.

I guess Aaron Winters went there for two of these reasons. He certainly liked the country, and it is said that he had killed two men in his time. He has certainly killed one since, and how he did it is worth telling. Mr. Aaron Winters, it may be said, was a highly respected member of the most exclusive social circle of the desert.

In no way can I so well describe the class of men of which he is a type as by relating the stories I was told about him and the four or five who discovered the borax deposits in and about Death Valley.

In the year 1880, Winters was living with his wife Rosie in a valley known as Ash Meadows, just east of Death Valley. The name of the valley came from some stunted ash brush that once grew there. It was habitable for a family or two, because a little bunch-grass grew there on which a few cattle could feed; there were mesquite trees within twenty-five or thirty miles sufficient to supply an abundance of mesquite beans, which serve the Arabs in place of flour, and, more important than all the rest, there was a flowing spring of good water. Mr. C. M. Plumb, who visited it at the time, has preserved the following description of this odd frontier home of Aaron Winters:

"Close against the hill, one side half-hewn out of the rock, stood a low stone building, with a tule-thatched roof. The single room within was about fifteen feet square. In front was a canvas-covered addition of about the same size. The earth, somewhat cleared of broken rock originally there, served as a floor for both rooms. There was a door to the stone structure, and directly opposite this was a fireplace, while a cook stove stood on a projecting rock at one side of it. At the right was a bed, and at the foot of the bed a few shelves for dishes. A cotton curtain was stretched over some clothing hanging on wooden pegs in the corner.

"On the other side was the lady's boudoir—a curiosity in its way. There was a window with a deep ledge there. A newspaper with a towel covered the ledge, in the center of which was a starch box supporting a small looking glass. On each side of the mirror hung old brushes, badly worn bits of ribbon and some other fixings for the hair. Handy by was a lamp-mat, lying on another box, and covered with bottles of Hogan's Magnolia Balm, Felton's Gossamer for the Complexion, and Florida Water—all, alas, empty but still cherished by the wife, a comely, delicate Spanish-American woman with frail health and little fitted for the privations of the desert.

"The shelves about the room and the rude mantel over the fire-place were spread with covers made of notched sheets of newspaper. Two rocking chairs had little tidies on their backs. The low flat pillows were covered with pillow shams and the bed itself with a tawny spread. In place of a library there were a number of copies of the Police Gazette. There was a flour barrel against the wall, a small bag of rice nearby, and two or three sacks of horse feed in a corner. The sugar, coffee, and tea were kept under the bed.

"The water of the spring ran down the hill and formed a pool in front of the house, and here a number of ducks and chickens, with a pig and a big dog, formed a happy group, a group that rambled about in the house as well as romped beside the water of the spring.

A few cattle grazed on the bunchgrass of the valley that stretched away before the house, gray and desolate."

It was just 200 miles across the desert from this home to the nearest settlement or railroad station.

One day, about the year 1880, a strolling prospector—one of the desert tramps—came along, bound probably from some Nevada town to Resting Springs to eat up a grubstake. He tarried overnight at the Winters home, and told Winters a long story about the borax deposits up in Nevada, and what a great fortune awaited the man who could find more borax deposits. Winters was a shrewd fellow, and he asked many questions in a casual way and said nothing in return. Among other things, the prospector told him that one could test a supposed deposit of borax by pouring certain chemicals over some of the stuff and then firing the mixture. If it was borax the chemicals would burn with a green flame. Telling that was the only good thing that a tramp prospector ever did, so far as I learned.

When his guest had gone, Winters made haste to get chemicals. He had been in Death Valley more than once, had seen stuff there that answered the description of Nevada borax, and he was going to see what the Death Valley marsh held.

He took his wife with him, not only when he went after his chemicals but when he went prospecting in Death Valley. That was due to one of his peculiar characteristics. It happens sometimes that a long spell of rainy weather prevails over the desert in the spring of the year. When the rain at last clears off and the warm sun comes out, countless millions of plants spring up from the dust and sand, and the arid waste becomes one vast carpet of fragrant flowers. Aaron Winters was like the desert he lived on. His character was an arid waste in most respects, but he loved his wife.

Going over to Death Valley, this strange couple camped on Furnace Creek, and going down into the marsh gathered a small quantity of the most likely looking deposit they could find, Winters "talking all the while and teetering and wobbling about," as was his habit when excited. Then they went back to camp and got supper, for the fire test could not be made by daylight.

At last the sun went down and the flaming colors in the western sky faded and darkened until the shadows in the gorge of the Funeral Mountains where Winters was camped became absolutely black. By the faint glow of a few dying coals Winters and his wife sat down on the sand, put a saucer of the material on a rock between them, poured the chemicals and alcohol over it, and then Winters scratched a match to fire the mixture. How would it burn? For years they had lived as the Piutes live on the desert. Not only had the wife to do without the little luxuries and comforts dear to a woman's heart; they had both lived on mesquite beans and chahwallas when the flour and bacon were gone—they had even gone hungry for lack of either. Would the match change all that? Winters held the blaze to the mixture in the saucer with a trembling hand and then shouted at the top of his voice: "She burns green, Rosie! We're rich, by ———."

They had found borax. William T. Coleman, noted as the leader of the San Francisco Vigilance Committee, and in other ways as well, was then a borax magnate. So was Mr. F. M. Smith. Soon after the news that it had burned green had reached San Francisco, two agents were sent by the firm of Coleman & Smith to the rude home in Ash Meadows. They found Winters a tough-fibered man, short in stature, stout in frame, dark-haired and with a full, florid face—past sixty years of age, but well preserved—in fact in every way a rugged frontiersman. He was slow of speech, somewhat reserved and unapproachable in manner, but a hearty, square man, bluff, brave, and generous. When it was understood that the newcomers were there for business, Rosie got a bag of pine nuts somewhere in the camp, and while cracking and eating these around the camp fire the bargain was made. The deposit brought $20,000.

On getting his money, Winters went over to Pahrump oasis, in Nevada, and bought out one Charles Bennett, who had made a ranch there, bargaining to pay $20,000 for the outfit, of which $15,000 was cash in hand, the balance being covered by a fatal mortgage. Then he and Rosie sat down there and enjoyed life for a time, but the hardships previously endured had been too great for the wife. Prosperity came too late, and within two or three years she died.

One more characteristic story is related of Winters. It happened in the usual course that he had to go to Belmont, the county seat, one fall on business—among other things to pay his taxes. It was a journey of several hundred miles, and Winters rather expected that someone would "hold him up" for what money he had along, and prepared for it by putting a worthless pistol in a holster on the dashboard of his buckboard, and a first-class Navy revolver under the cushion.

Sure enough, at a convenient place as he neared Belmont, two men "got the drop on him," and he was obliged to get off the vehicle and deliver up his cash. This he did with much talk and palaver. He was going to Belmont to pay taxes, and it was all the money he had and all he could raise. If he didn't pay the taxes he'd be ruined, and wouldn't the gentlemen be kind to an old man and give it back. As

Twenty-Mule Teams

he talked, he was "wobbling and teetering about" beside the buggy in his most nervous fashion. It made the road agents laugh to see him, made them laugh so that after a little they were thrown off their guard. Then one of them saw the worthless pistol on the dashboard, and pulling it from the holster, turned and with a louder jeer than ever showed it to his partner.

At that, Winter's turn had come. In an instant he had drawn the revolver from under the cushion and shot one man dead, while the other, with his laugh turned into a chatter of fear, threw up his hands and begged for mercy.

Thereat, Winters disarmed him, made him put the corpse on the buckboard and then walk under the muzzle of the revolver into town. There the story was told and the robber, through the influence of Winters, was released, taken home to Pahrump and employed for more than a year as a ranch hand.

This was after the death of Rosie. They say that after Rosie died, Winters lost about all of his investment in the ranch.

The discovery of the Amargosa deposit followed naturally on that in Death Valley. Winters had a hand in this, but shared the good luck with two men named Parks and Ellis. Each of them got claims there, and the three sold out for $5,000. Parks took his money and went to his home in the East. Ellis died with his boots on at Pahrump the next year, 1883. It was in a characteristic desert row. Winters was then running the Pahrump ranch, and had a liquor store that was a resort for various kinds of citizens—white men, squaws, and bucks—who came sometimes a good deal more than 100 miles to have a spree. Ellis had previously killed a Spaniard in a mining camp, and in consequence carried a gun and a reputation as a bad man. One day, James Center, who had been a cook at the works then but recently established in Death Valley, went over to Pahrump to spend his accumulated wages, and there got into a game of poker in which Ellis had a hand. A quarrel over a jackpot of just one dollar followed. Because Center accused him of cheating, Ellis went after a revolver. He was intending to avenge the insult by killing Center, but Center grabbed a Henry rifle from behind the bar and went out to seek Ellis. Ellis was by this time returning, revolver in hand, and took shelter by crouching behind the wheels of a buckboard as soon as Center appeared. There he got the first shot, but he hit his man in the fleshy part of the right leg only, and Center was able to return the fire on the instant. His first shot pierced Ellis in the abdomen, through and through, and tumbled him over unconscious. He died two days later. Center was carried over to the Amargosa borax works a few days later, where Supt. Perry drew a silk handkerchief through the wound, dragged out the debris of drawers and dirt left there by the ball, and then cured him up. No arrest was ever made.

What is known as the Monte Blanco deposit of borates in the Furnace Creek Cañon was located by Philander Lee, Harry Spiller, and Billy Yount. Tradition does not make them noted in any other way. They never killed anybody, never got killed, never got wounded even. They just lived, found a deposit of borates and sold it for $4,000. Philander used his share in making a ranch at Resting Springs. The other two "went off somewheres." But Philander is an interesting fellow, for he has a squaw and several half-breeds, and a brother named Leander, who has another squaw with half-breed progeny, and two other brothers named Meander and Salamander, who have no regular squaws, but just live around among the Piutes.

THE TWENTY-

Spears rounded out his 1892 romance of Death Valley's borax bonanza in Illustrated Sketches of Death Valley *with this engaging tale of the great wagons, teams, and men that hauled it out.*

MULE TEAMS
by John Randolph Spears

THE "largest, most capacious, and most economical wagons ever built were manufactured on the Mojave Desert, for use in Death Valley."

The tourist among the deserts of Nevada and California will hear a good many curious statements from the scattered population he will find there—the one quoted above among the rest—and if he has any interest in horses or teaming, he will find the subject of desert transportation worth inquiry. There is probably nothing like it in all the world.

I got my first glimpse of desert transportation at the Nevada Salt & Borax Co.'s works, at Rhodes' Marsh, on the Carson & Colorado Railroad, Esmeralda County, Nevada. The works for producing borax from the crude material found in the marsh there used nut-pine as fuel, and the wood was cut on a mountaintop twelve miles away, piled up on a bench at the head of a cañon, and drawn thence in wagons to the works. One of these wagons was standing empty in a wood yard when I visited the marsh, and, although not the largest in use, it was a sight to make an Eastern teamster gasp. The tops of the wheels came just level with the eyes of a tall man.

Over the divide at Teels' Marsh, some nine miles away, I found more wagons of the same kind, and, finally, down at the mining camp of Candelaria and the little village of Columbus, where there is another borax marsh, I saw what they called wood trains—all loaded—trains, so to speak, of two great wagons coupled together and piled high with wood.

The woodsman of the East counts his load great when he had piled two cords on the easy-running bobsleds in wintertime, but here the wood-hauler piles from five to six cords on each wagon, couples two of them together, and draws the train down the rocky defiles and winding cañons of the mountainside and across the sandy plains, where the wheels of an ordinary Eastern farm-wagon, with its load, would cut in six inches deep.

Of course, no one pair of horses, nor any combination of

horses known to Eastern teamsters, could move, let alone haul, such a load. The swell young gentlemen who handle the ribbons over two pairs of horses in front of a Newport coach, and the dignified driver guiding four pairs of heavy grays before a New York City safe truck, think themselves drivers of rare skill, and so they are. But the fuel-hauler of the desert commonly drives twelve horses, with the aid of a single rope in place of reins, and never has less than ten before him.

And yet he is but "a rawhide" driver when compared with those who had charge of the Death Valley borax teams.

When, in 1883, the manufacture of borax was first undertaken at the marsh in Death Valley, one of the best-known men in the desert region was Charles Bennett. He had taken up a claim on an oasis in the Pahrump Valley, in Southern Nevada, and had made a ranch of it that he afterward sold for $20,000. Here he lived, hundreds of miles from the nearest town, with the Piutes only for neighbors, unless, indeed, the scattered white Arabs of the desert—renegade whites and squaw wives—and one or two white families who lived at springs from twenty to 100 miles away, could be called neighbors.

But in spite of this curious taste in the selection of a home, Bennett thrived on his ranch, and accumulated plenty of horses, mules, and cattle, with money in the bank at Los Angeles, through furnishing supplies to prospectors and trading with the Indians. He learned about the doings in Death Valley, and before the fire was built under the pans, had made a contract to haul the product over the desert to Mojave Station, on the Southern Pacific Railroad, as well as to freight the supplies from the railroad to the workmen in Death Valley.

Before the end of the year, when his contract expired, the company making the borax concluded they could do the freighting more satisfactorily with their own teams than by contract, and, accordingly, J. S. W. Perry, now superintendent of the Pacific Coast Borax Company's borate mines in the Calico Mountains, and who had before that been employed in Mojave in the borax business, was put at work organizing a system of transportation over the desert which should be adequate for the safe handling of all the product of the Death Valley region.

Some of the difficulties in the way of carrying out the company's plans may be mentioned, but scarce described so as to be fully comprehended by one who has not seen the desert to be crossed. Between Mojave and the valley proper there were but three springs of water. The road from the railway station led away over the sandy plain in an easterly direction, toward a peak locally known as Granite Mountain, but called Pilot Butte in the reports of the California State Mineralogist and by the early prospectors as well. It was just 50½ miles across this desert—a desert where the sand-laden wind forever blows and the sun pours down with intolerable fierceness in summer—to the first spring, which was called Black Water. Beyond Black Water, 6½ miles away, was Granite Spring, at the foot of Pilot Butte, and the next spring was Lone Willow, twenty-six miles away, at the foot of one of the peaks of the Pana-mint Range. These last two spaces between springs were compara-tively short distances between waters, but the next dry space was worst of all, for it was fifty-three miles to Mesquite Well, near the lower end of Death Valley.

And yet experience had demonstrated that a loaded team could only travel from fifteen to seventeen miles in a day. There was, of course, but one way in which those fifty-mile stretches could be crossed, and that was by hauling water for men and animals for the three days required in the passage between springs. Nor was that all. The desert does not produce a mouthful of food of any kind. Grain and hay had to be hauled as well as water.

There were other obstacles along the trail. It is a mountainous country. The road leaves Death Valley by what is known as Windy Gap. This gap is really what is known in that country as a wash. It is the bed of torrents that come pouring down after a cloudburst on the mountaintop. Volumes of water in foaming waves twenty feet high are said to be common enough, and others much higher are told about by the white Arabs. When a wave has passed, boulders are found scattered in all directions, gullies are cut out, and at the best only a bed of yielding sand is found for the wheels to roll over. Worse yet, this bed of sand rises on an average grade of one hundred feet to the mile for forty miles, while the grade for short distances is four times as much.

The entire length of this desert road between Death Valley and Mojave is 164½ miles. There was, of course, in all that distance no sign of human habitation. In case of sickness, accident or disaster, either to themselves or the teams, the men could not hope for help until some other team came along over the trail.

The first thing done by Mr. Perry was to obtain, by inspection or correspondence, the dimensions of all varieties of great wagons used by Pacific Coast freighters. With these and the load carried by each wagon spread out before him, he proceeded to design the wagons.

The task he had set for himself was the building of ten wagons so large that any of them would carry at least ten tons. The reader who is familiar with railroads, in fact any reader who has traveled at all by rail, must have seen these legends painted on the sides of freight cars: "Capacity 28,000 lbs." "Capacity 40,000 lbs." (rarely) "Capacity 50,000 lbs." With this in mind, consider that these wagons for hauling borax out of Death Valley were to haul ten tons, or half a carload each—that a train of two wagons was to carry a load, not for one of the old-style, but for one of the modern, well-built freight cars, and carry the load, too, not over a smooth iron tramway, but up and down the rocky defiles and cañons of one of the most precipitous mountain ranges in the world, the Panamint. Because these were probably the largest wagons ever used, and because they were and still are completely successful, space may well be given to their dimensions in detail. They were as follows:

The hind wheel was seven feet in diameter, and its tire was eight inches wide and an inch thick. The forward wheel was five feet in diameter, with a tire like that on the rear wheel. The hubs were eighteen inches in diameter by twenty-two inches long. The spokes were made of split oak, 5½ inches wide at the butt, and four inches wide at the point. The felloes were made double, each piece being four by four inches large in cross-section, and the two being edge-bolted together. The forward axletrees were made of solid steel bars, 3¼ inches square in cross-section, while the rear axles were 3½ inches square. The wagon beds were sixteen feet long, four feet wide, and six feet deep. The tread of the wagon—the width across the wheels—was six feet. Each wagon weighed 7,800 pounds, and the cost of the lot was about $9,000 or $900 each.

It is worthwhile to once more compare these wagons with the best modern freight car. The best freight car for use on a steel track weighs 27,000 pounds, and carried a load of 50,000 pounds. Note that the car weighs more than half the load. Two of these Death Valley wagons very often carried 45,000 pounds, and sometimes 46,000 pounds of cargo, exclusive of water and feed for men and team, while their combined weight was but 15,600 pounds, or about one-third of their load. Moreover, all of the ten were in constant use for five years without a single breakdown. The works in Death Valley were then closed down, but two of the wagons have been in constant use since, and are at this date (1892) running from the Borate Mine in the Calico Mountains to Daggett Station on the Atlantic & Pacific Railroad, where they bid fair to have an experience equal to that of the wonderful one-horse shay.

The building of the wagons was but the beginning of the work, though it should be said here that the building was all done in Mojave Village by men working by the day—it was not a contract job.

While the wagons were building, the road had to be divided up into what might be called days' journeys. The heavy loads were to be brought in from Death Valley, and since only supplies for the workmen were to be carried out, the wagons would have but light loads one way. Of course the teams would not travel so far in a day with a full load as with a light one. Moreover they could not travel so far on the long upgrade like that in Windy Gap as they could down the long grade from Granite Spring toward Mojave. So the matter was figured over, and ten stations were established at intervals along the whole route, where the teams could stop for the night when coming in loaded to Mojave, while certain other stations were established for resting places on the way out to Death Valley, these last being located with a view of making a team travel further when light than when loaded.

So far as possible these stations were established at the few springs found along the route. Elsewhere dry camps had to be made. Here the natural lack of water was overcome by a system of wheeled water-tanks, very much like the tanks of street sprinklers. These were made to hold 500 gallons each, and were towed by the teams from the springs to the dry camps, and from the dry camps back to the springs to be filled again when empty. They were necessarily made of iron, because a wooden tank would dry out and fall to pieces when partly empty.

Then, in the language of the desert Arab, the springs were developed. Some holes were cleaned out and enlarged. At others that were not easily accessible from the best trail to be followed by the wagons, pipes were put in and the water run down to convenient tanks. At all the stations from two to four feed boxes were built of lumber, each large enough to hold four bales of hay and six bags of barley, barley being the grain used on the desert as oats and corn are used in the East. The teams bound out to the valley filled the feed boxes, and then emptied them coming in. The greatest distance made by a team in cool winter weather, on a downgrade with no load, was twenty-two miles. The shortest run for hot weather was about fourteen miles.

But it should be said here that for the three months in the heat of the summer, from the middle of June until the middle of September, no teaming could be done at all. It was not possible for either man or beast to stand the terrific heat of even the Mojave Desert, not to mention Death Valley.

The teams consisted of eighteen mules and two horses. As was said, the man who handles four trained horses before a society coach, or eight huge Percherons before a safe-carrying truck, may think himself a pretty good driver, but in the desert, to use the desert term, he would be a sick rawhide beside the man who steers eighteen mules with a jerk-line. To compare the one with the other is like comparing a Corinthian yachtsman, or the deckhand of a harbor scow, to the captain of a Black Ball liner, if we may use a nautical simile in a story of the desert.

In building the desert freight train, the front wagon receives a tongue of ordinary length, while from the rear axle projects a little wrought-iron tongue about three feet long. The second wagon has a tongue, say six feet long, with a stout vertical ring on the end of it, which, when the two wagons are coupled together, slides over the three-foot tail of the front wagon. Then, to hold the two wagons together, a stout chain runs from the front axle of one to the front axle of the other.

The horses and mules are harnessed up in pairs. The horses are attached to the wagon at the tongue, and a great, handsome 2,800-pound team it is—gentle, obedient, and strong as a locomotive. Ahead of them stretch the mules, their double-trees geared to a chain that leads from a forward axle. The most civilized pair are placed in the lead and the next in intelligence just ahead of the tongue, while the sinful, the fun-loving, and the rawhides fill in between. The nigh leader has a bridle with the strap from the left jaw shorter than the other, and from this bridle runs a braided cotton rope a half an inch in diameter through fair-leaders on each mule to the hand of the driver, who sits on a perch on the front end of the wagon box just eight feet above the ground. That rope is known as the jerk-line, and its length is not far from 120 feet. The team that draws the desert freight train stretches out for more than 100 feet in front of the wagon.

If historians and poets have been justified in writing rapturously about the Arab and his steed, what may we not say of the Death Valley teamster and his mules? To see him soar up over the front wheel to his perch, tilt his hat back on a rear corner of his head, gather in the slack of a jerk-line, loosen the ponderous brake, and awaken the dormant energies of the team with "Git up, —— —— you; git up," is the experience of a tourist's lifetime. And when, at the end of a journey, the teamster pulls up beside the dump with the mules in a line so straight that a stretched string would touch the ear of every mule on either side of the chain, as has often been done, one wants to be introduced and shake hands as with "one whom lesser minds make boast of having seen." And when one sees the mules settle forward in their collars, feeling gently of their load until at last the chain stretches as firm as an iron bar, and with one accord start the train of well-nigh 60,000 pounds weight almost as though it was naught, he wants to be introduced and shake hands with the mules, too—that is, figuratively speaking. Their intelligence is such that he would be proud of a speaking acquaintance with them, but if he knew the mules he would be a little shy about getting within hand-shaking range.

It is wonderfully interesting, too, to watch the mules as they turn a sharp corner in a cañon, or on a trail where it rounds a sharp turn on the mountainside. Span after span, near the end of the tongue, often without a word from the driver, will jump over the long chain and pull away on a tangent that the heavy load may be dragged around. Even then the novice wonders how they succeed, for some of the curves are so sharp that the leaders pull in one direction while the wagons are traveling very nearly in an opposite one.

In their short journey after fuel, the drivers of the ten-horse teams often manage their outfits alone. It is but a day's trip from the village to the wood camp and back; but in freighting over the desert with a twenty-animal team, every driver has an assistant called a swamper. The swamper's duties are multifarious. On a downgrade, he climbs to a perch on the rear wagon and puts on the brake; on the upgrade, he reasons with and throws rocks at the indolent and obstreperous mules. As mealtime approaches he kicks dead branches from the grease-brush along the route, and pulls up sagebrush roots for fuel. When the outfit stops, he cooks the food while the driver feeds the animals, and when the meal is over washes the dishes, which, with the food, are carried in a convenient box in the wagon.

The mules get their grain from boxes which are arranged to be secured to the wagon tongue and between the wheels when feeding. They eat their hay from the ground. Beyond feeding and watering, the animals get no care—they curry themselves by rolling on the sand, and rolling with cyclonic vigor, at that. The cloud of dust raised when an outfit of mules starts in for a lark is suggestive of a Death Valley sandstorm, and there is nothing to compare with their cries of glee after the rolling is done. The work is not wearing on the animals. It is common and polite to say to a driver when a thin or scrawny mule is seen in a big team: "Been getting a rawhide, hey?" which, being interpreted, means: "Ah, I observe you have recently purchased an animal unaccustomed to the work."

Quite as interesting as the teams and the freight trains of the desert are the men who handle them. The drivers receive from $100 to $120 per month, and the swampers about $75. They furnish their own food and bedding. The bill of fare served at a desert freight camp includes bacon, bread, and beans for a foundation, with every variety of canned goods known to the grocery trade for the upper strata. They carry Dutch ovens for their baking, pans for frying, and tin kettles for stewing. On the whole, however, they do not eat much fancy canned stuff, and a cobbler made of canned peaches serves for both pie and cake.

"We don't care much for gimcracks, but we're hell on grub. The gimcracks don't stay by ye," as one said. They rarely carry liquor for use on the road. I observed that empty bottles on some of the desert trails were as thick as good resolutions on the road to sheol, but the teamster did not empty or leave them there. They had served to cheer the road for gentlemen en route to inspect Breyfogle, Gunsight lead, and Peg-Leg mines discovered by enthusiastic eaters of grubstakes.

This is not to say, however, that the teamster is a disciple of Neal Dow, or the Woman's Christian Temperance Union. While the five trains were running regularly between Death Valley and Mojave, the chief care of Superintendent Perry was to keep them moving regularly. He had the road so divided that the teams went out to the valley, got loaded, and returned to Mojave on the twentieth day at three o'clock with a precision that was remarkable. At Mojave the teamster was allowed to have the rest of the day and night to himself, and it usually happened that when the hour of starting came next day, he rolled in instead of soared to his perch, and then, as he blinked his eyes and pawed the jerk-line, said:

"Git hep-th-th-th-th yougithop."

It is a matter of record that the mules understood him, nevertheless—that, in fact, these long-eared, brush-tailed tugs of the desert never did but once fail to understand the driver, no matter what his condition. On that occasion the driver, instead of getting drunk, had gone to hear an evangelist preach, and had been converted. Next morning, it is said, when he mounted the wagon and invited the team to go on, the mules with one accord turned their heads over their shoulders, cocked forward their ears and stared at him. He had omitted the customary *emphasis* from his command.

It is a curious fact—a fact that a thoroughbred Kansas boomer will scarcely believe in—that the building of a railroad to a desert mining camp invariably decreases the life and activity seen on the streets and among the business houses. The railroad benefits the mine owners, but injures everyone else. The explanation is simple, however. Before the railroad reaches the active camp, all the supplies are brought by teams, and so are the mails and the passengers. When the railroad comes, the teamsters and swampers drive away to return no more, and the railroad brings none to take their place. In

Twenty-Mule Teams

fact, it would take a pretty lively citizen to fill the place of a departed teamster, in any event.

"There was a faro bank running most of the time at Mojave. It was a good thing for us, for the teamsters could go broke in one night and be ready to go out over the road in the morning," said Supt. Perry. That was by no means a heartless remark, as it seems to be at first blush, for if the teamster did not gamble away his money, he was sure to get drunk and spend it in ways more harmful, while if by any chance he got the wages of two months in his pocket at once, he would rush off to Los Angeles for a spree that would take a fortnight or more to recover from. The teamsters are, with rare exceptions, unmarried men.

The life of a teamster on the desert is not only one of hardship, it is in places extremely dangerous. Mention has been made of the grades up which the loads must be dragged. There are other grades down the mountains, like the one, for instance, on the road from Granite Spring toward Mojave, where the plunge is not only steep, but the roadbed is as hard as a turnpike. The load must go down, and so when the brink is reached the driver throws his weight on the brake of the front wagon, the swamper handles the brake on the rear one, and away they go, creaking and groaning and sliding, till the bottom is reached. If the brake holds, all is well, but now and then a brake-block gives way, and such a race with death as then begins cannot be seen elsewhere. With yells and curses, the long team is started in a gallop, an effort is made to swing them around up the mountainside, a curve is reached, an animal falls or a wheel strikes a rock or a rut, and, with thunderous crash, over go the great wagons, and the teamster who has stuck to his post goes with them. There are many graves on the desert of men who died with their boots on, but some of them hold men who were killed while striving to guide a runaway freight-team in a wild dash down the side of desert mountain.

As one may suppose, the effect of desert life upon the teamsters is almost every way deteriorating. The men who drove from Mojave were out twenty days for each half day in the settlement, and the settlement itself was but a collection of shanties on as arid a part of the desert as can be found outside of Death Valley. They were not men of education or very wide experience. Their topics of conversation were few. The driver and his swamper had very little to say to each other. To all intents and purposes each lived a solitary life. Being thus alone they grew morose and sullen. Their discomforts by night and their misery by day in the desert heat added to their ill nature. They became in a way insane. It was necessary whenever a team came in to inquire of each man separately whether he was perfectly satisfied with the other, and whether a change was desired or would be objected to. If the least ill will was displayed by one toward the other, a new swamper was provided, lest a fight follow on the desert and one kill the other. Even the greatest precaution could not prevent murder. The soil at Saratoga Springs in the Amargosa Valley is stained with blood, a human corpse once swung from a telegraph pole in Daggett, and a rounded pile of stones in Windy Gap is marked "Grave of W. M. Shadley"—all because human flesh and human brain could not endure the awful strife of life on the desert. Because these are phases, and illustrative phases, of life on the desert, the stories of these crimes should be told.

Fortunately the stories are but brief. A team was coming in to the railroad from the borax works in the Amargosa Valley. At Saratoga Springs they stopped for the night. There the teamster and swamper quarreled, and the swamper hit the teamster on the back of the head with a shovel as he sat by the camp fire, killing him at once.

Then the swamper buried the body close by the spring and lay down to sleep by the grave. In the morning he hitched up the team and started to drive in. But he was no teamster, and soon had the mules in a tangle, and the wagons, big as they were, overturned, the fall breaking the swamper's leg. In this condition he crawled about among the animals and turned them all loose save one horse, which he somehow mounted and rode away over the long, hot divide, with the broken limb swinging about and the broken bones grinding together, till he reached the works once more.

His terrible condition and untrue story of the trouble with the teamster awakened the deepest sympathy—a feeling which lasted until he had been sent in a buckboard, a journey of 105 miles over the desert, to a surgeon. When the workmen came to dig up the body of the teamster, that it might be removed to a healthful distance from the spring, they found he had been foully struck from behind, and they wanted to lynch the murderer. But they did not do it, and because of the discomforts and dangers of a trip over the desert, neither the coroner or the district attorney of the county would investigate the matter.

Daggett's only lynching was due to the murder of a teamster. His swamper, for some fancied wrong, was moping about the village, drowning his care in liquor. Another teamster advised him to kill the offender. Early next morning someone passing the blacksmith shop heard groans behind it, and there was found the offending teamster, alive but with his skull crushed. Beside him lay one of

Twenty-Mule Teams

the huge spokes used in building wheels for desert wagons. One end was covered with blood and the hair of the dying teamster.

Two nights later, when it appeared that the justice was about to turn the swamper loose for want of direct evidence of guilt, a masked mob took both the swamper and the teamster who had advised the crime from the lockup. The telegraph poles at Daggett have a single cross-arm. Two ropes were thrown over one of these arms, and nooses in the ends were put about the necks of the two prisoners. Both men had until this time thought the movement a bluff to frighten them into confession. Now they would have begged for mercy, but before the trembling lips could gasp half a sentence the tightening ropes lifted them from the ground.

However, it was really but a bluff on the teamster. He was soon lowered to the ground and advised to leave town. He left. The swamper now "holds down a six-foot claim on the mesa," just beyond the village limits.

Death in the Valley

*T*HE DEADLY IMAGE OF THE VALLEY IS
its grandest illusion, born of the cursed name given it by the forty-niners who
were mourning the death of one of their companions—Richard Culverwell.
But once branded, the name demanded much more than the loss of a single
argonaut to justify it. So a terrible legend of the annihilation of a whole
wagon train grew up around it. By the turn of the century, the legend had
such a hold that one popular writer, George Wharton James, after devoting
one chapter of his book Heroes of California to the Jayhawkers, devoted
another entire chapter to the imaginary "Unknown Heroes of Death
Valley"—quoting the Sunday supplement version of the tale, reprinted here.
All was not entirely illusion, however, for the valley can be truly deadly in
the summer, especially for the overconfident and the unprepared. But the very
real deaths of hapless prospectors who succumbed to the desiccating summer
heat only added to the legendary horrors. So too did those of others who died
not by the processes of nature, but by the hand of man.

THE LOST

The wholly mythical tale of the slaughter of an entire wagon train, that grew up around the name Death Valley, was told most dramatically by feature writer Robert Rinehart in the Los Angeles Times *of August 16, 1908. This version was elevated to popular history by George Wharton James in his* Heroes of California *two years later.*

WAGON TRAIN
by Robert E. Rinehart

THREE ERRORS of judgment furnished Death Valley with the party that gave it its name. The lost wagon train attempted to cross the desert and the valley in the height of summer.

Reaching the valley, the emigrants, ignorant of the preternatural dryness of the spot in summer, entered the hot hollow with only an ordinary supply of water; and last and most fatal of all, instead of going south as the Jayhawkers had done, they went north. Yet their mistakes, outside the ill-chosen summer, were excusable. In truth their mistakes would normally have occurred to any party in the same position. The two serious errors had a large element of bad luck, a sort of Nemesis. The party was doomed.

But who were the members of this wretched party? Whence did they come? What friends and relatives had they abandoned in the East at the lure of California gold?

These are unanswered questions. A few names, alleged victims of this party, have been preserved by Death Valley tradition; but who can say tradition has been accurate? It has run riot with the number of victims. Sometimes the death toll is thirty; again it is thirteen. Indeed, little is known about the doomed wagon train beyond its wretched climb of the Funeral Range, its pitiful, plucky progress down Furnace Creek Canyon, its dreadful death march up the furnacelike valley and the horror of the end up among the desolate sand dunes of Death Valley. Overland history, bitter as it is with desert hardship and suffering, has no equal to this last chapter of the death party that named Death Valley.

Uncertainty shrouds the early movements of the ill-fated wagon train. It probably set out from Salt Lake City sometime in the early summer of 1850. Manifestly it was ill-advised and under poor guidance or it would never have attempted the southern trail at that time of year. To all appearances no seasoned desert man was with it. But it had courage. This courage and its desert ignorance carried it far in face of great hardship and handicap—carried it to Death Valley and death.

Vague as was the early travel of these emigrants, their later trail is plain. In the great heat of the summer they reached Ash Meadows and the Amargossa Wash. Probably they had been drawn from the regular trail by the wheel marks of the Jayhawkers and their followers. At Ash Meadows they found plenty of water, and in good condition and good spirits, still following the Jayhawker wagon ruts, set out for the divide over the Funeral Range clearly apparent ahead on the western horizon.

During this trip began their distress. The journey to the summit proved longer and steeper than it looked. The rough trail taxed the oxen cruelly, plodding along with the great lumbering wagons. The midsummer desert sun blazed hotter with every pull. It was a good forty-mile drag uphill. The last half was a bitter trail.

Here the doomed emigrants began to write their tragedy on the desert floor. The oxen from sheer exhaustion could not draw the heavy wagons. To lessen the loads, household articles were cast along the trail. Women as well as men walked beside the wagons.

In a deplorable state the party reached the summit from which the trail leading downward gave an easier way. But it had been on short water supply for many an hour, because since leaving Ash Meadows no water was to be had. Water-famished, the emigrants toiled down Furnace Creek Wash. To add to their trials a band of Indians waylaid them at a bend in the wash and killed a number of their oxen. The emigrants beat off their assailants and plodded on down the trail, arriving finally at Furnace Creek Canyon; and at last, none too soon, at the rippling, rushing little Furnace Creek. The water was very hot, but it was good spring water and Good Samaritan water to the distressed wagon train.

That the party stopped a few days at Furnace Creek to recuperate is certain. From its scouts it learned that the canyon opened into a valley white-hot. It must have appreciated that the worst lay ahead, for which was needed every ounce of strength and fortitude. It could not go back. It had to go forward into the forbidding unknown. So one morning it stood at the Furnace Creek Canyon gateway and gazed out into the bowl-like Death Valley, red, fiery-red around the rim; white, withering-white at the bottom's dip.

The emigrants had the choice of the south or the north, safety or death. No Jayhawkers' wagon ruts were there to mark the way to the south and safety. That trail had been buried beneath the rocky spew flushed down Furnace Creek Canyon by the spring and summer cloudbursts. To the south lay the long length of the valley, with its glaring, ominous salt marsh. Banked on the other side was a seemingly unsurmountable mountain range. To the north, around the rim of the valley, ran what seemed level ground for the wagons. True, far up in the north the hollow ended with an embankment of buttes. This was more or less discouraging, but beyond them the barricading mountain range appeared to break and give a passage out to the west. Moreover, the north way avoided the salt marsh. This way promised release. They chose the north, and death.

Appreciating the long burning road ahead, the emigrants filled every available keg, bucket, camp pot and kettle with water from Furnace Creek. They feared that water might run low in the toil up the valley. They reasoned that perhaps that water supply might have to hold over until the next day. With such a generous store of it, however, they were more than hopeful of withstanding even the thirst attacks of two days. They reasoned well, for how could they know the deadly, sinister character of that deep hot hollow ahead?

To understand the torture of that last day's travel, the unlooked-for vanishing of that generous supply of water, and the mysterious exhaustion of man and beast, one must know Death Valley in summer. One must know that this furnace spot, the lowest dry land in the western hemisphere, perhaps in the world, is also the most arid. The hot, withering desert winds, dry as an oven blast, blow into the south entrance of the valley and sweep northward as up a chimney. They blow over the surface of the sizzling salt marsh. These winds, already low in moisture, as they slip over the griddlelike marsh are roasted. By the time they reach the north end of the valley they are destitute of moisture as a cinder. It is asserted that in August the air at the north end of Death Valley has less than 5 percent humidity. When one considers that 70 percent humidity is pleasantly normal, the terrible strain of Death Valley's 5 percent humidity can be rated for all its evil. A pedestrian cannot walk half a mile through this blasting atmosphere without several generous draughts of water. Desert nomads, seasoned desert travelers—for no others venture on a Death Valley tramp in summer—have drunk a gallon of water in going two miles. The arid air when drawn into the lungs fairly licks the moisture from the body's tissues.

Picture, then, the anguish of the day and night after the band of doomed emigrants set out from the mouth of Furnace Creek Canyon on their death march around the northeast segment of Death Valley. Along the broiling rocky floor the tired oxen, stumbling, dragged the wobbly wagons. Men and women in anguish tramped a trail so blistering that in these days a desert man wraps his feet in moistened sacks before he trusts himself to the same scorching way. The evil sun poured down its heat rays upon the travelers and shriveled their very skin. The withering desert air, breathed into their lungs, inflamed their tissues. Mental and bodily lassitude seized them. In helpless horror they saw their water store dwindling before the unrestrainable call of man and beast. Yet, driven by despair, that death party pushed on more than twenty-five miles through sun and sand, and at night camped beyond the North Buttes among the sand dunes. They reached their journey's objective point as planned in the morning, and found ahead of them the divide through the Panamints. To this day they call the place Emigrants' Pass. But the emigrants never passed over it.

Wonderful was the persistent pluck of that doomed party. With an order worthy of bright promise rather than impending destruction, the men made their last camp. Wagons were backed into the regulation circle, their tongues pointing outward, and chains and ox-yokes laid out in approved overland fashion. The cattle were turned loose to rustle. Camp fires were lit, built from the scant desert fuel. Supper was cooked and eaten, but it was a supper without water, for the supply was practically gone, and near the camp were no signs of water. Then all lay down in the mystery of the desert darkness.

In the gamut of desert hardship there is no horror such as the horror of a camp without water. Horses whine pitifully and cattle bawl hoarsely in their efforts to make known the unspeakable thirst torture they do not understand. Fantasy plays with the restless nerves and minds of men and women, and drives them to delirium. Thirst-maddened, men and women shriek for water. On that dreadful night Death Valley's christening party drank the bitterest cup of human woe.

Wretched as was the night, the dawn that broke on the luckless camp was worse. Madness, thirst madness, had set in. Men and women in frenzy fled the camp and scattered at random over the trackless sand waste in search of water. Some too weak to leave the wagons, abandoned by their fellows, perished miserably in camp. Bookish altruism had vanished with the water. Fugitives flying in vain, a foe within them, scoured the sun-scorched sand of Lost Valley. The strongest reached the canyons of the Panamint Mountains and found water, only to die of starvation in the valleys and mountains beyond. Others, crazed, came to the bitter ripples of Salt Creek and in their delirium gulped down the brackish, poisonous water. They died beside the stream. Lone wanderers, lost among the sand dunes, dropped in their steps and passed over the Great Divide. All round the somber site of that last camp were strewn the shining skeletons of man and beast—skeletons, for the watchful coyotes saw to that.

Death in the Valley

VICTIMS OF

Reporter Orin Merrill found a real basis for the valley's deadly image in the tragic fate of a few prospectors who challenged its fiery summers and he spread the word in his 1906 paperback "Mysterious Scott," The Monte Cristo of Death Valley, and Tracks of a Tenderfoot.

DEATH VALLEY
by Orin S. Merrill

DEATH VALLEY and Funeral Range are still entitled to hold their names—given to them years ago on account of the perishing of so many emigrants—and will continue so, if prospectors do not give up the idea of prospecting this region during the summer months as a few have attempted to do this summer, 1905.

I have interviewed several of the old-timers who have crossed Death Valley. One old prospector said if a person considers his life worth six-bits he has no business to attempt to cross Death Valley during the heated summer. Another prospector, whose acquaintance I made, was in town under medical treatment for his eyes. He got into the Sinks of Death Valley where it was so hot he burned his eyeballs. Another one says he would not consider crossing it for any amount of money, while another one says he has crossed it at all times and is going to do it again this summer, but one should pick his way and be prepared. In all I have interviewed a score, and *as a man* they all say it is a foolhardy piece of business for most anyone, that they are taking their lives in their own hands, and it was the universal opinion of all that it is no place for a tenderfoot during the heated period.

If one has an ample supply of water—and that means just what it says, ample supply, nothing less—then the chances are far more in one's favor than otherwise. So in case he does not find the spring he is looking for or that it has gone dry since he visited it the month before, that he still has plenty of water left. The lack of water has been the cause of many a lost life. They think they know where there is a spring—in fact they know they do, they have been there before. They have plenty of water to take them. When they get there the spring has gone dry, which many of them do during the summer. Their water supply is exhausted. They are left to the mercies of the heat and the desert. Nobody knows what it means to be without water with these conditions staring him in the face until he has been through it himself, and no pen will ever be able to describe it so the reader will be able to live it over in his mind.

My reader may think "O! Fudge! Show me the man—the able-bodied man, even if he is out of water—who cannot make fifteen, twenty, twenty-five, or even thirty-five miles to water if necessary." That is all right to lay down by a spring under the shade of a tree and talk, but it is an entirely different matter when you are out of water and on the desert. Many a person has given up and perished when they were within two miles or less of water.

It is peculiar but it is true; if one has water with him he does not get nearly as thirsty as when one is out and doesn't know exactly when he will be able to get the next drink.

The water is not the only factor in Death Valley that should cause one to avoid it during the summer. Many a corpse has been found with a canteen beside him half full of water. The heat is so intense that it has its list of victims also. The water anyway becomes so heated that it is of little service to anyone to satisfy thirst.

A great part of Death Valley lies below the level of the sea; in fact, very little of Death Valley proper lies above, and some parts are, as government statistics will show, as far as 300 feet below sea level. Then on each side is the high range of mountains—the Funeral Range on the east, or towards the Nevada side, and Panamint on the west. . . . With this abrupt change of elevation of from less than nothing to over a mile in height on one side, and in some cases on the California side over two miles in height, with the sun's hot rays beating down, who can expect anything but heat—heat unadulterated.

That is not all about Death Valley. When it is wet, the ground is of a slimy, mushy composition, wagons will mire in up to their hubs, and at places it seems to have no bottom. In dry weather this becomes hard, white, and dazzling to the eye. The greatest borax works in the world lie in Death Valley, and the dust of this together with the soil causes this white composition.

Those who have gone through during the summer months claim one cannot see 100 yards in front of himself on account of the dazzling soil and the very dense blue air that is continually rising from the ground caused by the almost intolerable heat.

At Rhyolite, while it may be cool and comfortable there on account of the elevation, at any time during the summer one can look southward across the few miles' stretch of valley and see the Funeral Range veiled in this blue air that has come out of the valley beyond.

There is little doubt that the Death Valley region is rich with precious metals, but prospectors cannot do much during the dry summer months, even if they had assurance that they could stand the heat. Instead of looking for minerals they would spend their time, and more than probably their lives, looking for water.

There are but very few consecutive days that pass during the extremely heated summer months but that someone is picked up in Death Valley in a deplorable condition, either out of their head or exhausted with the heat.

Here are three cases, where more than probably three prospectors are dead and the survivors in each case didn't have much margin to go on. The survivors of these three cases all got into this one camp—the Bullfrog District, at the time of the writing of this story—within the last week.

The sum and substance of one, as told by John Mullan, the survivor, is practically as follows:

A party of three, composed of John Mullan, Morris Titus, and Earl C. Weller—the latter two brothers-in-law, home Telluride, Colorado, and ages twenty-nine and twenty-five respectively—started out from Bullfrog, June 20th, on a prospecting tour to the Panamint Range—across Death Valley. They had with them nineteen head of burros and two saddle horses and first went to Wood Camp, a distance of twenty miles, where they expected to find water. They found the spring had recently dried up so they redoubled their tracks as far back as Mud Springs. Upon leaving Mud Springs they were told where they could find a water hole in Death Valley. Upon breaking camp the next morning, they only had twenty gallons of water for themselves and their twenty-one head of stock and the water hole to locate yet. They went down a canyon as directed but could not get out and as they got out of water in the meanwhile things commenced to look serious. Finally about two o'clock in the afternoon they did come to a moist place where by digging out a hole they could catch about a cupful every four hours. What did that mean when they had themselves and so much stock to look out for. Mullan and Weller stopped, but Titus pushed on so as to look for a few hours longer for the water that they were directed to. He told them he would be back at the camp for the night. He never came.

The next morning Weller took the stock, two of the burros saddled, and started out to look for Titus and water. Neither one has been seen since and they are thought to be dead, as Weller had no water in his canteen when he went out and had no food, as they left all provisions at their last camping place; also several of the burros three or four weeks later came back to one of the springs above Rhyolite a few miles.

The next morning after Weller left, Mullan went out to look for his partners but got sunstruck and lost himself. He wandered about the balance of the day and far into the night before he finally wound up at his camp, more dead than alive. He became so far gone this last day that he had to resort to moistening his tongue and lips with his urine.

He made several attempts at various times to get out of the canyon and locate his partners, but he was so weak, both mentally and physically, that his attempts were all unsuccessful. Finally, a fortnight later, a Mexican happened along and brought him back to Bullfrog where he became able to relate his story. He said the heat was intense and his suffering indescribable.

At one time when the three were together, while they were going down the canyon, the burros refused to go. They turned around several times and wanted to go up a by-canyon. Another prospector, who was a few hours behind them, noticed the place where they had had trouble with the burros. He afterwards was relating the incident and said if they had gone up the by-canyon, as the burros desired, that they would have found water as there was a spring up there, and it was more than probable they would be alive today. The burros had never been over the ground before as they had just been brought here from Colorado by Weller and Titus. The two horses died within the first few days out.

The second story is this:

A German, Gerard Schaeffel, and wife were camping on the east side of Funeral Range but desired to go to Furnace Creek Ranch, via Death Valley, so as to put their horses out on pasture. They were warned by friends against attempting to go at this time of the year, but regardless of that they started out with their two packhorses to make the trip. They arrived at Keane Springs all right, but after leaving there their troubles commenced. Their supply of water gave out, but they kept on going as far as they dared to in hopes of finding other springs. They could not locate them and finally turned around and attempted to get back to the springs. They became so exhausted that they let the horses loose but finally got back to the springs after being without water for nineteen hours. The man fainted three different times on the return trip and, but for the assistance of his wife, would surely have perished. The horses returned to the springs still five hours later, but their dog dropped on the wayside and hasn't been seen since.

The lady says she can go where any man can, but a million dollars would be no inducement for her to again attempt to make the trip under the same circumstances.

The other story is this:

Two carpenters by the names of Jensen and James Riff went out in the mountains near Death Valley. They were camped at a spring

176   *Death in the Valley*

and prospected out from there, but one day lost it and ran out of water. They finally got within about four miles of the camp when the larger one—Riff—gave out and refused to continue. The other one succeeded in making the spring and afterwards went back for his partner but he had gone. Jensen then came to town, a distance of fifty miles, arriving at midnight and together with a couple of friends of Riff's and a team immediately returned in search for his unfortunate partner.

They found places where he had been lying with his head under greasewood bushes so as to keep out of the sun. One place where he had been lying quite a while they could see his prints in the sand where he had shifted his position around the frail bush, making a semicircle in his endeavor to shade his head as much as possible from the sun's hot rays. The last signs they were able to discover of him were footprints, and as they were a goodly distance apart it looked as though he had been running at the time. The footprints showed he was making towards the middle of Death Valley, and of course the search would have been fruitless from then on.

Old-timers say these thirst-driven-mad men, after they get to a certain stage, the first thing they do is to strip stark naked and commence to run, afterwards they drop down on the sand and vigorously paw into it, like a dog.

Jensen says before he left, Riff always wanted to go in the wrong direction and the way he eventually did go.

These are only a few of the incidents where there are survivors left to tell the story. This is just a little over a week's midsummer record of Death Valley. In all of these cases, the survivors returned to the camps of the Bullfrog District within a period of less than ten days' time. How many more cases where the survivors managed to get to other localities, to the west or to the south, is hard to tell, or how many more unfortunates whose bones are bleaching in the sun, where there is no one left to tell the story is still a harder matter. It is estimated that thirty or forty have given up their lives to Death Valley this summer, with the season not more than half over.

Steps are being taken by several of the cities of southern California to lessen the deaths in prospecting Death Valley, which lies in California, and their other desert lands. The main thing they will do is to discover all the good springs and have permanent signposts placed along the trails directing one to these watering places. Also to discover the poisonous springs and mark them such.

There are numerous springs, but it is an easy matter for a person to get within a half a mile of a spring in this mountainous country and, if they don't know it is there, to miss it.

Some of Death Valley's deaths were from quite unnatural causes, as M. R. MacLeod, editor of the Skidoo News, reveals in his coverage of the sensational lynching of murderer Hootch Simpson in April of 1908. There were also grisly sequels to this episode, including a yarn about digging up Hootch's body so that he could be re-lynched for Los Angeles news photographers, a true story about the local doctor's decapitation of the corpse for study, and further facts and fantasies about the later adventures of both the skull and the headless skeleton.

MURDER IN CAMP
by M. R. MacLeod

THE TRAGEDY

THE COMPARATIVE quiet of Sunday morning was broken by a wild disturbance that resulted in the brutal murder of James Arnold, one of the most prominent citizens of the camp—the father of the camp in fact, inasmuch as he located the townsite—and ended in the lynching of his assailant, Joe Simpson, a local saloon keeper and gunfighter. It will go on record as one of the most remarkable lynchings that has taken place in the United States for many years. Joe Simpson, locally known as Joe "Hootch," owing to his fondness for the liquor known by that name, had been indulging in his favorite stimulant for some days and was in a highly inflamed state. Joe was out of funds, a condition not calculated to improve his usual bad temper, and to his disordered imagination the only practical way of getting it was to kill a banker. For this purpose he crossed the road from the Gold Seal saloon, which he owned in partnership with Fred Oakes, and entered the Skidoo Trading Co's. store, in which the Southern California Bank is located. He immediately covered the cashier, Ralph E. Dobbs, with his gun and demanded twenty dollars, under the penalty of instant death. In a moment the place was in a blaze of excitement. A wild rush ensued and before he could carry out his threat, he was overpowered by a crowd of citizens and disarmed by Dr. R. E. Macdonald and Fred Oakes, his partner. He became so abusive to everyone that Jim Arnold, the manager, eventually put him out of the store by force. In the meantime, Henry Sellers, the deputy sheriff, was on the scene with handcuffs with the intention of securing him to a telephone pole, there being no jail in camp. However, his partner and friends promised to keep guard over him until the necessary warrant could be sworn out for his arrest. He voluntarily went to bed and was soon asleep. His gun was hidden by Oakes in what was considered the most unlikely place to be searched, i.e., the bakeoven of the restaurant run in connection with the saloon. A messenger with a fast horse was dispatched to bring in Judge Thisse, who was prospecting in Nemo Canyon, some

179

twelve miles away, so that an order could be made to remove the prisoner to Independence, the county seat, for trial. But Judge Thisse came too late. At two o'clock, about two hours before he arrived, the crime was committed.

Simpson had evidently been thinking on the seriousness of his position. He knew that if he went up to Independence he would probably get a term of years on the rockpile. Holding up a bank is no light offense, despite the proverbial wooliness of mining camps, and further, he was still under a bond of good behavior from the court at Independence, having shot up a hotel there on his last visit a few months ago. Dwelling on these things and rankling under his sense of injury from his forcible ejectment from the store earlier in the day, he armed himself with his gun, which he had discovered hidden in the oven, and crossed the street. He was seen entering the store with the gun in his hip pocket but it was too late. He passed the bank counter, and approaching Jim Arnold, asked, "Have you got anything against me, Jim?" and Arnold answered, "No Joe, I've got nothing against you." "Yes you have—your end has come—prepare to die" and with that, he raised his gun and shot Arnold just below the heart. Turning quickly, he threw his gun on Mr. Dobbs behind the bank counter and commanded him to come out and die, but before he could fulfill his threat, he realized his own danger and backed out into the street. Simpson's entrance to the store and the crack of the shot caused a scene that, for a moment, was more dramatically tense than ever pictured in play or story. Constable Sellers, who was reading a newspaper in the Club saloon, snatched up a shotgun and loaded as he ran. The shells wedged! Flinging it down, he leaned over and grabbed a six-shooter from beneath the bar. The rapidity of his actions can be judged from the fact that he was up with the murderer before he had crossed the street. Others were equally quick. At the sound of the shot, Dr. Macdonald dashed into Pfluger's saloon and snatched up a long-barrelled Winchester rifle. It was a great moment. Two minutes before the street was deserted; everything was still; even the dogs slept in the blinding glare of the noonday sun. Simpson, unnoticed, quickly crossed the street and the shot rang out, the echoes of which were drowned in the death cry of the victim. In a moment the camp was in an uproar. As rabbits from a warren, armed men sprang from every direction in every state of clothing and carrying arms every size and vintage, from the half-toy derringer to the mammoth shotgun that tears a man in two; from the hoary flintlock to cruel Colt Automatic 41 that cuts the bone like cheese. As they dashed up, they stopped transfixed at the scene before them.

The Capture

Gordon McBain, stupid with liquor and unarmed in any way, attempted to arrest Joe as he stepped from the store, calling on the others not to shoot. Less that fifty yards away, Doc Macdonald, kneeling in the dirt with levelled rifle, again and again called on McBain to stand aside or take the consequences of the bullet meant for Simpson. From the other corner came the constable, with his six-shooter raised, running like a deer and calling on Simpson, who was moving slowly, crouching behind McBain, to submit. With a sudden rush they were in the restaurant, where Sellers felled Simpson with a blow on the head. McBain still blundered between the constable and his prisoner. Simpson made a last effort to wrench his hand free, which still clasped his gun, and the constable, realizing that all would be killed in a minute, slipped his gun barrel into McBain's ear and threatened to blow his brains out. Nor was he a second too soon, for Simpson discharged his last three shots at that moment, one bullet passing within an inch of Sellers' stomach. Before the zing of the last bullet had silenced, the constable had Simpson overpowered and his gun was taken from him by Ben Epstein. McBain (still too drunk to clearly understand) was placed under arrest, charged with obstructing officers in the exercise of their duty, and locked up in Sheehy's Pool Room, where he remained until the night of the lynching. Constable Sellers should be highly commended for the great bravery he displayed throughout the action. He virtually carried his life in his hand, from the time he appeared upon the street until he had subdued the murderer. He showed great patience, too, with McBain. Many officers would have shot him down without argument.

Simpson, handcuffed but jubilant at his cowardly crime and at the hot fight he had put up, was taken to the Club saloon until a guardhouse could be decided upon.

Death of Arnold

When Simpson's first bullet tore its way through Arnold's vitals, he sank to the floor crying, "For God's sake don't shoot again Joe. You've got me now," and in the excitement of the dramatic events of Simpson's capture, he was, for a moment, half-forgotten. Like a dying animal that hides itself, Arnold crawled on hands and knees into the cellar below, his life ebbing away from internal hemorrhage. He was found and carried down to Dr. Macdonald's surgery. A cursory examination convinced the doctor that the chances were against the patient. The bullet had entered just below the heart, and passing beneath the ninth rib, punctured the corner of the liver, severed the spinal artery, and passed out of the body in the small of the back. The doctor put the question to Arnold, "Jim, do you think that you are going to die?" and he replied, "No." A copy was then made of Arnold's last statement as follows:

Skidoo. Cal.
April 19, 1908

Dr. Macdonald's office. Jim Arnold on cot. Dr. Macdonald asked Arnold, "Who shot you, Jim?" Arnold replied, "Joe Simpson." The doctor asked, "How did he come to shoot you?" Arnold replied, "Joe came in and asked, 'What grievance have you against me?' I replied, 'None.' 'Well,' he says, 'your time has come' and shot."

(Signed) James Arnold.

The following witnesses were present: Phil Forg, Fred Oakes, and J. H. McCormick.

If the details of the cowardly crime and the condition of the dying man were not enough to inflame the citizens to mete out swift justice to the bloodthirsty ruffian who did the deed and who has been the cause of more gunscrapes than any man in camp, his demeanor might have settled the question. He was in a jocular mood and proud of his prowess. He laughingly proclaimed himself a "Hero," a "True Blue," and a "Bohemian." When his partner, Fred Oakes, came in and said, "Joe I didn't think you would do it," he replied, "Hell, look at the fun I had doing it!" and in reply to the information that Arnold was dying, he observed, "I'm glad to hear it." The feeling ran very high, and there were open threats of lynching if Arnold died. Dr. Grigsby of Rhyolite was telephoned for immediately the examination was over. He made the trip in a fast auto, covering the journey in less than six hours. But the combined efforts of the two doctors could do nothing for the dying man, who passed away at eleven forty-five the same evening.

On Monday an inquest was held over the remains in the office of Judge Thisse, who acted as coroner. The evidence adduced simply covered the above facts. Some witnesses were cross-examined, notably the doctor, Fred Oakes, and Gordon McBain. Questions to Dr. Macdonald were mainly of a technical character. Oakes was questioned rather sharply as to the care he promised to exercise over his partner and why, in hiding the gun, he did not first remove the cartridges. The most searching questioning was reserved for Gordon McBain. This witness was still in a semi-stupor from his long spree and could give no coherent replies to questions about his inter-

ference that so nearly resulted in other deaths. After due delibera-
tion, the jury, consisting of W. B. Follansbee, M. Gavelstad, A. H.
Swinerton, J. H. Wilson, C. J. Shackett, A. T. Hall, J. J. Sheehy,
F. Pfluger and W. McCoy, brought in a verdict "that the deceased,
James Arnold, had died from the effects of a gunshot wound inflicted
by Joseph L. Simpson."

Early in the day, the district attorney was telegraphed for to
take charge of the case. The funeral was arranged for the following
day, and it was then the widespread feeling of regret and deep respect in which the deceased was held manifested itself.

A Desert Funeral

At noon on Tuesday the victim was buried, with a simplicity
and pathos unknown in larger communities. The casket, fashioned
with loving hands in the carpenter's shop of the Skidoo Mines Co.,
was placed on a wagon suitably draped, and drawn out to the cemetery. In the absence of a cleric, A. T. Hall conducted the service,
which was opened by the singing of "Rock of Ages" by a male
quartet composed of Charles J. Shackett, Thorleif Olsen, S. W.
Kline, and Judge Frank Thisse. Following this, Mr. Hall read the
Burial Service of the Church of England. No atmosphere of surplice
and candles could be more appealingly simple than this rough mining camp service, the first public divine service ever held in the
camp. The stalwart figure of Hall, with his flowing grey locks and
suntanned face, reading in vibrant tones, half-hushed by the subdued sobbing of the women, the never-to-be-forgotten "ashes to
ashes, dust to dust" associated with such terrifying significance in
our childish memories, lifted the whole scene out of the materi-
alistic circumstance of common day.

As if in keeping with the fitness of things, the day was dull and
cloudy, filling the valley with somber shadows. No pen can ade-
quately describe the solemn impressiveness of the scene. In the little
basin, green with its short-lived vegetation, hemmed in by the everlasting hills that on the one side shut out the scorching winds of that
wilderness of desolation, Death Valley, on the other blocking the
dreary vista of the saline wastes of Panamint Valley and the grandeur
of the mighty snowcapped Sierras, the little company were gathered
together. Prospectors from their camps in lonely gulches and canyons for miles round had gathered to pay tribute to the remains of
one who had proved a friend in need to so many of them. They
stood around the grave in groups, picturesque in their various garb.
The black of the pall and coffin was relieved by two beautiful floral

emblems made under the superintendence of Mrs. Arthur Holliday. They consisted of a wreath and plate, woven with infinite care and taste. These nameless desert wildflowers, bright-hued but scentless, were fitting ornament to this desert grave and for the man who for so long had sojourned in this desert land, wandering in its sun-drenched valleys and snow-clad peaks. He was buried, too, as he would have wished, among the hills that had rung with the echo of his prospecting hammer and within a few feet of the townsite located by himself. When the last murmur of the Lord's Prayer had died away, the coffin was gently lowered into the grave. After the quartet had rendered "Nearer My God to Thee," the party dispersed in twos and threes, slowly wending their way back to camp. But the spell of reverence was of short duration. There was other and sterner work to do.

The Lynching

The lynching took place on Wednesday night. Henry Sellers, when interviewed, described the occurrence as follows. "In the early part of the week, I feared violence, but as the days went on I felt that the ill feeling had cooled off. On Wednesday evening, shortly before midnight, the door was broken in and Deputy Heath and myself were overpowered. A dozen guns were pressed against us, and we were told that if we made a sound we would have to take the consequence. The guardhouse was a one-roomed building of thin corrugated iron, in poor repair. The walls could be kicked in anywhere. Resistance was useless. The night was so dark I was unable to recognize one man from another. There was a large number present, about fifty I judge. Only two of the party spoke. I could not recognize either voice. The prisoner was awakened and taken from us. Guards remained at the door and window to prevent us from coming out. We saw nothing of the lynching."

The body was discovered early next day, hanging, and Judge Thisse advised of the fact. He immediately ordered the body to be cut down. An inquest was held later in the day, but no information could be obtained as to who the people were who did it. While there was a general feeling of levity outside the court, investigation was conducted with due dignity. The judge evidently felt his position very keenly. Outside the court, several references were made that provoked a smile. One bystander remarked that he had been awakened twenty-three times during the night, to be told that some persons had hanged Joe Simpson, and in his own words, "I was surprised every time." Another suggested that the jury return a verdict that the deceased "died by the visitation of man." A third remarked that Joe was a "true Bohemian" until the last, having at his "positively last public appearance hung around all night" as was his custom.

After the inquest, the body was disposed of.

Ghostly Footsteps

It is somewhat surprising that such an occurrence as a public hanging could be conducted so quietly. The only sound heard during the night was that of McBain fleeing from his imaginary pursuers. Sometime before midnight some person was heard to open the poolroom in which McBain was confined and to whisper hoarsely:

"They're hanging Joe to a telephone pole. Run, Gordon. Run like Hell."

McBain needed no second bidding. He made a beeline for the mill gulch, the pounding of his iron shoe-rivets making ghostly thunder in the narrow canyon. It is generally supposed that he is still running. If so, he should be somewhere about Mexico by this time, which is certainly rough on Mexico. He was seen on the following morning passing Stovepipe Springs in Death Valley at a dog trot, a little lame in the near hind fetlock.

The Lesson

To those living in settled communities, the facts of this man's death at the hands of his fellows will be looked upon as a crime. To the people of Skidoo, it was looked upon as a regrettable necessity. To permit this murderous beast to be at large, when no man's life was safe without he went about with his hand forever on his gun, was not to be tolerated. It had to end. That an end was not effected until a useful and honorable citizen had been foully murdered is too pitiful for calm consideration.

The removal of this pest by a method so excellent has caused a feeling of relief throughout the camp. In the two days immediately previous to that of the murder, he was out to kill four citizens—Frank Pfluger, Jack Sheehy, and Ralph Dobbs, as well as the victim James Arnold. On the previous evening he entered Pfluger's saloon twice. On the first occasion he contented himself with abuse and threats, owing to the presence of Jim Glendining, Pfluger's partner, for whose gun-craft he (Simpson) has a wholesome respect.

At the second visit, he threatened gun and was told by Glendining that if he reached for his gun, he would not live long enough to pull the trigger. He thought it over and changed his mind. That Sheehy and Dobbs are still alive is due to what some term "Providence," others "Luck."

That lynching under any circumstances should be necessary is more than regrettable; it is deplorable. The moral injury is often greater than to the lynched. It may prove to be so in this case.

Had the murderer been sent for trial it would have cost the county thousands of dollars, which would have been nothing short of an imposition on long-suffering rate-payers. It would have cost some of the citizens of this community considerable inconvenience and expense, and, maybe, before it had dragged its way through, another case might have come up, perhaps involving the death of other innocent people. Further, a conviction might not have ensued, resulting in the prisoner being turned loose upon some other community. That such a man should be at large is not only a national shame but a national crime.

The method of disposing of such in the way that happened here is JUST, CHEAP, and SALUTARY in the lesson it conveys. Local gunmen are already in a chastened frame of mind. Would-be bad men, as they bowl along the road on their triumphal entry of Skidoo, will note the number, the stoutness, the great convenience of the telephone poles, and reflect thereon.

It is a matter of deep regret, but it was the will of the people.

The valley's legacy of death also had its practical uses, as Randsburg Miner *editor Clyde McDivitt recounted in March 1906, when one wily renegade simply tried to fake his death to save his skin.*

A BOGUS GRAVE
by Clyde J. McDivitt

THERE IS ABOUT to be written another chapter of the lone grave at Wingate Pass, that mark of the tragedy of the desert which has filled the heart of many a traveler with awe of the impending and mysterious dangers of Death Valley.

Dr. and Mrs. S. M. Slocum of Monrovia have started to the Death Valley country where "Doc," as he is familiarly known, will begin the active development of the King Midas prospect, the one which tempted William Dooley into Death Valley. And the headboard which was placed at this grave when it was fresh told that the body of William Dooley was laid there.

If Dr. Slocum was at all responsible for the death of William Dooley, his share in it was involuntary, but the very fact that fear of Slocum was the primal cause of the tragedy invests the ownership of the mines with a weird interest. William Dooley had an important interest in King Midas during the rush to Randsburg the fall after gold was discovered there. It was from Randsburg that he started on his fatal journey.

Dr. Slocum met at the "Steam Beer Club 2," then a saloon run by Billy Hevren, his old-time friend Billy Pender. Pender was a well-known mining engineer and he wanted his friend Slocum to go with him into the Death Valley country. While they sat over a glass of beer, Pender pointed out his present partner. He was one of the hardest looking characters in that hard-looking set of men—stout, heavily bearded, not a man to meet on a lonely road.

"How did you take up with that sort?" asked Slocum.

But this same black-browed, villainous-looking fellow had saved Pender's life in Mexico when he found the mining engineer half dead from fatigue and exposure. "Now he is in trouble," said Pender. "He and another fellow in Arizona had trouble on a claim—and the other fellow was left on the claim. He is afraid of the officers and I am going to take him out with me and do a friend's part," explained Pender.

Slocum was introduced to the man, who was none other than

William Dooley, but he was called plain Bill. And Bill didn't like Dr. Slocum, that was plain. So the two friends left him in his moroseness and arranged that Pender should be careful to leave a plain trail which Slocum could follow a few days later.

The second party across the trail was Slocum and Ned Saddler, and faithfully they followed Billy Pender. Three or four days out of Randsburg they ran into Pender's camp at the foot of Wingate Pass, and Slocum led.

The first thing to attract his attention was a new-made mound, standing near the road where the Coleman borax people got their water from a tank which was filled from Willow Springs above in the mountains. Startled, he ran up and read the inscription:

"Here lies the body of William Dooley, who came to his death from giving Billy Pender the damn lie." (Signed by) Charlie Bigby and William Delaney.

The men whose names were signed were well known on the desert. The signboard had been cut with infinite pains out of redwood boards from the support of the water tank, then abandoned. There were the marks of where the body was carried up the hill, and the interment had evidently been made with great labor in this repellant soil.

All the men were shocked and surprised. The tragedy hung like a pall over them, and it was anything but a cheerful party that made its way finally to their proposed permanent camp a few miles from that of Billy Pender at the head of Goler Canyon in the Panamint Mountains.

In spite of a heavy snow, a blinding one, Slocum and Saddler started for Billy Pender's camp next day. Halfway up to the camp a man came running down, waving his hat frantically. It was Billy Pender, pale, anxious, harassed. They shook hands and allowed him to precede them up the hills as he directed. He led them upward, upward into the Stone Cabin of Black Mountain, famous since the silver excitement of the '60s as a place of refuge.

"Now, you're safe," he said, "and I suppose you think I owe you an explanation. The probabilities are that since you turned on this trail you have been covered by a 50-Winchester. Old Bill Dooley."

"Who?" exclaimed his visitors.

Pender nodded. "Old Bill Dooley has taken a violent dislike to 'Doc.' He thinks he is an officer from Arizona, and it took me a long time to convince him that I was not going to give him up after you met him at the Steam Beer Club.

"The idea has haunted him until he is hardly sane. All the way he has talked nothing else; he has slept on his arms when he did

Death in the Valley

sleep, and he has fought my leaving clues for you. The night when we camped at Wingate Pass I went to sleep while he was whittling away on boards from the tank, and when I woke in the morning I found him standing at the grave there to fake which he had done almost superhuman labor. He has been watching for you. I am practically sure he has had his gun on you all the way up."

Billy Pender persuaded Bill Dooley to come in. He entered with his Winchester in the hollow of his arm. He took the hand of Slocum gingerly, and held onto his gun. Heartiness melted his caution not a whit. While the remainder of the party chatted, he sat on the bunk across the room with an ugly look on his face. The visitors rose to take leave. There was never a word from Bill Dooley, not good-bye or a cussword. And Billy Pender covered the rear on the trail down the mountain for fear that grouchy person would take a potshot at them.

Ned Saddler wanted to move at once across into Striped Butte Valley to camp. He thought it would come to a showdown between Slocum and Dooley and it didn't suit him at all. Dooley plainly had a dangerous delusion and he was a desperate man. But in two days Billy Pender came over.

"Some news for you," he announced. "Old Bill Dooley has vamoosed, and he has taken everything in camp. He has the teams and guns, and is heading for Funeral Range, across Death Valley. He didn't leave us a can of beans or a bacon rind, and I'll have to throw myself upon your hospitality for a few days."

That was nine years ago. Since then old Bill Dooley has not been heard of on the desert. The story of the lone grave spread among prospectors. Many of them were curious as to Bill Dooley's after movements. His claim on the King Midas property lapsed.

Somewhere on Death Valley's expanse his bones have gone to swell the number of unidentified dead, and the grave at Wingate Pass is the only one he ever had.

Catholics cross themselves at the emblem on the headboard on this mound of rock; the tenderfoot shudders at the hint of violent death on the unpoliced wilderness of sand; the hardened prospector muses upon the possibility that his bones may find such a dreary resting place.

But the fellow who was not afraid—he got the mine.

Rainbow Chasers

*T*HE PERSISTENT ILLUSION OF
boundless riches in lost ledges of silver and gold has drawn countless
prospectors into Death Valley to brave its deadly specter in the hopes of
finding fortune. Some fell victim to its infernal heat and most felt lucky just to
get back out alive. But a few did find real riches, although they didn't
always get to reap the profits. These rich strikes, of course,
only lured many more to try their luck.
The biggest pot of gold found by any of these rainbow chasers was in the
Bullfrog district, discovered in the summer of 1904 by Shorty Harris and a
partner. The ensuing rush to Bullfrog was the largest ever seen in the Death
Valley country as thousands of new hopefuls poured in to prospect every
canyon and ridge. These stories give glimpses of some of the hopes and
hardships of both greenhorns and greybeards.

PROSPECTING DEATH

*Bullfrog attorney and part-time journalist Paul DeLaney tells a lively tale,
replete with spooks and rattlesnakes, of his own prospecting venture into the
valley in the summer of 1907 guided by "poet-prospector" Eddy. DeLaney
published the story that fall in his short-lived
magazine, the* Death Valley Prospector.

VALLEY IN SUMMER
by Paul DeLaney

DEATH VALLEY was appropriately named. Furnace Creek burned it-self into the brain of the man who gave it its cognomen. It burns itself into the brain of every man who visits it in summer. All of the points in Death Valley are properly designated. The names are not poetic, but practical. There is no time for dreaming in that desolate region. Men are of but few words when there and they speak to the point. Elsewhere men may walk in the valley of the shadow of death, but there they walk in the valley of death itself. There may be fiery furnaces in the world beyond, but there are furnaces of fire at Furnace Creek.

A great deal has been written about Death Valley and volumes will be written about that mysterious spot on the earth, or in the earth, as time drags on, but it can never be accurately described. The best descriptive writer of ancient or modern times would feel his incompetency when he attempts to tell what he saw and experienced, if he should live to try to tell what he saw and experienced in that desolate country in midsummer. It is only the person who has been there that knows what is encountered; others may only read and imagine.

There are only three trails that cross Death Valley. Along the line of these trails a few daring prospectors have traveled. They can in a measure tell what, in a maudlin state of mind, they saw. The silent mounds along the way are still fresh in their memory. Like the few points where slimy water seeps from the salt marshes, cooling in taste and sickening in results, they stand out as landmarks in the seared memory of the man who has dared that death-hole in the earth.

The graves are not those of tenderfeet, either. The tenderfoot never gets beyond the danger line, unless he is piloted by those suffi-ciently experienced to carry him over. The silent mounds contain the last remains of the pioneers who became so inured to the hard-ships of the valley that they knew not the grasp of death when it was upon them. The tenderfoot falls by the wayside and is rescued while he is still upon its borders; the pioneer is beyond the remotest hand of aid before he falls—he never surrenders—and is later found by one of his kind, a hardy prospector, almost as grim as the grim monster himself, who performs the last sad rites over the remains in the solitudes of the burning desert at the dead of night, for no mortal hand is strong enough to wield a shovel or spade in the withering fire of a Death Valley sun.

Gold! It is all for gold. Nature appears to always hide her treasures in such secluded spots, and the more secluded the greater the temptation to the adventurous prospector. Wild seas around the earth by way of the Horn, the limitless plains beset with hordes of murderous savages, were the barriers in the way of the prospector in 1849. Oceans of ice floes, glaciers, impassable mountain passes, snowcapped peaks, and the treacherous rapids of the Yukon barred their way toward the North Pole in 1898; and the sand dunes, salt marshes, burning winds of Death Valley—a veritable hell presided over by Satan himself—all fought them back in the year 1907.

But they have always found the way, and the terrors of Death Valley will be overcome, though many will fall as they have fallen before. The gold, which jets out from the rocks of the Funeral, the Grapevine, and Panamint ranges of mountains hangs out over the smoking furnace known as Death Valley like fountains of cold water and limitless oases of vineyards and gardens to the thirsty and famishing prospector, will finally be reached by him, and plucked and distributed into the coffers of mankind.

False reports may come, disappointments may follow, lives may be lost, poverty may still stalk abroad in the wake of many in the Nevada-California gold belt for years to come, but more wealth lies in the mountains bordering on Death Valley than in anyplace yet discovered upon the face of the earth, and the years to come will find an activity there unprecedented in the history of the world's mining.

It was the report of 10,000 ounces of silver to the ton, big pannings of gold, and mountains of the precious metals that lured our party to the Panamints and caused us to brave Death Valley in midsummer, despite the warnings of old-timers and the known risks to life.

Knowing of necessity that we must travel by night, we left Rhyolite late in the afternoon of July 17th. Our party consisted of five persons. Clarence E. Eddy, the poet-prospector who had made three round-trips to the very point of our destination was chosen guide and pilot, and A. H. Dickson and Frank Hargett, two experienced desert prospectors, were placed in command of the expedition. G. T. Keene, a Rhyolite newspaperman, was the fourth member of our party.

A two-horse wagon loaded down with provisions and horse feed, water and mining supplies, drawn by two strong horses, with an extra saddle horse tied behind the wagon, constituted our principal equipment. Every man carried a large canteen holding from a gallon and a half to two gallons of water, which was securely wrapped with blanket material and encased in strips from gunnysacks in order that the water might be kept cool through the evaporation process introduced into this country by deported members of the Boer army. This and the South African water bags are the only systems yet discovered for keeping water in a condition for drinking purposes while traveling in the Death Valley country.

Wherever you see a prospector, you see pending from his neck a canteen thus wrapped, and in his wagon are barrels or cans of water to refill his canteen whenever the same becomes empty. Without water and plenty of it, death is certain in a few hours in the valley.

Nearly every member of the party carried a revolver upon his person or close at hand, for these are the main signals of distress on the desert. Three timed shots ringing out on the air of that region will always bring response if the man who hears is able to pull a trigger or come to the rescue.

The entire trip lay in a southerly and southwesterly direction. As a railroad time card emphasizes its divisions, the prospector "black-letters" the watering places on his route. From Rhyolite to Eddy's camp in the Panamints there are but four watering places, and only one of these is safe to quench the thirst of man. With Daylight Springs, Furnace Creek, Tule Holes, and Bennett's Holes, only Furnace Creek furnishes water safe for man. This covers a distance of over 70 miles and requires three whole nights in which to make the journey.

The first few hours out from Rhyolite was like a picnic excursion. Rhyolite was in plain view for the ten miles across Amargosa desert and until we reached the summit of the gorge between the Funeral and Grapevine ranges. At this point, where the government geological stake indicates about 4,000 feet altitude, is Daylight Springs, at a distance of twelve miles from the Bullfrog metropolis. Here we spread our first meal on the ground and ate sumptuously, while we looked down upon the lights in Rhyolite, with the moon rising over the summit of the Funeral mountains. Daylight Springs, which have quenched so many thirsts and saved so many lives long before the Bullfrog district was discovered, consists of a tunnel dug into the side of the mountains about eight feet with sufficient dip to hold the water that slowly oozes into the bed of the tunnel. It has such a brackish taste that it is only relished by horses and burros and by man when reduced to the last stages of thirst.

Down into Death Valley

In the early evening we were again on the road for an all-night drive toward Furnace Creek. From Daylight Springs the descent is gradual. From an altitude of 4,000 feet a descent is made of 170 feet below sea level. For several hours we traveled through the gorge that separates the two ranges. Down, down, down the wheels crashed over the gravel and ground through the sands, the heavy wagon fairly pushing the team along with its weight. All eyes were constantly strained in the moonlight for a sight of the great hole in the ground ahead which marks the place of one of the wonders of the world. But the walls of the crooked gorge obscured it for a long time.

The night was so still that scarcely a breath of air was stirring. The cool mountain breeze had been shut off as if by the closing of an air valve. An oppressive heat settled down upon us, and the horses became sluggish and timed their steps.

"We will soon see Death Valley," said Eddy in a smothered voice that sounded ominous. "There is a whiff of it," he continued, as a hot wave of air rose up from the earth and passed by, leaving a burning sensation on our faces.

Then another, still stronger and warmer, arose and passed on up the mountain to mingle with the cooler breeze of the high altitude. These increased with regularity, strength, and heat until we found ourselves facing a stiff current of air that burned our faces and hands and made breathing difficult. One would turn his back upon the unwelcome gusts only to find that it played upon the back of the head and neck with more damaging results. The head began to ache and the brain was dizzy.

Then it was right about face and gulp down the stifling breeze and expand the lungs and long for just one breath of pure mountain air again. But men are men, and silently we adjusted ourselves to the situation, waiting for the other fellow to complain, with the secret feeling that "If he can stand it, I can."

"There it is," said Eddy, pointing across to the left.

And there it was, and we were not out of sight of it for many days. Over in the direction we were traveling a dark place appeared in the earth, and over on the other side the Panamints rose high into the heavens, many of their peaks bearing the white marks of the snow which lay in the gulches and cañons.

We were heading slowly for this dark cavern. When we had gone a few miles further it opened up before us, and to the right and left it looked like a bottomless pit, and from it poured up that same suffocating heat which had been making breathing difficult for several hours, and which was now increasing with warmth and strength every step.

The moon, which was in its first quarter, began to sink over the lower range to the west, and the darkness of the cavern increased. At midnight, on the brink of this cavern, we stopped and fed our horses and gave them a small allowance of water from a barrel in the wagon. We made coffee to keep us awake and drank a great deal of the water. Already the hot winds had dried our bodies until thirst became a constant companion. The horses would look longingly at the barrels, and the men kept their canteens closely about their necks and would touch their lips to them sparingly like a petted child clinging on to its last morsel of candy. It made them jealous to see a companion take more than one swallow at a time, and if he took a large swallow all eyes were turned upon him appealingly.

It is here that water is placed at its real value and does not need the indorsement of a temperance lecturer. But it becomes an idol later, which men worship with madness.

Only a short halt was made, for Furnace Creek lay many miles ahead, somewhere down in that hole in the earth, and it must be reached before the morning sun should rise high enough to send its rays down into the place to add its heat to that of the earth. It was probably three o'clock in the morning when we reached the level ground at the bottom, or the bed of Death Valley. The hot breeze had burned our faces and hands until they were no longer sensitive to it. A long white line lay to our right. This we were told was the salt marsh. It looked like a stream of water a portion of the time and then it looked like a snowbank. On our right and on our left a silent mound now and then appeared. We were told that some unknown prospector was taking his last rest at these places. An inscription on a piece of cracker box often told the story of the burial, but in few instances did the scrawling handwriting tell who the victim was. So careless is the prospector in his search for gold that he often fails to carry anything about his person that would identify him if he were lost.

At the dawn of day we had the first view of Death Valley. The mountains stood above us in every direction and the white line of salt and borax lay along the bed of the valley in a northwesterly and southeasterly direction for a distance said to be nearly 150 miles. In the middle of this is Salt River, probably the greatest wonder in all this region.

We reach the edge of the salt marsh about sunrise and continue along its edge for many miles. We pass the staked-out claims of the borax workers of years ago and later reach the ruins of an old borax manufactory of "Borax" Smith, which is not running. The sun is now heating the wind to an intensity, water is getting scarcer and warmer, and the horses are lagging. The road winds around a point which extends from the mountains down into the valley, and the deep sands almost clog the wheels.

Furnace Creek Farm

But a long line of green willows in front wave and flaunt their boughs in the hot breeze, and we are told that this is Furnace Creek. Furnace Creek farm is a veritable oasis without the cool shades and enlivening breeze. It has flowing water, green trees, palms, willows, fig trees, grapes, melons, meadows and gardens, but there is no point not reached by the burning winds. A portion of the nights are passable, but the remainder of the nights and the days are spent in a torment not unlike that described as presided over by Satan.

A stream of water flows through the place like a millrace, day and night, from a spring above. This furnishes irrigation and produces the vegetation, but everything is hot, hot, hot, except the water, which is cooled in water bags and in a large earthen urn, which is filled early each evening. Red-meated watermelons, yellow musk-melons and dripping grapes and candied figs burn the mouth and stomach when not submitted to the complete process of cooling in the crude manner of being wrapped in rags and subjected to the evaporation plan with the use of the warm water which flows through the place.

Furnace Creek farm was established by "Borax Smith" to accommodate the men and horses employed at his borax works near the place, but is now kept up for the purpose of holding the ground and protecting the property. W. A. Northrup is in charge and supplies all persons who pass that way with a limited amount of horse feed, and provisions for men. He has none for sale, but does it in a spirit of humanity where the necessities justify it.

He has been there since the tragic death of Jack Dayton, the former manager. He spends most of his time alone, as few people pass that way, and it is practically impossible to keep help on the farm. Men sent there soon become dissatisfied and leave without warning. Some of them reach civilization again and some perish in the valley.

The farm is nearly 200 feet below sea level. The thermometer in summer stands at from 100 to 136 in the shade. In midsummer it rarely ever goes below 110 in the shade and runs up to 136 in the afternoon. It often stands at 110 at midnight. There is no hour, day or night, that is absolutely comfortable.

With the rising sun the heat rapidly increases and by two o'clock it is at its worst. By ten o'clock in the morning the wind begins to increase in strength and warmth and by two o'clock it blows a gale of scalding heat. At times no living thing would survive if it were subjected to its heat without shade and water. A good idea may be given of the heat at its worst stages in this manner. If one were caught and one's face held in front of a hot furnace for hours, with the hot blasts almost singeing one's eyebrows and hair all of this time, one would have a fair idea of what life is at Furnace Creek ranch about two o'clock on any midsummer day.

A Hell on Earth

An idea may also be given of the heat at this point in the daytime by stating the facts about an iron pipe that conveys water from a spring a quarter of a mile from the place. The pipe lies along the ground this distance and, of course, is exposed to the sun and wind. Early in the morning one may drink this water, which is fairly cool. By ten o'clock in the morning it is too warm for the bare hand, and by two o'clock in the afternoon it sputters forth a scalding stream, and an egg may be boiled in the tub into which the water runs from the pipe. It is to this kind of heat that one is exposed who travels in the daytime, and it, with the burning wind, has baked many a poor wretch's brains and sent him reeling to the ground with a canteen about his neck well filled with water, never to rise again. Many victims have been found dead with a canteen filled with water. The old-timer, when compelled to travel in daytime, keeps a wet handkerchief on top of his head and on the back of his neck, and uses more water in this manner than he does for drinking purposes.

Enervated from a day's fight with the hot winds and heat at Furnace Creek farm, we started out again at sunset for Bennett's Hole. The worst of our journey lay before us. With canteens and barrels filled with the tepid waters of Furnace, we started down the slight incline to the lowest depths of the valley where no human being has yet found his way. Furnace Creek is nearly 200 feet below sea level, while it is 278 feet below the sea at Bennett's Hole. Over next to the lake on the side of the Funeral range it is said to be still lower, but until man can invent some means of reaching this spot, the lowest parts will not be recorded.

A Trail of Death

The distance from Furnace to Bennett's is given as twenty-two miles, but the traveler is ready to dispute the point with his sworn statement. On this trip the great salt marsh is crossed, and in its center Salt River. These points would furnish food for scientists for years, and the pen of man is incapable of describing them.

With eight miles of "salt floes" and a river of salt brine of unknown depth, it took $20,000 of "Borax" Smith's money to even make a passable trail across this death trap. Driving a wagon across a mere crust, which if it should give way at any point would send the occupants of the wagon to the most horrible death imaginable, is not pleasant traveling to men who all night long have been viewing the silent beds of former victims of the desert.

Standing at the foot of an extinct volcanic crater, which bears the appearance of having been one of the world's recent eruptions, is Mushroom Rock, overlooking this roadway across the "stretch of death." Some have dubbed it the Death Valley Sphinx. On a slight pedestal, with a comparatively small stem, this rock, with well-formed "leaves" like those of a mushroom or toadstool, stands many feet above the surrounding debris. The whole is composed of volcanic lava, which still appears to be going through the cooling process.

Only a Crust Over Eternity

But we enter upon the trail across the salt marsh. For eight miles we travel through salt floes of every imaginable shape, made more uncanny by the growing moon which fights its way through the crags and peaks of the mountains overlooking that desolate region. This stretch is said to be over a lake of unknown depth. The hot sun and wind had for ages been forming a crust of salt upon the surface which has risen up like huge blisters upon the water. They have baked and rebaked and other crusts have formed, and with a kind of self-bracing architecture have formed a support that will bear up the weight of men, teams and wagons. This formation is beautiful, grand and awe-inspiring. It represents everything that the mind can picture.

The first appearance is that of a huge ice-covered lake, where the ice has been broken from beneath in blocks of from one foot square to several yards in dimensions of every kind. They are in squares, diamond shape, and present every angle known to mathematics.

Then as you proceed toward the center they increase in height, forming a still more picturesque landscape. Monuments, church steeples, tombs—every sort of awe-inspiring architecture is presented. It was only through blasting and the persistent use of pick and drill that the trail could be driven through, and now it is so rough that travel over a corduroy road is like an asphalt pavement compared to it.

All of this is over salt brine of great depth, and an occasional hole in the crust exposes the heavy liquid beneath. But the scene that causes the tired and weary prospector to stop and behold is Salt River. As white as snow, this solid stream of mock flow, about sixty feet in width in the main channel, stretches out as far as the eye can see lengthwise of the valley. A little bridge in the center protects man and beast from the only hole where the surface is soft enough to yield to weight.

In the moonlight, and but few see it otherwise, for no man can stand the heat of the sun at this point, it looks like a winter scene in the far north. While there is no flow, it bears every appearance of it, and one can imagine that one can see the ripples in the white mock stream. But it is all salt, hard and crystallized at some points, soft like putty at others, with now and then a hole in the surface where white brine is exposed. It may be that it flows in spring when the snows are melting in the mountains. Prospectors tell of how the whole is covered with water at certain seasons of the year.

Off of the salt marsh and onto the sands again, and Bennett's Hole many miles ahead. The stars forming the dipper are gradually dropping beneath the horizon, and the approach of morning gives alarm for fear that the sun may rise before the hole is reached. The water in the canteens is milk-warm, the hot breeze still burns into the exposed points of the body, and the horses lag along almost lifeless. A tired colt of one of the animals drawing the wagon lies down in front of its mother during a pause for rest and refuses to stir. To hurry through ahead of the sun, the colt is placed in the wagon and some of the men take to the road on foot.

But rattle, rattle, rattle! The deadly warning of the only inhabitant of the valley at this point is sounded at the feet of the pedestrian and he shys around with strained eyes and nervous tread. Only a few more steps are taken and another warning comes. Soon they sound like children in a toy store, and the pedestrians again mount the wagon and the colt is forced to the ground again and driven by a man mounted on the saddle horse.

The rattlesnakes crawl into the road at nights in order to rest and cool themselves in the soft dust cut fine by the travelers, and are ready to strike for the life of all invaders.

A Known Grave

On the left-hand side of the road a grave is passed. It bears the feature of being a known grave. Jack Dayton, former manager of the Furnace Creek farm, sleeps here. The story is the most pathetic I heard on the trip. A plank from a goods box tells the story. The skulls of six horses lie against the mound, three on each side. Jack, his six horses and a cat all perished at the same time. Only a dog survived, and it was found sitting by the side of its master's body, which it had guarded for twenty-two weary days.

Dayton had started from Furnace Creek for Daggett with an empty wagon to get supplies for the farm. He was drawn by four horses and tied two horses to the wagon in the rear. He had a cat in a box which he was taking to a friend at Daggett, and a dog followed along.

He had been due in Daggett for two weeks, and, not arriving, Frank Tilden and a Mexican by the name of Dolph started out in search. It was midsummer and they traveled by night. Within a mile and a half of the old Eagle borax works they came upon the wagon of Dayton, which was in the road about eight miles this side of Bennett's Hole. Around the wagon were six dead horses in harness. Dayton's body lay under a mesquite bush near the roadside and his dog sat by it as the only silent mourner. The cat in the box was also dead. They had been there twenty-two days.

A survey of the place told the story. Dayton had become deranged from the heat. He had left his wagon and sought a shade under the mesquite. He had died. The lead horse had drawn his companion around to the wagon to secure water or feed and became entangled with a standard projecting above the wagon body. They had stood there in a circle until they all perished. The dog had found his way to a pool of slimy water a mile and a half distant and sustained itself; he had kept off the vultures and coyotes from the body of his master for twenty-two days.

We passed by Tule Holes, four miles this side of Bennett's Hole, in the night. Eddy was asleep and we did not discover the place. But a little after sunrise we reached Bennett's. Bennett's Hole is in front of the wash, though many miles distant, of Johnson's Cañon. Some prospector, said to have been Bennett, dug a hole about eight feet deep and struck a slimy water in the sands. It is about one foot in depth in water and refills as fast as it is drawn out, though it never gets any deeper.

Dead bugs floated on the surface and a kangaroo rat sat complacently on a dry spot near the water's edge. He had fallen in and after an unexpected bath was taking his imprisonment philosophically. We draw the water from this hole, expecting purer water to enter. But it was all alike, briny, slimy and unwholesome. But our Furnace Creek water was exhausted and we had to drink.

Before the day was over the evidences of the excitement at home were presented. Three parties arrived in the sweltering sun and burning wind, who gulped down the water at Bennett's Hole as if it had been ice lemonade. A dozen men and burros were lined up later and photos were taken. Bennett's Hole has never seen such activity before, and may never see it again.

Ascent of the Panamints

The start for Eddy's camp was made at sundown. Wagons were cached and animals were packed and the men started out on foot. There were two trails to the camp, which is eighteen miles from Bennett's. A large patch of lime about ten miles distant up in the mountains is the main landmark. It is a number of miles in width. On the right-hand side of this, Willow Creek Cañon cuts its way to the summit of the mountains, and on the left-hand side, Johnson's Cañon winds its way.

Either trail is difficult of ascent. For ages waterspouts have formed up in the Panamints, and the waters come down in a flood, bringing with them boulders and heavy timbers from the mountain peaks. Either trail for eight miles from Bennett's lies among these boulders, and the way has to be picked slowly in a winding way that makes progress as slow as a snail's gait. The sun has baked the rocks also and the Death Valley burning wind is encountered on this trail for hours.

By ten o'clock at night the poison water from Bennett's has become hot in the canteens, and some of the trudging pedestrians become deathly sick from drinking it. A pack is removed from a horse and left by the trail and the sick man is hustled upon the animal's back, and the caravan moves slowly on.

The Willow Creek trail is taken so that Hidden Spring may be reached on the upward trip. A few miles up the cañon a trail leads off to the left and this is followed over precipices and deep gorges to a mountain of boulders, from beneath which a sluggish vein flows, depositing its sweetened water in a crevice among the rocks. Only a cupful can be obtained at a time, and while the men were in a measure satisfied, the horses were compelled to stand restlessly and content themselves with a few swallows during the night, dipped up and placed in a bucket.

The pack containing the provisions had been left behind and the men spent the night without eating. The horses nibbled at the small bits of vegetation which had sprung up about the seep called Hidden Spring.

The early morning found us on the trail again. We crossed over to Johnson's Cañon and at eleven o'clock we arrived at Eddy's camp.

The camp was deep down in the cañon by a garden of a quarter of an acre fenced in by a hedge of growing willows watered from a rapid stream of cool spring water which flowed from a fountain through a small irrigation ditch for a couple of miles. It is known as Hungry Bill's garden. Many years ago a white man by the name of Johnson is said to have settled the place. He died or moved away, and Hungry Bill, an Indian, settled there with his family some sixty years ago. He has lived upon the products of the garden, the game of the mountains, and from the sale of ore which he has found in pockets in the country since that time. He claims the whole country lives in a low, savage state, it is claimed.

A few days were spent in prospecting, but the enervated condition of the men was such that nothing but nuggets would have attracted their attention seriously. They soon responded to the call of the wealth hidden in the Funeral Range on the other side of the valley, and they left the place and Hungry Bill in the possession of his own.

Our last night in the Panamints proved an eventful one. We were treated to a frightful surprise which turned an occasion that had started out with hilarity into an uncanny evening of storytelling.

A majority of the prospectors had declared the camp below former estimates and we had decided to leave the following morning for the return trip across Death Valley. Eddy, the poet-prospector, maintained that the camp was all that he had ever estimated it to be, and said he would remain until he made thorough tests.

Indians had been seen climbing along the cliffs above the camp just before nightfall, but as they had frequently done this, it was believed that Hungry Bill had only sent his boys out to make a reconnoitre to assure himself that we were going to leave him again in the possession of that vast country.

In order that all wounds that had been made by adverse criticism of the camp should be healed, we gathered about a common camp fire for a social evening. In that camp, where seventeen prospectors of modern times had gathered in a rush for gold, there were musicians, actors, poets and public speakers. Eddy was made master of ceremonies, and was required to open the entertainment with a recitation of one of his own poems. Then came a song, then a recitation, and an impromptu address.

Rattlesnakes Call

The men were warming up to that interest that can only be reached in the solitude of the mountains. Another member of the party had been called upon to do his "stunt," and a moment of silence had just begun prior to his rising from his seat.

"Rattle, rattle, rattle!" broke the silence from the midst of the circle. Everyone knew that it was the signal from the deadly rattlesnake. We had heard this warning many times before on that trip.

To move was dangerous, but the party moved as one man. The exact place of the enemy was not discernible, but no one felt safe in that neighborhood when the tail of a rattler was vibrating in such close proximity.

He was just the color of the ground, and while he lay in his coils ready to strike, no one could see him. Men tried to get up into the air, as there was nothing else to mount.

"There he goes!" finally shouted a member of the party near a sage bush, and then his revolver rang out and reverberated up and down the cañon. But the snake coiled and gave the signal again. This time a rock well directed silenced him.

He was stretched out by the fire and besides measuring over two feet he had thirteen rattles and a "button."

"An unlucky number," remarked a member of the party who had otherwise been silent during the evening.

The dead snake was cast off in the nearest cañon and the entertainment proceeded, with less enthusiasm, however.

But soon another signal was given and another snake dispatched. This was followed by numerous rattles, and soon the camp appeared to be alive with the reptiles. Wherever one walked one provoked the signal of one of these deadly rattlers.

As we killed, their numbers increased, and a silence settled down among the men that was lonesome.

Whether or not Hungry Bill, the Indian, who owned the property or claimed to own the country thereabouts and who was jealous of the prospectors, had caught a nest of the rattlers and brought them to the edge of the camp in the darkness and released them, we did not know, but it was the first time that a snake had been seen in the camp, which had been established for over a month, and the men were of the opinion that it was the work of the Indians.

Told Ghost Stories

There was but little sleeping the remainder of the night. The prospectors huddled close together in a common circle and talked in low voices, glancing at every shadow on the ground and expecting at any time to feel the fangs of a rattlesnake.

"Did you men see the ghosts of Death Valley?" inquired one of the prospectors who had been the first to cross the valley.

"No," replied the party in a sort of chorus. "Did you?"

"Yes," said the first speaker, and then he detailed how the spooks had lined up with torches and "paraded" out in the salt marshes by the thousands.

He said that it had been witnessed for years by people crossing the valley in the nighttime, and said it almost always occurred about midnight. He was under the impression that it was the spirits of departed immigrants who had perished in Death Valley in the early days when men did not know any better than attempt to cross it in the daytime.

We listened to his gruesome description of the "Death Valley spooks" until late in the night. With imaginary visions of these and the constant dread of rattlesnakes, we slept but little.

The early morning found us on the trail. We reached the edge of Death Valley at noon, and the heat was so intense that we hovered together in the shadow of our wagons the remainder of the day, trying to withstand the burning winds and stifling heat.

As soon as the sun sank we started on the journey to Furnace Creek, knowing that if we did not reach that place before sunrise that with our meager supply of water we should perish. Along the alkali trail the horses plodded in a stillness that is indescribable. We moved like snails, so thirsty and tired were the animals.

It was getting on toward midnight and this reminded us that it was the hour for the "spooks." No one seriously believed in it, but the stories of the previous night and the lonely graves we had seen during the night along the trail, of unfortunate prospectors who had attempted to cross in the daytime, had not stimulated our nerves to any considerable extent.

Spooks Appear

The many nights of sleeplessness and the heat of the previous trip across Death Valley had told on our nerves. The hardiest and nerviest of men may be brought to a state through hardships that will make cowards of them. With common interest we were watching for the "spooks." And we did not have long to wait, though at first we thought it was artificial instead of natural phenomena.

We were somewhere about the center of the sink when we saw a blaze of fire suddenly rise up in the desert far to the south. It appeared to be considerably above the ground and moving. My companions saw it at the same time, and one of them remarked in wonder that an automobile should be passing along in that portion of Death Valley at such an hour. We stopped our team and watched the light. We soon discovered that it was not moving, but that it was giving forth a flame not unlike a Chinese "spitter." The fire fairly shot forth as if blown out of the gooseneck of a plumber's furnace.

"It is somebody with a torch, and probably lost," remarked a member of our party.

We shouted at the top of our voices, but the flame flared on, and there was no change in its position. We started to drive out that way, but remembered the treachery of the valley and decided to wait.

While we were watching another light appeared a little to the west. It was dim at first, but soon began to flare like the other. Then another and another appeared, following each other in quick succession until the sink looked like a torchlight procession, but they were all stationary. When we would drive on they looked as if they were moving, too.

"It looks like a demonstration of a flambeau club," said one of the men.

"It looks more like a spook procession," replied another.

It was a sultry night. We had traveled by night on account of the hot day that preceded. A suffocating heat seemed to rise up from the earth. You could feel it like the hot air coming from a house furnace through the door. We had our revolvers buckled about our waists, and one more nervous than the others reached for his rifle. Then we smiled grimly at each other as we could see from the dim light from the phenomena which lighted up our faces.

We were not afraid, and yet the stories of Death Valley loomed up in our minds; that is, in my mind, and others afterward acknowledged the same thing, and we could imagine all kinds of things. We had passed a number of mounds that night, and while we could not read the inscriptions on the little headboards by the light from the stars, we remembered many of them, as we had read them going over. One told about an unknown prospector being found with skull crushed, and how the partner found the body and buried him. Another told the story of death from thirst, and another told how the companions had fallen out in that desolate country, and how one had murdered his companion and fled.

Wholesale Massacres

Then the stories of the wholesale massacres of immigrants by Indians in early days came up in our minds. We saw all kinds of visions, and the lights flickered about the desert like so many jack-o'-lanterns. We were in a breathless mood. Neither spoke for several minutes. We would watch a new light appear, and then watch another exhaust itself. The whole valley, so far as we could see, was a panorama of dying and rekindling lights. The team was restless, and finally walked on, drawing us along with them, though we paid but little attention to them.

I was looking away to the south at a new blaze of fire, when suddenly the place lighted up right in front of us, blinding our eyes and frightening the team. For a moment the "hair fairly rose on my head," and I saw from the pale faces of my companions that they were in no easy mood. We looked in front of the lead mule and saw a ball of fire lying on the ground. We got out to investigate. We found a blaze that made a sizzling noise. It was coming from a round substance as large as a man's fist. We kicked it about, and as the fragments would fall apart the blaze would continue. We discovered that it was composed of a whitish substance and that the fire had come from spontaneous combustion. It was saltpetre, or some substance formed from the salt and other chemical matter of that region, and the processes had caused the flame. We ran across plenty of the phenomena within the next few hours. In fact, it became so frequent that we quit investigating and came to pay no attention to it.

SOUTHWEST

Rufus Steele's poem, which captures the spirit of the prospector's timeless quest in the manner of Robert Service, appeared in the San Francisco Pacific Monthly *of October 1907.*

FROM BULLFROG
by Rufus Milas Steele

Out there in the land o' sagebrush, in the brown horn-toad's
    domain,
Where the clouds float 'round moth-eaten—in the land of stingy
    rain:
Where the birds are only sagehens, where the gray coyote slinks:
Where each little drop o' water is a shinin' pearl that stinks:
Where the trailless, silent desert like a windin' sheet has grown—
Alkali made even whiter; redhot sunshine crumbles bone!
Where you swing a pick in anguish, probe the bowels of a hill,
P'raps you'll hear the nuggets callin'—then it's time to scrawl your
    will.

Out there in the land of gamble, where the chance is swift and
    steep,
Where each man gives in his little so that some may take a heap:
Where the life rips off the covers, stamps his breed upon each
    lad—
Where a man is clean and quiet, or is rotten, shoutin' bad:
Where the fightin' ground is ready for the man who cannot wait,
Where he sheds his extry linen, has his battle out with Fate:
Where a man may win a fortune, where he'll lose all but his name,
I have cut the deck for dealer, tried to play a white man's game.

I recall when I first saw it, saw this hidin' ground of gold;
It's not hard to recollect it—these gray hairs don't mean I'm old.
Stood above a new rag village on a bit of risin' ground—
You could hear the clink of glasses, roulette wheels a-clickin' round.
But my thoughts were on the desert, shimmerin' in devil's breath,
On the bare hills that meandered to the valley they call Death.
Any man can be a hero, gladly go to eat his dirt,
When he's got a proper purpose buttoned in his flannel shirt.

Bushy Pete made me an offer—Peter Bush had been his name:
So I followed him at sunset, packed my blankets to his claim;

215

To a staked-out patch o' hillside where, he hadn't any doubt,
When he'd dug in all his savings he should dig a fortune out.
Coaxed my muscles with the hammer, swung the pick with growin'
    might,
Came to know the faintest colors, how to fuse the dynamite:
Learned the things that might be useful—how to tunnel, stope and
    shelf—
In that wondrous time when I could go prospectin' for myself.

Learned a mite of human nature from the men who came and
    went,
Men of fifty occupations on one occupation bent.
Learned that overalls and whiskers do not make a sameness when
They are part of ev'ry feller: dogs are dogs, and men are men.
Had my share of sour moments: it will sometimes turn your head,
This hard life among the raw things, too much flesh, too little
    bread.
But I carried with me somethin' that could banish ache and pain—
Just a mem'ry of a someone wavin' good-bye to a train.

Bushy Pete was not a liar; when his stake could stand alone
Peter handed me a nugget, sent me forth to find my own.
Then I purchased Bill, the burro—you could shove him in a
    sack—
And I strapped an outfit weighin' more than him upon his back.
Found out all that men could tell me 'bout the desert, always
    strange;
Mostly 'bout the pools of water: struck out to'rds the Fun'ral Range,
Little knowin' as I punched Bill out o' sight across the hill
That the truest friend I'd ever find was this same burro, Bill.

Morning stillness in the desert, seems to pierce your very ear:
Only crunchin' of your bootheels saves you from the deaf man fear.
Not a livin' creature stirrin': oh, if rock or bush would move!
Unseen sand imps blot your footprints, leave you no retreatin'
    groove.
White-hot noontime in the desert; shadows flee as if afraid:
Now you reach the broadest yucca, sink and pant in its thin shade.
Hours, ages; then it's ev'ning: you and faithful burro roll
With your last strength down a hillside, sprawl beside the water
    hole.

Ev'ry day gnawed at my courage, ev'ry day the luck was strained.
Could I always make the water when the canteen had been
    drained?
Learned that sand and desolation try to smite you with their curse:
Learned that where there are no panthers somethin' trails you that
    is worse.
Came to know this desert dragon, tried to dodge it ev'ry way:
Fell down on my face in terror when the Thing brought me to bay.
Out there in the quiet judgment, where a man is just a mole,
Where there's not a leaf to hide you, you have got to face your
    soul.

Cinched my belt and punched the burro—was it anything so
    strange?
Gold was waitin' at the grass-roots over in the Fun'ral Range!
When the night had shut the sun out, Bill and me would cool our
    tongues,
Almost burst our sides a-breathin' air that did not scorch our lungs.
Have a scanty bite o' supper, eat together, man and mule,
Rub our noses just for comp'ny, throw ourselves down by the pool.
Soon we two would be a-dreamin', one asleep upon his side,
With the other seein' visions, dreamin' with eyes open wide.

Pond'rous animals a-stalkin', all in sheaths like coats-o'-mail:
Man whose claws reached out to tear things while he sat back on
    his tail:
Big fish crawlin' from the water; snakes that stood up, birds in fur:
They all hissed the man in passin'—course no such freaks there
    ever were.
Came another, sweeter vision, in a twilight, in a shade—
Bread an' butter to the starvin', courage to a man afraid.
Though I hadn't seen Her dress so, though She turned Her face
    away,
Still I saw Her, felt Her, knew Her—hear the burro's mornin' bray!

Came a day just like the others, saw a far-off ugly hill,
Guessed that in its side was water, in a pocket, glassy still.
Carried just enough to last us till we reached the new supply—
Makes your legs a bit more willin' when you've got to move or die.
Staggered to the pool at sunset, knelt and waited to see Bill
Plunge his nose in to the eyelids, from the bottom drink his fill.
Saw the burro sniff and leave it. It was like a body blow.
Knew this was the poison water. Bill could read the warning: Go!

Turned from danger and temptation, headed Bill out on the plain:
Shut my teeth to stop the curses, beat my legs to ease the pain.
Marched a mile and fell exhausted, realized it with a start,
That I had been stepping, stepping to the poundin' of my heart.
Tried to weigh the situation: way back there was water, true;
Two days on the Fun'rals beckoned, with a chance of water, too.
Burnin' lips were pleadin' "Backward!" "Gold!" I heard the silence
    cry:
Slapped the burro, started forward for an all-night journey—dry!

Giant ships run by machinery churn the oceans till they boil,
All because the shaft and socket have a little drop of oil.
Just a little sip of water would have gone straight to the points,
Kept the heart and lungs from grindin', bones from raspin' in their
    joints.
Came the awful freaks of night-time, came the things that never
    were,
Came the mammoth walkin' serpents, came the ostriches in fur:
Lined up front and back and sideways, had no feelin' for our pain:
Made poor Bill and me go marchin' to their stride that shook the
    plain.

Lookin' over I could see the hairy man a-swingin' long;
Felt I'd give some of those nuggets just to be a half as strong.
By and by I saw him heavin', his mouth, too, was full of fire;
Poor old thing, he wasn't human; not a trained slave of Desire.
Saw him stoop and gather pebbles, roll them far back on his tongue,
Saw his jaws a-munchin', munchin'; saw him brace up as if stung.
Cunningly I snatched up pebbles, placed them, forced the jaws
    to go,
Tasted blessed crazy water, felt redhot saliva flow.

Marchin', grindin' all to nothin', ages strung out just like gum:
Stumbled, staggered, kept on fallin', struck the sand and lay there
    dumb.
Slept, oh sweetness; but the silence woke me up, pried open eyes.
All the freaks were stopped and waitin', watchin' to see if I'd rise.
Pressed my palms to raise my shoulders, lifted, heard the muscles
    crack:
Realized one of the biggest things was perched upon my back.
Then She came and brushed it from me, set me on my feet a man:
Turned to touch Her, She had vanished: clutched Bill's ear and ran
    and ran.

Far behind an enemy was softly climbin' up a hill:
From the summit saw me, 'way off; saw me draggin', almost still.
Sent an arrow at my hatbrim like a bullet from a gun;
Struck me, whirled me round to face him—oh, the grinnin'
    mornin' sun!
Cruel blow, but it revived me, from the darkness set me free.
Though it meant prepare for battle, you can fight when you can see.
Give a man free limbs and daylight, he will tell you it is well,
Even with the canteen empty just about a mile from hell.

Strained my eyes in all directions; water holes were scarce as
    grass—
Only sand, and sand a-bakin', charmed, or it would turn to glass.
Bill could tell it without lookin', only looked 'round at his pack,
So I tusseled with the cinches, threw off all but pick and sack.
Marked a beeline for the Fun'rals, punched Bill almost to a lope,
Had n't gone a mile till it was just like walkin' on a rope;
With a thousand teasin' devils poundin' anvils in my ears;
With my tongue creepin', creepin', reachin', beggin', but no tears.

Buried in the sand a shirtsleeve, saw it eaten up by ants:
By and by came on the pieces of a garment men call pants:
Little further found a canteen, just an achin' empty hull:
Held my breath and went a-huntin' till I found it—found a skull.
Told the poor thing I was sorry, heard it laugh just like a clown.
Hastened onward, almost smothered, peeled my shirt and threw it
    down.
Joy, oh joy! to lose the burden, wanted to burst into song:
Stopped, all frightened, crawled back to it, bound it on me with a
    thong.

Thought of hairy man and pebbles, grabbed one; I would get a
    swig;
Tried to place it, but it tumbled; couldn't do it, tongue too big.
Got down in a shadeless hollow, went a-hoppin' like a frog,
Clawed a well to hunt for water, not as man would, that was dog.
Come on, Bill, let's make the Fun'rals! Straight ahead I saw the sun
With his one big eye a-squintin' down the barrel of his gun.
Bill came close, together huddled, so the sun could pot his own.
Jesus, pity little babies when the breasts are bleachin' bone!

Put my arms around the burro, begged him to work out a plan;
Bill must henceforth be the leader, this was not the land of man.

Southwest from Bullfrog   219

Begged him just to do one favor, promised him a palace, strawed;
Begged him just to lead to water, begged him by the livin' Gawd!
But he wouldn't understand me, and he wouldn't seem to see;
Bill had strength and instinct left him and he wouldn't share
    with me.
He could spare the moisture diamonds on his hangin' tongue at
    least:
Out there in the treasure desert dying man robbed dying beast.

Water, water, water, water. On my burnin' face a flood.
Reached down in the dark before me, fingers clutched the juicy
    mud.
Found my tongue was in the water, lappin', lappin' as I could.
Knew salvation had come some way: knew that Gawd was mighty
    good.
Heard old Bill a-snorin' by me; went on sleepin' while I wept:
Woke up, forced another swaller, rolled into the pool and slept.
How we ever found the water, how he led a wild man through,
Only Bill knew, Bill was silent: burros don't boast what they do.

Lay two days beside the water, even then 't was hard to go,
But the Fun'rals were a-smilin' and the grub was gettin' low.
Sagebrush nodded as we passed it, even cactus seemed to bend:
Slim brown lizard came a-scootin' like he'd just lief be our friend.
P'raps it's what a little suff'rin' brings to ev'ry man some time—
And I even thought about Her without feelin' 't was a crime.
So we reached the barren Fun'rals, found a spring where rocks rose
    bold:
Spent a sleepless night before we'd set out searchin' for Her gold.

Somehow things look bright and easy 'way off in a soft'ning light:
Gold was waitin' at the grass-roots, but the grass was not in sight!
Ev'ry day I went prospectin'; in the rocks the pick would ring.
Tried out all the likely places, came at night back to the spring.
Ev'ry day a bigger circle; little fears soon grew so thick
That I'd dig on in the darkness till the points wore off the pick.
I could see Her waitin', trustin': She had b'lieved my golden tales:
I would get it if I had to dig it with my fingernails!

Found an old ravine that wound up through the hills and on and on;
Torrents had rushed down it sometime, now the smallest drop was
    gone.
Yelled to find a trace of color, knew that I was on the track.

Worked on through the hottest hours—blisters cannot break your
  back.
Yard and rod and mile I furrowed up the narrow steep ravine,
Grudgin' time it took to go back with the burro and canteen:
Grudgin' each dip in the grubsack, grudgin' time it took to nap;
Grudgin' anything that kept me from that wearin' tap, tap, tap.

Colors, traces: Where the nuggets? Surely we must be most there!
Turned from each new empty pickhole, swung to lay the next yard
  bare.
Any stroke might end the tension, any stroke might make Her rich!
Gawd be in the nerves and muscles, help 'em just to keep the pitch.
Six miles back of us is water—old canteen is scorchin' tin:
Nuggets first, and then we'll go back; yes, we'll go back; not till
  then!
Prayed and shouted as I sweated; burro shivered, not with cold.
Patience, Bill, a little longer: *we will drink and eat the gold!*

Bushy Pete had gone prospectin' to forget his gamblin' loss.
Wise Pete went around the desert as the shortest way across:
Wandered in the Fun'ral Mountains, down an old ravine he rolled:
Found a madman with his fingers, mouth and bootlegs stuffed with
  gold!
Water—water by the spoonful—saved his reason, brought him
  through:
He had found a pocket that would be a lifetime stake for two.
Peter fed him, nursed him, lead him, childlike, back to town again,
Where he'd put old Bill on barley, shave his beard, and then—and
  then!

Wandered weak out to the sand-edge just to tell the thing good-bye;
I was grinnin' glad to leave it, but somehow it made me cry.
Cursed the roastin' devil's kingdom, knelt to kiss the thing so dear:
And the desert shrieked with laughter—bein' deaf I couldn't hear.
Wrung the rough true hand of Peter, had a private talk with Bill,
Took the train a-flyin' eastward—wish I was as happy still!
Wish I never could have found Her: wish I'd never had to know:
Gawd, ain't women *ever* faithful? Gawd, what made me work so
  slow?

Hello Bill. Why, hello, Peter. Yes, it's me you see back here.
P'raps I'll keep on stayin' with you, kind o' like the atmosphere.
Bill, I think we'll go prospectin', though we've got enough o' wealth:

Southwest from Bullfrog   221

Guess we'll drill around the desert for a while just for our health.
Wonder will it seem like Heaven when we stagger to a pool?
Wonder will the freaks come night-times just to giggle at a fool?
Wonder will another vision—Pshaw! I guess that's at an end.
Hear the little lizard callin'! Come on, Bill: ol' friend, ol' friend!

HALF A CENTURY

Shorty Harris, one of the last of the jackass prospectors and a classic gabby braggart, recalled his life story to Philip Johnston in the October 1930 issue of Touring Topics, *now known as* Westways. *Even at age 73, Shorty was still looking forward to making just one more big strike.*

CHASING RAINBOWS

by Frank Shorty Harris

as told to Philip Johnston

BALLARAT is a long way from Rhode Island, and a lot of strangers that come through these parts think it's queer that I should have strayed so far from the place where I was born. But even a maverick jackass can go a long way from his home range if he starts out for better grass, or to find a place where there ain't no danger of someone putting a rope and a pack saddle on him.

Anyhow, it was on the twenty-first day of July, 1857, that the baby who was to be Shorty Harris first opened his eyes in New England. My father, Richard M. Harris, was an Irishman who had started to work in Providence as a shoemaker, and finally built up a shoe factory. My mother was Scotch, but I didn't inherit much of her ways, or I wouldn't be living in this old adobe today. I don't remember much about them—they both died when I was seven years old, and I was adopted by my aunt, Alice Cooney. She was very poor, and father lost all he had before he died; so I had to go to work when I was eleven years old. I got a job in a calico mill dipping cotton into dye, and my wages were nine dollars a month.

There were several of us orphans in that mill, and we used to get together sometimes of an evening, and plan how we might go someplace else where we could earn more money and not have to work such long hours. I had only one pair of shoes and wore them to church on Sunday; the rest of the time I went barefoot.

A kind old priest, whose name was Father Andy Gibson, took pity on us boys, and we went to his house two hours a week, where we learned how to read and write. That was the only schooling I ever had, but it was enough; for I got fitchered up on big words and could read the newspapers like anyone else.

When I was fourteen years old, I ran away from my aunt's home and turned my hand to different kinds of work in Massachusetts and Connecticut—farm work, section work, and anything else that I could get. Then I went to firing boilers in a factory, and after I had saved up about eighty dollars, went to Philadelphia to see the Centennial Exposition. This was in 1876. But my little stake did not last long, and jobs were scarce, so I shined shoes and sold papers on the streets. After a few months of this, I got the notion to go west. I started out, beating my way on trains and stopping for a day or two to work when I got too hungry to keep going.

One day I got off the train at a little town in Kansas—Dodge City—and found that I was really "out West." Around the station were piles of buffalo hides as big as houses, and down by the railroad yards were thousands of cattle that the cowboys were loading into cars. There were saloons and dance halls a-plenty, and they did a rushing business day and night. Those cowboys from Texas who drove the cattle across the plains were a wild lot. They were all mighty quick on the trigger, and most of their arguments were settled with bullets. Hardly a night passed that there wasn't a man laid out cold after the guns got through popping. But at that they were all bighearted fellows, and would split their last dollar with a man who was down and out.

I soon made up my mind that I didn't want to stay in Dodge City. There was too much lead flying around of an evening; and besides, I kept hearing wonderful stories about the rich mines that were being found farther west by fellows who were just ordinary punks like me. Here, I thought, was a chance to make my fortune; so one night I climbed on the rods and started out. Between keeping the cinders out of my eyes, dodging brakemen and rustling food, I was plenty busy on that trip. Finally I wound up at Yuma where a big husky brakeman told me about plenty that would happen if he found me on his train again. I walked down by the river and took a long nap under a cottonwood. When I went back to the station there was a big crowd on the platform. I gathered from what they were saying that a train was coming through with General Grant and his son. Pretty soon there came the whistle of a locomotive, and the crowd let out a cheer that sounded like a war whoop. The train rolled in and stopped. General Grant was on the hind platform, and gave a short speech. While all this was going on, I found a good place to ride under the General's car, and when the train pulled out that crowd waved good bye to Shorty as well as General Grant!

The next day, when we got to Colton, I was as dirty as a coal miner and as hungry as a wolf. Walking along the platform, I bumped into the General and Fred; they were stretching their legs and talking to each other. I told Fred that I had come west on his train to make my fortune, but my luck had not been very good so far. He could see that I was telling him the truth, because I looked like a

226   *Rainbow Chasers*

scarecrow. I braced him for a road stake, and he gave me seven dollars! That was a lot in those days of schooners and free lunch.

Los Angeles was just a small place in '77. There were no pavements like those in Philadelphia, and most of the people in the streets were farmers and cowboys. I worked at different things for several months, and then decided that I'd better go somewhere else. At this time, news was coming in of big strikes in Colorado, so I hopped the trains again, and beat it to Leadville. Here I got my first experience in mining—and the life of a mining town that was a rip-snorter!

It was easy to get a job, and pay was good. A man got four dollars a day for working in a dry mine and five dollars for working in a wet one. Most of the deep mines, or shafts, were wet, and the tunnels were dry. Here I made the first real money that I had ever seen in my life, but I did not keep a dollar of it. The other miners showed me how to gamble and spend, and believe me it didn't take long to learn how to do it! Every Saturday night when we got our pay, we would buy a few rounds of drinks at a saloon—and there were more saloons than anything else in Leadville. . . .

I soon decided that I'd rather prospect than work for wages. No one ever got rich working for four dollars a day, and there was plenty of country that had not been hunted over. I had heard some wonderful stories about the Coeur d'Alene district in Idaho, and took a notion to go there. When I had saved up a small stake, I left Colorado to try my luck in the new diggings. It was late in the fall when I got to Wallace, and plenty of snow lay on the ground. I got acquainted with a couple of men who were going to start out for Thompson Flats, and the three of us decided to go together. We made some sleds out of barrel staves, and hauled our outfits more than sixty miles. It was tough, and several times I wished that we had burros to do it.

A man always takes a big chance when he goes prospecting. He may spend months or years without finding anything worth looking at; so when we found a man who had some good ground to lease, it looked like a good way to clean up some ready money. It was a placer proposition, and after six weeks' work we had washed out about 400 in gold apiece. But when the snow went off, I got restless and made up my mind to try my luck in Montana. The other boys figured that they'd better stay on the Coeur d'Alene, so I went out alone. For nearly a year I prospected and worked for wages around the Montana camps without getting much ahead; then a letter from one of my Idaho partners told me that I had left too soon—they had found some claims that showed wonderful pay-ore, and sold out for a fortune.

Half a Century Chasing Rainbows

Good reports were coming in from the camps in Utah, and I went to Tintic to look things over. There was plenty of work in the mines, and I put in about two years there and at Frisco, which was a live place if there ever was one. I hear that Frisco is a ghost town now—abandoned and the buildings falling to ruin. That is what happened to many of the towns where I worked in the early days, but nobody then would have thought it was possible. Even now, it's hard for me to believe that owls are roosting over those old bars where we lined up for drinks, and sagebrush is growing in the streets.

In '85, I went from Frisco to Tombstone, and she was a beauty in those days. I've read quite a bit lately about some of the old-timers going back there and staging some of the exciting things that were pulled off forty-five years ago. They would have to go some if they made it as lively as it was then, for Tombstone was almost as hell-roaring a place as Leadville. The boys were all decorated with six-guns, and believe me, they knew how to use them. The handiest on the draw stayed in town, but those that were too slow made a one-way trip to Boot Hill. Killings were so common that the *Tombstone Epitaph* didn't have much to say about them—just a short paragraph for each one. And the streets had names that sounded interesting—there were Toughnut Street and Trigger Alley, and both of them were good places to make a start for Boot Hill. That camp had plenty of musicians, men who could play mighty well on the Winchester violin—a fiddle that can be tuned up damn quick!

Most of the country around Tombstone was plastered with claims, and I didn't find anything worth staking out. Miners from California and Nevada told me of the big strikes that were being made there, and of the Lost Gunsight, the Lost Breyfogle, the Lost Pegleg, and other lost mines that were sure to be found sometime. They told me of other places like Tombstone—wide-open camps that never slept, where fortunes were taken out of the ground every day. After I had heard those stories, I made up my mind that that was the country for the Short Man, and I was on my way.

During the next seven or eight years I went from one good mining center to another, working long enough to get a stake, and then going out to prospect. For a while I was in Virginia City, then I went to Bodie while she was still going strong. The Silver Peak country in Nevada was mighty good in those days. I blew into town one day, completely broke and hungry as a coyote. The first job that I struck was peeling potatoes in a restaurant for three dollars a day, but it was a fine job at that because I got plenty to eat. And while I was saving up enough money from my pay to start out prospecting again, I put on enough flesh to carry me over some of the hungry days that were sure to come.

Finally, I got an outfit together and went out to find a claim. Luck was with me in those days, for I struck it rich before long. I located ground that showed some of the best values ever seen in that country, and got $7,000 for it. That was the most money that I had ever owned, and it meant plenty of good times for Shorty. After I had blown most of it, I was ready to start out to find another claim.

All this time I was hearing more stories of lost mines, especially about the Lost Breyfogle. The old-timers told me that it was somewhere east of Death Valley, and that the man who found it would get enough gold to pay the national debt. Then there were other stories of the Panamints, west of Death Valley, where a gang of road agents had found some wonderful bodies of silver-lead and sold them to Senator Stewart. It's a funny thing, and something that I can't explain, but the country that is far away always looks best to a prospector. Somehow he feels that over the big range of mountains are better formations than those around him; and a hundred miles away is a rich outcropping that is just waiting to be staked out. Well, that's the way I felt as I listened to those tales of Death Valley, and I decided to look it over.

Since I first started prospecting in Colorado fifteen years before this, I had seen plenty of wild country and had learned plenty about long trips with a burro. But when I got into Inyo County, I had to learn a lot more. Right from my front door I can see where I first camped in Panamint Valley, under the mesquite at Postoffice Spring long before Ballarat or Randsburg was on the map. I saw this town grow to a good size, with over a thousand people, and big shipments of bullion going out on the stages every day. And now I'm still living here, watching the 'dobe ruins crumble around me. But you can see that I have a pretty good place to live. When the town was going strong, this was the schoolhouse, and when all the people went away and there was no school, I just moved in.

But when I first came to Panamint Valley, about the only inhabitants of those mountains were the mountain sheep, and the Short Man followed their trails through the canyons and over the peaks looking for gold. And there is some wonderful ore up there— some of the prettiest that I ever saw. Most of the formations are broken up, and there are no large bodies that you can count on. I have found pockets that held as much as $1,600 in gold, and some small veins have been almost pure stuff.

John Lambert came into this country in '92 after I had been here quite a while, and we worked as partners. One day—it was St. Patrick's Day—we were climbing over the ledges of Pleasant Canyon, trying to find the place where some rich float had come from. Well, we located it, and believe me, it was the kind that, as the miners say, "has the eagle stamped right on it."

With our picks we broke about fifteen pounds of that rock loose and carried it down to camp. There we ground it up and panned it out in a wash tub. Talk about your coarse gold—it was there, all right! Out would come a five-dollar chunk and then one that would run two or three dollars, and the dollar pieces kept pouring out of the pan almost in a yellow stream. The small batch of ore had $360 in it, and that was only a start of what we found in the St. Patrick mine; for we panned out a fair-sized stake for each of us, and then sold the mine while the showing was still good. The buyer took out just about what he paid us, which meant that we got all there was in the St. Patrick without having to do all the work!

After this, I found more claims in the Panamints. Some of them were good enough to wash out free gold and others were only good to sell. In those days I was called "Shorty the Peddler" because I had so many claims and prospects that I wanted to dispose of, and I sure know how to do it. Once I had a fine showing up in Pleasant Canyon, and R. W. Harrison of the Radcliffe Mining Company looked it over. When he asked my price, I said:

"Well, it has all the earmarks of a good mine, and I think that I'd be making you a present of it for fifteen thousand."

Harrison said that he would see other officers of the company and find out what they would do. Two weeks went by and I didn't hear a word from them, so I said to myself, "They must be getting cold feet; I'll have to give them the rush act!" One day I found them all together at dinner, and I went in with a long face and a letter in my hand.

"I've just got bad news from the East," I told them, "and I've got to get away quick. My father is dying and my aunt is in the hospital. There is some money to be divided up among their relatives, and I must be on the spot when this thing is pulled off. I'll take eleven hundred for that claim right now."

"That's quite a fall from fifteen thousand," Harrison said.

"Well, I mean business, but you'll have to act quick if you want it."

When he had threshed out all the details, I had signed up for a price of $1,000, which was just what I had intended to get in the first place, but a man always has to start with a higher figure.

230   *Rainbow Chasers*

I could usually find some way to put a deal over, but sometimes it took some real work. There was another time that a man got interested in a property I had for sale, and went out with me to look it over. He thought the showing was pretty good, and asked me how much I'd take. I told him that the price on this one was $2,000. I could see that I'd started too high, because he began to move away like he didn't want to talk about it anymore. I needed money pretty badly and wanted the deal to go through.

"How much money have you got on you now?" I asked him.

"About a hundred and seventy-five or eighty dollars," he said.

"Well, that's my money, and you've got a mine!"

But he kept walking off, so I said again:

"If that price won't hold you, I'll put a bell and a pair of hobbles on you and see if they won't keep you from getting away!"

But I couldn't make it stick, and my buyer escaped from me after all.

I never was much of a hand to grubstake. Most men would expect a prospector to find a mine worth a hundred thousand with his first $50 or $100 stake, and not one in a million will stay with you. When I got down to bedrock, I'd sell a claim, or, if I couldn't sell one, I'd work a while for wages or do tunneling by contract. I always found it a damn sight better to go on my own.

All my traveling in this country was done on the hurricane deck of a jackass, and believe me, that's the way all the big strikes have been made. A jack can go almost anywhere that a mountain sheep can, and carry all that a man needs for several weeks. You've heard it said that "gold is where you find it." I can tell you that it's usually found in places that are hard to get to, and a burro can get there when a horse or a mule would be stalled for good.

I believe that a jackass is the wisest animal in the world. He can work for a long time on slim pickings and get by where a horse would starve, but he likes to dodge hard work as much as possible and he sure knows how to do it. When I made a camp where I planned to stay for a week or two, the jacks would wander around close, and part of the time they'd almost be in the way. But as soon as I'd start to get the outfit together like I was thinking of moving on, they'd sneak off and I sometimes had fifteen or twenty miles to hike before I found them. When I did locate them they were in an out-of-the-way place, well hidden. A prospector once told me that his burros hid out on him and he couldn't find them for several days. He was about to give up the search, when he saw one of them carrying something in his mouth. It was a five-gallon oil can with a wire bail in it that the burro had filled with water which he was carrying to his pals. By following him and keeping out of sight, the prospector found the rest of them in a small valley.

Some burros are great thieves, and you have to watch 'em close if you don't want to lose your grub. I knew a couple of men—Doctor Trotter and Frank McAlister—who went on a long prospecting trip with five burros, one black and four grays. The black one was named Honest John, because he was such an expert camp robber. When the men found a place where they wanted to stay for a few days and look around, they unpacked their outfit and got ready to go back into the canyons afoot.

"Frank," said Doc, "we had better fix up our camp so Honest John can't rob us; he'll clean us out if he gets a chance!"

So they spread a tarp over their grub and weighted it down with big stones. That afternoon when they came back, McAlister let out a yell:

"Gee whiz, Doc, they're all white burros; what in hell has happened?"

They ran to camp, wondering what could be the matter, and found that Honest John had rolled those stones off the tarp and the five burros had helped themselves to two sacks of flour—eaten what they could and scattered the rest over the ground where they had rolled in it. Those men had a hard time to gather up enough to make one mess of flapjacks.

I know a miner by the name of Dusty Rhodes over in the Hidden Spring country, who told me a good story of this kind. He had a burro that he called Rustler Billy, and he had to keep things out of reach or he'd lose them. One morning he put a loaf of bread in the Dutch oven, figuring that it'd be perfectly safe there, but Rustler Billy cleaned him of that loaf by lifting the lid and grabbing the bread. These jackasses are educated devils!

Sometimes when I sold a claim and wanted to put on a real celebration, I'd go to Tonopah, which was the biggest camp in this part of the country, and the livest. There were always plenty of games going on, and if a fellow asked the dealer what the limit was, he'd point to the ceiling. The most exciting times came on the Fourth of July, when the whole town turned out to have a good time. There were drilling matches, where one man swung a double jack, and another handled the drill, and the first prize was usually a thousand dollars. It was about this time that the pneumatic drill began to be used, and the miners called them "wiggle tails." But it didn't take as much skill and teamwork to handle them as it did the double jack, and they were not used in contests then.

I prospected most of the country east of Death Valley, around the Johnny Mine and Goodsprings, and located some pretty good claims in that district. One day when I stopped at Resting Springs, Fi Lee, a squaw man who lived there, told me that he had heard of some good showings over at Greenwater, and I decided to see what I could find. That was one of the hardest trips I ever made. It was in the middle of the summer, and many of the springs were dry. When I got into the Funeral Mountains at Greenwater, I found an old shaft that must have been dug by the "forty-niners." There were old powder cans in it that had rusted to pieces. It looked as if an accident had happened to the outfit that made the discovery, for there was some rich ore in that shaft. I put up my monuments and started back to Ballarat, but ran out of water before I had gone far. I knew the burros could find some—a burro can smell water several miles away—so I turned 'em loose, and sure enough they led me to a hole in the rocks that held a little water. But it was the worst I ever saw, full of dead rats and birds, and the burros wouldn't touch it. When a jackass won't drink water, a man had better let it alone if he values his life and health. But I was so damn dry that I was ready to take a chance at anything wet, so I strained it through a gunny sack and filled my canteens.

When I got to Furnace Creek it was one of the hottest days anyone had seen in Death Valley. I found three men lying on the porch of the ranch house with cottonwood leaves over their faces. One of them raised up and said to me: "God, partner, ain't it hot?"

"Hell no," I said, "I've got my overcoat tied on my packsaddle!"

I went from the ranch across Death Valley, through Townsend Pass, and on to Ballarat. When I got there I was all in and about ready to quit. I sent Jud Decker, a partner of mine, to Independence with the notice. But before he put it on record he went on a big spree, and forgot what he had made the trip for. The next year some miners discovered that my Greenwater claim had not been recorded, and they filed on it. Later on, it turned out to be one of the richest in that part of the country, and I figured that I was the loser to the tune of $1,000,000—for that's what was taken from that mine!

But Inyo is a big county, and I knew there was plenty more gold for the man who found it, so I didn't worry. As long as a fellow has plenty of bacon and beans and a few good claims to sell, he is not so badly off. I had some pretty good ground around Ballarat—and the town was going strong then. Stages were running to the inside every day, and they carried plenty of bullion from the mines. There was plenty of money in the camp, too, and she was a hummer. But there wasn't much powder burned in Ballarat. The boys managed to have their good times without getting too rough. They were a mighty fine bunch for the most part, and free spenders, too. When a man walked into a saloon with coin, the others didn't need an invitation. Somebody would yell:

"Hey, what's the matter with you fellows sitting back there? Money on the bar!" And they'd all march up to get theirs.

But if a gent came in the front door with jack, and didn't come clean with the fellows, he'd go out the back door "light," without stopping long inside. And we fired all the "sleepers" down the cellar in those days.

I knew a girl in Ballarat by the name of Bessie Hart. She was a mighty fine woman and a good cook. No one in camp dared to pull any rough stuff around her—she was six feet tall, weighed 210 pounds, and could lick a husky man. I don't know why a little hammered-down fellow like me should fall in love with a woman like that—but I did just the same.

One day I was up by the Stone Corral sharpening picks in the blacksmith shop, and Bessie was blowing the bellows for me. Two of her best friends, Dean Harrison and Tom Walker, had gone to Tonopah, and she was missing them a lot, and I thought this would be a good chance for me.

"Miss Bessie," I said, "I guess you're kind of lonesome now since Dean and Tom are gone?"

"Oh, a little," she said.

"Well now, we've been kind of friendly for several years, and since they aren't likely to come back, what's the matter with me and you getting married?"

She didn't say anything for a minute or two—just looked me over from head to foot—just gave me the top and bottom stuff, and I wondered if she was going to speak.

"Shorty," she said finally, "I like you. . . . You're a good friend and a handy little fellow to play with. But you're too little for hard work!"

That was all I needed to show me that I was out of luck when it came to getting a wife, and I've never tried since. Plenty of my friends have got married, and from their experiences I've learned quite a lot about the business of matrimony. Flattery costs nothing, and one way to keep your wife from spending too much time and money at the beauty parlor is to tell her now and then how young and pretty she looks. When a man can't offer a woman dollars and cents he'll often be surprised to see how far a little flattery and incense will go.

But even if I've never been lucky at the game of love, I've had some good breaks when I was looking for gold. The best strike I ever made was in 1904 when I discovered the Rhyolite and Bullfrog district. I went into Boundary Canyon with five burros and plenty of grub, figuring to look over the country northeast of there. When I stopped at Keene Wonder Mine, Ed Cross was there waiting for his partner, Frank Howard, to bring some supplies from the inside. For some reason Howard had been delayed, and Cross was low on grub.

"Shorty," he said, "I'm up against it, and the Lord knows when Howard will come back. How are chances of going with you?"

"Sure, come right along," I told him. "I've got enough to keep us eating for a couple of months."

So we left the Keene Wonder, went through Boundary Canyon, and made camp at Buck Springs, five miles from a ranch on the Amargosa where a squaw man by the name of Monte Beatty lived. The next morning while Ed was cooking, I went after the burros. They were feeding on the side of a mountain near our camp and about half a mile from the spring. I carried my pick, as all prospectors do, even when they are looking for their jacks—a man never knows just when he is going to locate pay-ore. When I reached the burros, they were right on the spot where the Bullfrog mine was afterwards located. Two hundred feet away was a ledge of rock with some copper stains on it. I walked over and broke off a piece with my pick—and gosh, I couldn't believe my own eyes. The chunks of gold were so big that I could see them at arm's length—regular jewelry stone! In fact, a lot of that ore was sent to jewelers in this country and England, and they set it in rings, it was that pretty! Right then, it seemed to me that the whole mountain was gold.

I let out a yell, and Ed knew something had happened; so he came running up as fast as he could. When he got close enough to hear, I yelled again:

"Ed, we've got the world by the tail, or else we're coppered!"

We broke off several more pieces, and they were like the first— just lousy with gold. The rock was green, almost like turquoise, spotted with big chunks of yellow metal, and looked a lot like the back of a frog. This gave us an idea for naming our claim, so we called it the Bullfrog. The formation had a good dip, too. It looked like a real fissure vein; the kind that goes deep and has lots of real stuff in it. We hunted over that mountain for more outcroppings, but there were no others like that one the burros led me to. We had tumbled into the cream pitcher on the first one, so why waste time looking for skimmed milk?

That night we built a hot fire with greasewood and melted the gold out of the specimens. We wanted to see how much was copper and how much was the real stuff. And when the pan got red hot and that gold ran out and formed a button, we knew that our strike was a big one and that we were rich.

"How many claims do you figure on staking out?" Ed asked me.

"One ought to be plenty," I told him. "If there ain't enough money in one claim, there ain't enough in the whole country. If other fellows put extensions on that claim of ours and find good stuff, it will help us sell out for big money."

Ed saw that this was a good argument, so he agreed with me.

After the monuments were placed, we got some more rich samples and went to the county seat to record our claim. Then we marched into Goldfield and went to an eating house. Ed finished his meal before I did and went out into the street where he met Bob Montgomery, a miner that both of us knew. Ed showed him a sample of our ore, and Bob couldn't believe his eyes.

"Where did you get that?" he asked.

"Shorty and I found a ledge of it southwest of Bill Beatty's ranch," Ed told him.

Bob thought he was having some fun with him and said so.

"Oh, that's just a piece of float that you picked up somewhere. It's damn seldom ledges like that are found!"

Just then I came walking up, and Ed said, "Ask Shorty if I ain't telling you the truth."

"Bob," I said, "that's the biggest strike made since Goldfield was found. If you've got any sense at all, you'll go down there as fast as you can and get in on the ground floor!"

That seemed to be proof enough for him, and he went away in a hurry to get his outfit together—one horse and a cart to haul his tools and grub. He had an Indian with him by the name of Shoshone Johnny, who was a good prospector. Later on, it was this Indian who set the monuments on the claim that was to become the famous Montgomery-Shoshone Mine.

It's a mighty strange thing how fast the news of a strike travels. You can go into a town after you've made one, meet a friend on the street, and take him into your hotel room and lock the door. Then, after he has taken a nip from your bottle, you can whisper the news very softly in his ear. Before you can get out on the street, you'll see men running around like excited ants that have had a handful of sugar poured on their nest. Ed and I didn't try to keep our strike a secret, but we were surprised how the news of it spread. Men swarmed around us and asked to see our specimens. They took one look at them, and then started off on the run to get their outfits together.

I've seen some gold rushes in my time that were hummers, but nothing like that stampede. Men were leaving town in a steady stream with buckboards, buggies, wagons, and burros. It looked like the whole population of Goldfield was trying to move at once. Miners who were working for the big companies dropped their tools and got ready to leave town in a hurry. Timekeepers and clerks, waiters and cooks—they all got the fever and milled around, wild-eyed, trying to find a way to get out to the new "strike." In a little while there wasn't a horse or a wagon in town, outside of a few owned by the big companies, and the price of burros took a big jump. I saw one man who was about ready to cry because he couldn't buy a jackass for $500.

A lot of fellows loaded their stuff on two-wheeled carts—grub, tools, and cooking utensils—and away they went across the desert, two or three pulling a cart and the pots and pans rattling. When all the carts were gone, men who didn't have anything else started out on that seventy-five-mile hike with wheelbarrows, and a lot of 'em made it alright—but they had a hell of a time!

When Ed and I got back to our claim a week later, more than a thousand men were camped around it, and they were coming in every day. A few had tents, but most of 'em were in open camps. One man had brought a wagon load of whiskey, pitched a tent, and made a bar by laying a plank across two barrels. He was serving the liquor in tin cups, and doing a fine business.

That was the start of Rhyolite, and from then on things moved so fast that it made even us old-timers dizzy. Men were swarming all over the mountains like ants, staking out claims, digging and blasting, and hurrying back to the county seat to record their holdings. There were extensions on all sides of our claim, and other claims covering the country in all directions.

In a few days, wagon loads of lumber began to arrive, and the first buildings were put up. These were called rag-houses because they were half boards and half canvas. But this building material was so expensive that lots of men made dugouts, which didn't cost much more than plenty of sweat and blisters.

When the engineers and promoters began to come out, Ed and I got offers every day for our claim. But we just sat tight and watched the camp grow. We knew the price would go up after some of the others started to ship bullion. And as time went on, we saw that we were right. Frame shacks went up in the place of raghouses, and stores, saloons, and dance halls were being opened up every day.

Bids for our property got better and better. The man who wanted to buy would treat with plenty of liquor before he talked business, and in that way I got all I wanted to drink without spending a bean. Ed was wiser, though, and let the stuff alone—and it paid him to do it too, for when he did sell, he got much more for his half than I got for mine.

One night when I was pretty well lit up, a man by the name of Bryan took me to his room and put me to bed. The next morning when I woke up, I had a bad headache and wanted more liquor. Bryan had left several bottles of whiskey on a chair beside the bed and locked the door. I helped myself and went back to sleep. That was the start of the longest jag I ever went on; it lasted six days. When I came to, Bryan showed me a bill of sale for the Bullfrog, and the price was only $25,000. I got plenty sore, but it didn't do any good. There was my signature on the paper, and beside it the signatures of seven witnesses and the notary's seal. And I felt a lot worse when I found out that Ed had been paid a hundred and twenty-five thousand for his half, and had lit right out for Lone Pine, where he got married. Today he's living in San Diego County, has a fine ranch, and is very well fixed.

As soon as I got the money, I went out for a good time. All the girls ate regularly while old Shorty had the dough. As long as my stake lasted I could move and keep the band playing. And friends— I never knew I had so many! They'd jam a saloon to the doors, and every round of drinks cost me thirty or forty dollars. I'd have gone clean through the pay in a few weeks if Dave Driscol hadn't given me hell. Dave and I had been partners in Colorado and Utah, and I thought a great deal of him. Today he's living over in Wildrose Canyon, and going blind. Well, I had seven or eight thousand left when Dave talked to me.

"Shorty," he said, "if you don't cut this out you'll be broke in a damn short time and won't have the price of a meal ticket!"

I saw that he was right, and jumped on the water wagon then and there—and I haven't fallen off since.

Rhyolite grew like a mushroom. Gold Center was started four miles away, and Beatty's ranch became a town within a few months. There were 12,000 people in the three places, and two railroads were built out to Rhyolite. Shipments of gold were made every day, and some of the ore was so rich that it was sent by express with armed guards. And then a lot of cash came into Rhyolite—more than went out from the mines. It was this sucker money that put the town on the map quick. The stock exchange was doing a big business, and I remember that the price of Montgomery-Shoshone got up to ten dollars a share.

Businessmen of Rhyolite were live ones, alright. They decided to make the town the finest in Nevada—and they came mighty near doing it. Overbury built a three-story office building out of cut stone—it must have cost him fifty thousand. The bank building had three stories, too, and the bank was finished with marble and bronze. There were plenty of other fine business houses, and a railroad station that would look mighty good in any city.

Money was easy to get and easy to spend in those days. The miners and muckers threw it right and left when they had it. Many a time I've seen 'em eating bacon and beans and drinking champagne. Wages were just a sideline with them—most of their money was made in mining stock.

Rhyolite was a great town, and no mistake—as live as the Colorado camps were thirty years before, but not so bad. We had a few gunfights and several tough characters got their lights shot out, which didn't make the rest of us sore. We were glad enough to spare 'em. I saw some of those fights myself, but never took any part in the fireworks. "Shorty, the foot racer" was what they called me, because I always ducked around the corner when the bullets began to fly. I knew they were not meant for me; but I wasn't taking any chances.

There was plenty of gold in those mountains when I discovered the original Bullfrog, and there's plenty there yet. A lot of it was taken out while Rhyolite was going strong—$6,000,000 or $7,000,000—but they quit before they got the best of it. Stock speculation—that's what killed Rhyolite! The promoters got impatient. They figured that money could be made faster by getting gold from the pockets of suckers than by digging it out of the hills. And so, when the operators of the Montgomery-Shoshone had a little trouble—when they ran into water and struck a sulphite ore which is refractory and has to be cut and roasted to be turned into money—then the bottom dropped out of the stock market and the town was busted wide open. She died quick, too. Most of the tinhorns lit out for other parts, and that's a sure sign a mining camp is going on the rocks.

If the right people ever get hold of Rhyolite they'll make a killing; but they'll have to be real hard rock miners and not the kind that do their work only on paper. Rhyolite is dead now—dead as she was before I made the big strike. Those fine buildings are standing out there on the desert, with the coyotes and jackrabbits playing hide and seek around them.

My last big strike was made over in the Panamints at Harrisburg while Rhyolite was going strong. I crossed Death Valley with a jackass outfit and went into Townsend Pass. From there I climbed the range and found an outcropping where Skidoo was afterward located, that showed some values. But it was not good enough to start a stampede, so I followed the belt south for ten miles and picked up some ore that looked wonderful. I formed a partnership with a man by the name of Crawford, and he put up a mill and worked ore. The mine paid "from the grass roots down," as the saying goes. Crawford took out $25,000 from the first milling, and it looked like the ore went deep. But you never can tell when a vein like that will pinch out, and when a man representing a company in San Francisco offered Crawford and me a fair price, we decided to sell. I got ten thousand in cash and 165,000 shares of stock, and Crawford got the same. Fifty thousand shares of the stock I put away, and sold the rest at from thirty-five to fifty cents a share.

With plenty of money in my bank account, I decided to have a good time, so I made two trips east, and scattered that coin around in Kansas City, Chicago, New York, and Philadelphia. Nothing was too good for old Shorty when he had the money. And I was surprised to know how many friends I had. Fellows that I had never seen or heard of before gave me the glad hand and helped me to spend my jack.

When I got back from my last trip east, I heard some bad news. The company that owned the Harrisburg property had levied a big assessment on the stock—more than I figured it was worth. It was just a "freeze-out" game, but I let my stock go instead of paying the assessment. Promoters can always find some way to take the prospector's share away from him without paying for it.

Then I heard some more news that showed me how close I had come to making a strike at Skidoo. Thompson and Ramsay prospected over the same ground I had covered before I located Harrisburg, and struck some pay rock that was almost the pure stuff. I had missed it by half a mile when I found the low grade and decided to follow the belt south. Well, Thompson and Ramsay cleaned out sixty-five thousand each, and they didn't have a ten-foot hole! That was the cream of the strike, and they sold out to Bob Montgomery, who spent $300,000 before he took out an ounce. But he got all that back and plenty besides, for Skidoo paid him about a million. And

Rainbow Chasers

after he pulled out, the leasers worked the mine for several hundred thousand more.

Since Skidoo, Greenwater, and Rhyolite went down, there hasn't been so much doing in the mining game around here. The war started a few years after those camps hit bottom, and that was a death blow to a lot of gold mines. When the cost of labor and machinery went up, it meant that the value of gold went down. Properties that were operating and paying dividends on low grade ore before the war are not being worked now.

There hasn't been a real strike made since the jackass men dropped out of sight. These flivver prospectors are just a bunch of four-flushers—they have never made a strike and, take it from me, they never will. If any more good stuff is found in this country, it will be the ass men who turn the trick, and you can bank on that!

I never had much use for a flivver. Several years ago, a friend gave me one and thought he was doing me a favor, but it turned out that he just let me in for a lot of trouble. I didn't know how to run the thing, so I got a young chap to drive it for me. This fellow said that he had been chauffeur for the Kaiser, but he couldn't keep that car on the road. Over by the Furnace Creek, he ran it off a small bridge and mussed it up considerable. It cost me plenty to fix it up, and then I had the devil's own time getting it back to Ballarat. For several weeks it stood by my house and I didn't know what to do with it, then something happened that gave me a fine idea, and I got rid of the thing and had some fun too.

An Indian, whose name was Tim, had run my burros off and hid them in a canyon. Then he came to me after I had hunted for them several days, and said:

"Mebbe so I see your burros; for ten dollars I find them."

"You fetch 'em in to me and I'll pay you," I said.

Well, he stayed out for three days, and then brought them in and got the money I had promised. After that, the story went about that I had it in for Tim. One day after I got the flivver back to Ballarat, I saw Tim and asked him how much he'd pay me for it. He said that ten dollars was all he had, and I told him that the car was his. So he drove it away, thinking he had a wonderful bargain—but he didn't know what he was in for. That was three years ago, and ever since then the car has kept him and his whole tribe broke. All the money they have made has been spent for tires and parts. I got even with that Indian, and no mistake!

Well, this brings me to the end of my story. Gold mining is down in the dumps and prospecting ain't what it used to be. While things were going strong I made several fortunes—and spent 'em all.

The interest from all that money, if I had it now, would put me up with some of the big fellows in the city; but I'm a lot happier out here in the desert where I've always lived. I do some work on the road for the county, and earn enough to buy grub, and my rent doesn't cost me a cent, because I live in the old schoolhouse and don't have to pay any taxes. These old wheels of mine get pretty flat with the rheumatism, but I'm still able to keep going and have a good time. And I have some wonderful friends out here, prospectors and miners who speak the same language that I do—the kind that the old-timers understand.

But one of these days something is going to happen, something that will make them all sit up and take notice—old Shorty Harris is going to make the biggest strike of his life! Not far from Death Valley is a district that hasn't been touched. I've picked up some of the richest float over there that has ever been seen in these parts, and sometime I'll find just where that float came from. After that happens, there'll be a real party pulled off in Paris. All these years I've heard a lot about the mademoiselles, the Eiffel Tower, and Notre Dame, and I'm going to give them the once-over before I retire for good.

THE STORY OF

Price 25 Cents.

"Scotty"

AND HIS GREAT WESTERN DRAMA

BY CHARLES A. TAYLOR.

A.T.&S.F.

WALTER SCOTT

SPHINX OF THE AMERICAN DESERT

KING OF THE DESERT MINE

Death Valley Scotty

*N*O ONE HAS BETTER EXPLOITED
*or promoted the illusions of Death Valley's unfathomable mystery and
boundless wealth than that born showman and conscienceless con man,
Walter Edward Scott—known to all as Death Valley Scotty. He became, in
fact, the very personification of those illusions.
He began by conning money from Eastern innocents on claims that he had
found a fabulously rich gold mine in the heart of Death Valley. And to help
convince them of its riches, he put on a grand show of throwing money
around, culminating in his hiring a train to make a record-breaking run from
Los Angeles to Chicago in 1905. It was such a good show, in fact, that
before he was through he had nearly sold the whole nation on his moonshine.
Playwrights and poets also helped sell the fantasy and although many saw
through the charade, the indomitable mystery man finally captured a
permanent place in the imagination of the nation when his backer, Albert
Johnson, built the mansion that is now known as Scotty's Castle.*

SCOTTY, KING OF

Playwright Charles Alonzo Taylor, the creator of such cliché classics as "Through Fire and Water" and "From Rags to Riches," brought out this romantic tale in 1906 as a two-bit paperback, The Story of "Scotty" . . . King of the Desert Mine, *to promote his play of the same name, in which the Death Valley Mystery himself would star.*

THE DESERT MINE
by Charles Alonzo Taylor

IN COMPILING these few incidents relating to the life of my friend, Walter Scott, I strive to do not more than what I have done with my plays. I aim to tell a plain, unvarnished tale, as related to me by this now famous "man of the earth." . . .

"Scotty's" Early Life

Scotty was born in Harrison County, Kentucky, in 1876. His father was a breeder of thoroughbred horses. His mother, soon after the birth of her youngest child, died and the family moved west to Nevada, where he was raised on the frontier by an old lady by the name of Mugs. Scotty became a cowboy as soon as he was old enough to stride a horse. His brother Bill, some years older, was later appointed overseer of a big cattle ranch in California, and it was there Buffalo Bill saw Scotty's riding and induced him to join his aggregation of rough riders. Scotty traveled with that organization some seven years, distinguishing himself abroad by his daring feats of horsemanship. On his return to this country he went to prospecting, and was not again brought into the public eye until his discovery of gold in the Funeral Mountains, June, 1905. In California the legend runs that he has rediscovered the famous Peg-leg Mine, one of the lost mines of the West and known to be the most fabulously rich piece of land in the world.

There is nothing improbable in the theory that it has been located by Scott, as my story will show.

Scott has two friends who stuck to him through all his adversity, and who now share his good fortune. One is Mr. Rol King, his confidential adviser, and the other is his mule, Slim. . . .

Rol King was born in New Bedford, Massachusetts, 1863. He left home for the West at sixteen. He has been catering to the public for twenty-six years, and is now manager of one of the leading hotel cafes in Los Angeles, where Scotty makes his headquarters and leaves his bullion and private papers. Only Scotty knows when and where the mule was born, but he is old enough to know things other mules don't know, and Scotty owes his life to this fact. . . .

Discovery of the Mine

"Get a move on, Slim! We got ter make a water hole today or it's the boneyard for us both!"

Slim, being only a mule, made no reply, but at the sharp command of his master, visibly struggled to accelerate his laborious gait. The man's eyes softened as he noted the feeble response of the faithful animal, and, throwing his arms around the neck of the beast, he rubbed his cheek against his sun-parched coat. "We've bin good companions, you and me," he continued hoarsely. "I ain't good enough ter die yet, Slim, and, besides, I ain't ready fur it—I kin hold out if you kin. Keep your eye on them hills, Slim, and keep your heart up, fur there's water in them. Aye, and bright, shining gold that's only waitin' fur our pick."

Slim threw his ears back as if listening to these colloquial remarks, and, tossing his head, he gave vent to a long, dismal bray—indicative of despair, but an inclination to do the best he could.

The sun was slowly climbing toward its meridian, and Death Valley fairly baked under its scorching rays. Not a vestige of life—insect or animal—interrupted the grim, awful silence of this lonely solitude. To the half-dead traveler the place seemed shunned by nature and even the God that created it. The sand glistened, yellow and gold, beneath his feet—fading to brown and old rose in the distances, as seen through the reeking miasma that rose from its torrid depths. He had dismounted to lighten the burden of the weary animal, and together they plodded, side by side.

To cross the Mohave desert at any point by foot or horse is heroic—to penetrate Death Valley is certain death, ten cases out of twelve. It is generally the last resort of a prospector—a brave miner's method of committing suicide—the final throw in the game of chance that frontiersmen call life. It takes more than an ordinary display of nerve to make the venture, and Walter Scott had more than his share. One glimpse of the resolute face, now drawn from suffering the terrible tortures of thirst, and the student of character would readily affirm that here was a man who would never turn back when once he entered on a project—no matter what the danger might be. The fine, steel-blue eye looked far out to the horizon, where rose majestically the Funeral Mountains—blending in misty purple and blue in the shadow, bleached to white like Arab turbans where they reared their tall peaks to the sun. He knew from experience how deceitful was distance on prairie, desert, and plain. For two days he

Death Valley Scotty

had traveled in their direction and yet they seemed scarcely nearer than when he started. He shook his fist at them and smiled, grimly: "There's gold in them hills, Slim," he muttered. "Gold and water—bright, sparkling water to lave our burning throats, yellow shining gold to buy happiness fur you and me, Slim, old friend, and by God we're going to reach them!" The teeth snapped together in the firm, handsome jaw. Scotty had made up his mind—it meant success or death.

He stumbled and, pausing for a moment, looked down to see what his feet had encountered. There it lay, grinning up at him as if in mockery of his half-audible boast—a human skull, blown by the winds and separated from a pile of bones both human and animal that lay in a gruesome, porous heap, bleaching and baking in the sun.

A perceptible shudder shook his sturdy frame. He reached down and picked up the ghastly relic and noted the direction the fore part of the skeleton of the beast was pointing.

"Yer war goin' my way, pard," he mumbled incoherently, half delirious from the heat. "But yer found another road—got caught in the great round-up and they roped yer in with yer boots on." He grew to ruminating on the possible owner of the uncanny monument of a brave man's daring. Had he a wife—children? Someone surely loved him and was watching for his return. He placed the skull tenderly and reverently in one of the saddlebags. He scarcely knew why, only it seemed a sacrilege to leave it there at the mercy of the elements. He had a vague idea that in some way, by medium of the skull, he might possibly learn something of the owner's identity.

Higher and higher rose the sun in the cloudless sky until it hung like a seething, burnished ball of brass in the blue dome of heaven, withering the limbs of these two—man and beast—yet they tramped wearily on. The shifting sands under their feet fairly palpitated with the heat. All was one shimmering mass, unbroken by even so much as a rock or a cactus stump. The twigs of the speckled gray sagebrush snapped like macaroni beneath their feet—except when the young shoots, which gathered their sap from heaven knows where, bent like springs when the weight was lifted and sprinkled the ankles of the travelers with a fine cloud of sifted sand.

The man unloosed his blue flannel shirt at the collar and bared his breast as he drew himself to his full height, gasping for breath. The respiration of the mule sounded dry and harsh as he staggered under the weight of the miner's kit and a month's provisions. It was a battle to the death for the joy of living—a tournament supreme, with the elements on one side and a determined man on the other.

He loosened the heavy pickaxe, pans and camping articles

from the mule's back to lighten its load, and then mounted the animal, for a strange, airy sensation was stealing over him. His limbs had begun to totter and some weird, sweet music was ringing in his ears. Ha! he remembered it now—it was a cradle song—a plaintive, mournful tune he had once heard among the Apache Indians. Visions of his childhood floated before his gaze—his home in Kentucky where he was born—his father and the blooded horses where he took his first lesson in breaking ponies—Colonel Cody and his wild riders with whom he had worked, and in the pride of his manhood had given exhibitions of his marvelous skill in reckless daring with horse and lariat—old mother Mugs, who had raised him—ha! it was she who was crooning the slumber song.

"My God, Slim!" he murmured, pathetically, "the sun has burnt its way to my brain! On! on! old friend—make those hills and water and there ain't any dust in them mountains kin buy you!"

Slowly the sun faded to a deep and fiery red, tinting the distant hills with the glory of a Western sunset. Blue and purple faded to a pearl, smoky gray; on the ridges and in the deeper seams of hollow and canyon the great master-painter wielded his brush steeped with sepia and India ink, until the whole took on the semblance of a great wash-drawing silhouetted against the pale orange and old gold of the setting sun. Its beauty was lost, however, on the now silent figure that hung limply in the saddle with arms folded around the neck of his faithful Slim, for Scott's mind was a blank. His wealth of tousled hair mingled with the stump of mane on the mule; his eyes red and swollen; the tongue protruding from the mouth, shrivelled and brown from the terrible ordeal. Suffering had long since passed beyond endurance—Nature in pity had touched him with her wand and spread the mantle of unconsciousness over him in an endeavor to protect his scorching brain.

Not so the mule. Shortly after Scotty had lapsed into insensibility, Slim had been given a new lease of life. For hours the faithful brute had struggled on, groaning under his heavy burden, the flecks of foam baked on his forelegs and glistening like salt crystals in the sun. He received new inspiration, however, from the warning hiss of a rattler that reared its head from a small clump of cactus that was now beginning to dot the way. Slim knew the sign, and never were convent bells sweeter to a pilgrim than that rattling sound. Slim knew all about "sidewinders" and their habits. Sidewinders is the name for the rattlesnake of the desert, gained from its mode of travel, which is sideways, like a crab. They move rapidly, head and tail on equal footing. They are small and very venomous. Instinct plainly told him that where there were snakes water was not far off. For a moment he paused and sniffed the air, and then veering to the right, with a wary eye on his arch enemy, he broke into a jerky, irregular canter, and inside of an hour gained the foot of the hills. There he encountered a "livelie"—a species of lizard of large proportions—who disappeared up a narrow canyon, evidently astounded at the appearance of anything short of another "livelie" or a "sidewinder."

Now, all intelligent mules know that "livelies" hunt the water at dusk—ready to plunge in when attacked by their smaller but deadlier enemies, the tarantulas. Therefore, Slim cautiously followed this desert denizen, and to his great joy found a cool and rippling stream, clear and transparent, that bounded joyously over a little waterfall and emptied itself into a scoop-shaped basin that nestled in a cranny in the rocks.

As he leaned over in feverish haste to drink, the unconscious miner was precipitated into the shallow water on the edge of the spring. The shock of the fall and the cool water brought him to his senses. His first thought was of his terrible thirst and he plunged his swollen lips and face again in the spring, and when his protruding tongue relaxed so he could swallow he drank sparingly, knowing the danger of a too copious draught. His next thought was for the mule, who was in danger of foundering. Faithful Slim had made ninety-six miles in sixteen hours without a drop of water, a feat unprecedented, and to this day a marvel of animal endurance. Although somewhat in a dazed condition, Scotty led the beast away from the spring and with a lariat and stake he secured her at a safe distance from the water. He tried to talk, but found his mouth and throat too swollen for utterance. He could only throw his arms around the brute's neck and sob, and then and there he vowed in his mind that Slim and he should never be parted. The mule had saved his life, and come what may of their adventure, henceforth they should be inseparable.

Darkness had fallen and the stars came out in the clear blue sky in all their majestic splendor. Rough miner as he was, he could appreciate their beauty, for Scotty was a child of nature and had grown to love it through long association with it. An innate refinement lay thin-coated by his rugged brown skin. Philosophy in an embryo state was largely an element of his being, and coupled with native wit and a keen insight into human nature, there were few of his more civilized acquaintances that had not felt the impotency of their college educations when brain matched brain in satire or repartee.

He muttered a silent prayer of thankfulness up to where the peaceful lamps of night dotted the ether. Life never felt so sweet as he lay there reflecting on the goodness of the Maker of all things who had guided his mule out of the wilderness. He drew long breaths of the pure, dry ozone, and awed by the majesty of the vast illimitable silence around him he sank into deep, soft, and refreshing slumber, at peace with the world and his God. When he awoke the following morning he found he had slept upon a bed of gold. He will say little about this great day of his life, when, gazing about him, he beheld sparkling in the gravel of the stream, that for which so many have sought, for which millions have bled and died—gold, virgin gold. Suddenly it dawned upon him that he was rich—wealthier than a Midas—a modern Crœsus with a mine that rivaled the description of the famous legendary grottoes of Plutus. The man that but a week before hadn't the price of a grubstake could now vie with the great financiers of the globe and set the pace for the social world, if so he chose, for it was here, there, everywhere that he turned. Not a vision—not a dream—but gold in nuggets, large and small, and in such abundance that the knowledge overwhelmed him.

Coming Events

It was a full two weeks after the events recorded that Scotty dropped into Barstow and proceeded to hunt up old friends. The same motley crowd hung around the miner's favorite groggery. A cayuse, thick with the alkali of the desert, stood hitched to a post by the cowboys' retreat, lazily flicking the flies off his back with his tail and pawing the ground in a restless desire to be off and rid of his buzzing tormentors. Scotty knew the animal by the thick leather pouch that hung to the saddle. It belonged to the postmaster, who was making his daily call in search of the usual dose of "red-eye." There was the little news stall stacked up with the daily papers from Los Angeles, the general store where he had loaded Slim with provisions on the day that he had set forth on his memorable ride. Nothing seemed changed excepting Scotty himself. He had converted his bullion into currency of the realm and his pockets bulged suspiciously by reason of various bundles of bills that safely reposed within their skin-lined depths.

The newsboy recognized him, and hailed him with:

"'Lo, Scotty! Glad ter see yer back. Want a paper?"

Scotty nodded in the affirmative. It was the first familiar voice he had heard since his arrival. He gave the boy a hundred-dollar bill and told him to keep the change. The young news vendor hadn't any words left in him for thanks. The shock knocked the breath completely out of him. Scotty left him scratching his head in consternation, turning the bill over and over in his hand as if he wasn't quite sure whether it was a counterfeit, or whether the miner hadn't gone crazy and it was a shame to take the money.

With the air of a Pierpont Morgan, the good-natured miner sauntered into the building that did service for a hostelry in the lazy little town. The prospector says to this day that it was the cheapest hundred dollars' worth of advertising he has received since he made his meteoric entrance into California affairs. Within fifteen minutes after the miner's magnanimous display of generosity, the enterprising young street merchant had covered every principal business portion of the town and all Barstow knew that Scotty had "struck it rich."

Entering the barroom of the hotel, the prospector threw a five-hundred-dollar bill down on the counter and told the barkeeper to "get busy." "Wine for the crowd," he ordered, "and let that bill lay till we drink it up."

The barkeeper reached for his gun and looked to see what was coming next. The poker players seated around the small side tables sat up with a start and took notice.

Scotty never realized until then how popular he had been with the citizens of Barstow. The number that had missed him and were concerned about his health was appalling. They made him feel so ashamed of his neglect of them that he promised them henceforth when he took another trip across the valley he would have bulletins posted in the town announcing his temperature and every detail with reference to his physical welfare. Yes, even if he had to string couriers from the meetinghouse to the Funeral Mountains.

Others flocked in—in threes, in fours, and dozens. Such hand-shaking! It brought tears to the eyes of the hard frontiersman, but they were tears of fun. He was laughing inwardly. It was the tale of the pied piper of Hamlin being enacted over again, but the notes that came from Scotty's pipe were certificates of good United States coin—the tune was one older than any in print: "A fool and his money's soon parted."

However, there are fools who are born to it and those who are fools by choice. Scotty belonged to the latter. He reveled in the power of his newly found wealth. He scattered money right and left like a drunken sailor, but with a purpose—to feel the pulse of humanity, so to speak. Native philosopher as he was, he was trying to diagnose the makeup of their souls. As men are intoxicated by strong drink, so are they affected by the sight of gold. Now, humanity in a state of intoxication throws off its mask of social conventionalism. The real being comes to the surface, and Scotty, who was a judge of character, took a keen enjoyment in noting the "ills and virtues that men fall heir to." He hoped to profit by the knowledge. What if the more sober element of society looked aghast at his wanton extravagance; they knew not the set purpose deeply rooted in his mind. He could well spare the money, for his supply was almost inexhaustible. In time he would show them that he was not the fool they had taken him for. Until then they could think as they pleased.

After a short stay in Barstow, he once more started for the lonesome hills. He bought every little luxury needed to make him comfortable, and with a train of burros loaded down with every necessity for a long sojourn at the mines, he again started on a perilous trip across the desert. He no longer feared the privations of the treacherous trail. His former experience had taught him that he was immune from the poisonous gases and the usual terrors that inhabited Death Valley.

None saw him depart, as the start was made in the dead of night, with only compass and stars to guide him. His worst fear now was not the desert, but the many desperadoes that frequent the frontier towns. They would undoubtedly attempt to follow his trail, for all the West was gold mad on learning his unusual streak of good luck.

Of this second trip the miner will speak little. Many rumors are to the effect that more than one enterprising prospector who undertook to follow him was turned back by the determined young Crœsus. Scotty says it was impossible to shadow him, as he never took the same trail twice.

"There ain't no place to hide," he averred, "and with Long Range Rifle I could pick them off at two miles or more. I have a powerful glass that brings close to me objects that are miles away. Well, it's my business—if ever I send a man over the divide yer kin bet he deserved it, and it was a case of my life or his. I'm not taking any chances when a man puts his hand down on his holster."

The next time the world heard from Scotty was at Goldfield— one of the many towns on the edge of the desert. A dance was in progress that evening, and Scotty was given an invitation to attend. To use his own words he was "there in a minute," and "up and doing."

With true gentlemanly instinct he was loath to cut up the waxed floor with his hob-nailed mountain boots, and the girls laughingly took them off him, making him dance in his stocking feet.

His genial, smiling face was seen on every hand, and many of the poorer residents of the town who sought his pity found reason to bless him and wish him Godspeed on his departure next morning.

Not all the money spent on his frolics went to wine-bibbing and noisy revelry. This man of mystery, "Sphinx of the desert" (so called on account of the secretiveness attending his arrival and departure), has done many a charitable deed, as many who have been the beneficiaries can attest to, but in each case a promise has been exacted that the amount and circumstances of his bequests be kept from the ears of reporters and others who are constantly seeking items of interest concerning the doings of this modern Monte Cristo.

It was a few weeks later when Barstow saw him again. By this time the fame of his discovery in the hills had traveled all over the world. He was besieged on all hands by the representatives of the papers concerning his movements and his proposed plans for the future. Each morning found stacks upon stacks of mail from ambitious ladies, young and old, rich and poor, who offered him their hand in marriage—not for his wealth, they assured him, but just for love of his manliness and reckless bravery in penetrating the forbidding solitude of Death Valley. They craved a little remembrance if he refused them—a lock of hair or some little token of sentiment such as a nugget or a spoonful of dust—just to show he was not angry at their presumption. Scotty politely answered those he could, assuring them that, brave man as they thought him, he balked at bigamy, being already married. So much had been written about the strength of his wild wealth of unkempt hair that in a spirit of fun he sent many of them a few broom straws tied with a piece of baby ribbon, apologizing for the size of the bequest and pleading insufficient hair to go round.

Cranks wrote him from all parts of the States offering their services, eager to advise him where he could best invest his colossal wealth for the benefit of the country and themselves. Within a month his mail had grown to such proportions that Scotty found it necessary to hire two men to attend to it.

He first came into national prominence, however, through the outcome of a remark that was at first intended as a joke. He was drinking in front of a prominent bar at Barstow when someone asked him when he was going back to the mines.

"Not for a while," he answered. "I'm going to take a trip to New York. I've an engagement with them fellers as runs Wall Street. I want to make Pierpont Morgan look like a tallow dip on a sunny day when I shove some of my pile into a bank there. I'm going to hire John D. Rockefeller to shine my shoes and have the Flatiron Building moved over to Los Angeles. And I ain't going there on the cheap, either," he continued. "I'm going ter take a special train with one of them swell tenderfeet outfits that the magnates ride in and break all records. Say! them hoboes along the track will climb a tree when they see me coming, fur I'll make more wind than a cyclone. None of yer sixty-mile-an-hour gait fur me. I'm going to open her to the limit when I start, break off the throttle and draw fires to ease her when I see the lights of Chicago."

The assembled citizens of Barstow gazed in open-mouthed wonder when they heard this announcement. The clever ones of course took it as it was meant, but there were others who took it literally. Scotty was known to be a man of his word and for daring— well, there wasn't anything he wouldn't do if he set his mind on it. All agreed to that.

One of the youths assembled, who did service as a correspondent to one of the Los Angeles dailies, immediately wired his paper the news of the proposed trip, and within an hour all Los Angeles rang with the tidings that Scotty was going East on a run against time.

This ballad by cowboy poet Earl Alonzo Brininstool, appearing in the Los Angeles Examiner *of July 12, 1905, was the best of the instant homages inspired by Scotty's first grandstand play.*

SCOTTY'S RIDE

by *Earl Alonzo Brininstool*

HAVE YOU HEARD the story that's told with pride
Through the Western borders, of Scotty's ride?

This Scott was a cowboy, you understand,
A feller of muscle an' grit an' sand,
Who'd rode th' ranges fer years an' years,
At thirty a month, a-punchin' steers;

A fearless cuss, an' a rider bold,
With nerves of steel an' a heart of gold;
A diamond rough, but a man all through,
An' every feller that Scotty knew
Could bank on him to the last red cent,
Fer Scotty's promises allers went.

No, 'tain't a story—this Scotty's ride
On the afterdeck of a bronc' astride.
Scott left th' range an' th' ranch, you know,
Ter cut a swath with a wild west show.
But Scotty tired; he said th' pace
Wa'n't jest his style of a whirlwind race.

An' he dropped from sight fer a few short years—
Give up ridin' an' punchin' steers
To trail th' hills an' th' canyons rough
Fer a dead-blind lead on th' yaller stuff.
In other words, so his friends was told,
Scott dug an' delved fer th' hidden gold.

An' dog my cats! if he didn't make
A strike that—well, it jest took th' cake!
An' th' next we knew it wuz said that Scott
Was th' only Johnny-upon-th'-spot.

He'd dough to burn, an' he burned it, too,
In th' Angel City, where Scotty blew
In frum th' desert, one summer's day,
An' durin' a short but excitin' stay
Folks got th' notion that Scotty's pile
Was one that lasted a blame long while.

But Scotty's ride—he was bound ter make
A record that nobody else could break.
A railroad record, an' Scotty went
To th' Santy Fay, with th' bold intent
Of runnin' a train on a record trip
If th' plans held out as he'd laid th' tip.

Five thousan' bucks, an' a leetle more
Was th' price they mentioned, but Scotty swore
Th' money would cut no ice if they
Would run th' layout in Scotty's way.
An' they thought him locoed, yes, plumb insane,
When Scotty hollered: "Trot out yer train!"

From Los to th' Windy City's gate
Was th' course where Scotty was temptin' fate.
Two thousan' miles on a record run,
A fool thing nobody else had done.

He paid th' money with many a grin,
Remarkin', "I reckon it's well blowed in;
I'll make a record that no one's got
Er bust th' b'iler," said Walter Scott.

Th' "Coyote Special"—an engine bright
That gleamed an' steamed in th' fair sunlight;
A Pullman sleeper; a diner grand,
With vittles an' lickers enough on hand,
An' a baggage car. An' this was th' way
That Scotty started that summer's day.

Scott waved his hand in a fond farewell,
Th' whistle tooted, an' then th' bell
Clanged madly, an' out of th' depot flew
Th' "Coyote Special," one aim in view:

To smash all records in railroad speed,
An' to make th' run in th' time agreed.

Rockin' an' swayin' past bridge an' street,
Th' "Coyote" flew like a courser fleet.
She lunged an' plunged down th' steepest grade—
Laid former records clean in th' shade.
She ripped past towns with a rush an' roar,
Like a Kansas twister with death in store.

She shot down canyons with reckless pace,
An' Scotty smiled as he watched th' race.
Now in th' Pullman, now in th' cab,
With watch in hand, fer a short confab
With th' engineer. An' each dizzy curve
Was taken with many a jolt an' swerve.

Th' thick, black smoke from th' smokestack flew,
As Scotty hollered to "put er through!"
Milestones faded. Gosh! what a pace
Th' "Coyote" kept in that crazy race.

An' back in the diner th' dishes crashed.
At every curve there was something smashed.
Th' waiters, cuss 'em, were skeered to death,
While th' cooks jest trembled an' held their breath
When a sudden jolt er a grindin' jar
Went like a shudder through every car.

But Scotty would holler above th' roar,
To "pull out yer throttle a little more!"
Th' "Coyote" leaped o'er th' clickin' steel,
An' at every jump she would rock an' reel.
Folks gazed in wonder, an' trainmen cussed
As th' "Coyote" vanished in clouds of dust.

She bucked an' pranced like th' bronc', in ways
Remindin' Scotty of cowboy days.
She danced an' tore with a frenzied glee,
As she reeled off miles with alacrity.

She covered distance with fearful greed,
Through gorges plunged without slackin' speed.

Scotty's Ride   263

She sped o'er mountains by night an' day,
In th' same nerve-killin' an' reckless way,
An' when on th' levels she'd fairly hum,
Then Scotty would yell: "We're travelin some!"

Speed-mad was Scotty. They couldn't go
Half fast enough fer th' cuss, you know.
At every stop of a second's length,
He'd bawl with all of his brawny strength:
"Blankety-blank! what's the matter now?
What ails ol' 'Coyote' anyhow?

Come, rip things open, an' turn 'er loose;
Open yer throttle thar; what th' deuce
Is th' reason yer runnin' so cussed slow?
You can't fly any too fast, yer know."
Then over th' tender he'd briskly climb,
To note th' gains or th' loss in time.

States came an' went as th' "Coyote" flew.
Landscapes were blotted an' blurred from view.
Into th' blackness of inky night
Th' "Coyote" lurched in her frenzied flight.

Allers ahead in th' red-hot race,
Keepin' th' same ol' reckless pace,
An' Scotty grinned as he cried: "You bet
We're a-goin' ter bust th' record yet!"

An' bust it they did, thirteen hours, too,
As th' Windy City swung into view.
Then Scotty crawled from his Pullman car
An' drawled: "Gosh, hang it! well, here we are.
I told 'em I'd make it a record run,
An' I'll be switched if th' job ain't done."

This is th' story that's told with pride
Through th' western country, of Scotty's ride.

CHASING RAINBOWS

After being personally burned by Scotty, Sydney Norman, the Los Angeles Times *mining editor, penned this blistering exposé for the July 19, 1908, issue of the paper, and for good measure published it as a pamphlet the following year.*

266

IN DEATH VALLEY
by Sydney Norman

I HAVE RECENTLY returned from a three weeks' trip to the scene of
Death Valley Scotty's alleged mine, impelled thitherward by thirst
for a "story," induced by Scotty's promise that he had tired of the
desert life and was ready to show his great wealth-producer to a
quivering world. To say I was disgusted would be putting it mildly.
I was disgusted, sure, and footsore to boot. My disgust was not
brought on by the fact that I did not see the mine (that goes without
saying) but because the whole business was so coarse, so cheap and
so palpably rotten. I had expected to meet a clever man with a clever
scheme, but alas! I met but a penny Dare-Devil-Dick of the Desert,
woefully lacking in ingenuity of the high-class kind, clutching a
whiskey bottle by the neck and posing like a five-cent hero in a five-
cent drama on the Barbary Coast.

Poor Scotty; I pity him. The strain of nursing an attenuated
and feeble wraith of his former mystery has told upon him and even
he can only see suggestions of its existence through the magnifying
glass of a bottle inverted at an angle of forty-five degrees. It is too
bad that he has not devoted himself to legitimate pursuits, instead of
permitting himself to become the derision of the desert and the joke
of ribald jesters. Time was when Los Angeles theater-goers rose up
and cheered him; I fear he must now take to the back streets and
can-strewn alleys to attract the attention of even the dogs. It's too
bad. There are worse fellows than Scotty and in all my mining per-
egrinations I have never met a better companion in the desert. He
can cook an appetizing meal with one hand, grease the axles of the
wagons with the other, and at the same time use both feet to per-
suade his mules to do his bidding. And through it all he hands out a
line of picturesque slang that would put a western Checkers to the
blush. He might have made a good parson, a successful promoter,
or both.

What He Looks Like

In physique he is as nearly perfect as a man of his size (175 to
180 pounds) can be, with hands and feet more like a woman's than a

267

bad, bold man's. He has a keen, grey-blue eye, but one which seems to avoid his vis-a-vis and which carries the furtive look of the always-suspicious. He is extremely nervous at all times and in the course of our trip I never saw him sit down quietly, even to a meal. He claims to be a native of Cynthiana, Kentucky, and says that he first saw Death Valley seventeen years ago as a member of a geological survey party under a man named St. Clair. How he has crowded all the experience he described into thirty-seven ordinary years I don't know, but I do know that he is not unknown at Cody, Wyoming, that he has been existing on this alleged mystery for eight years, and that he spent several years as a bronco-buster with Buffalo Bill. It was during the latter experience that he met "Jack," his wife, a former New York girl whose partnership in his imaginary mystery has told upon her, too, and who is now ready to exchange the mysteries of the desert for the mysteries of housekeeping and the problem of making income meet the demands of the butcher, the baker, and the candlestick maker. Alas, poor Jack, hers is the really pathetic side of this ludicrous "mystery."

How the Play Came Up

It was about a month ago that the pangs of poverty, or the lack of notoriety, drove Scotty to make one more effort to resurrect his meal-ticket mystery and his near approach (on a brake-beam this time, I believe) was heralded to a few intimate friends in Los Angeles. Although Scotty did not know it, the sheriff of San Bernardino County was also notified that there was something in the wind and one of his deputies, detailed to watch developments, has since given me information which tends to prove what fools we mortals be.

At any rate, he was in desperate straits, and approached at least one of his old confederates in an effort to enlist aid in finding a man with money who would accompany him back to the desert and pay the expense necessary to outfit the "steenth" expedition to the scene of the mystery. This man refused to have anything to do with the plan, which involved the salting and faking of a mine, and Scotty was therefore compelled to fall back upon Rol King, proprietor of the Hollenbeck bar, who managed the stage gaucherie of this ex-cowboy in the palmy days and who has honestly clung to belief in a real mine through all the exposures his protege has been subjected to.

Father of Goldfield Falls

The latter unfolded a plan to A. D. Myers, locator of the famous Mohawk mine, who received his check for $400,000 for 100,000 shares of stock when the mine was sold to the Goldfield

Consolidated, and who is generally known as the "Father of Gold-field." A few months previous Myers had met Scotty in Rhyolite and had given him the chastisement of his life. That is where the element of danger entered into the trip, and I shall always believe, in the face of later developments, that the memory of that licking still rankled and that had opportunity presented, Scotty would have wiped out the score. But Myers is not a coward and, scenting an adventure at worst, he consented to finance the expedition and I, in the dual role of newspaperman and friend, was invited to join him. Rol King finally decided to accompany us to satisfy himself once and for all. And I think he is satisfied now. Ask him. Anyway, the necessary arrangements were quickly perfected and we left Los Angeles on June 1 for Barstow, where a start was to be made.

That Impressive Cavalcade

I shall always harbor resentment against the people of Barstow. I feel that they were not properly impressed with the picturesque side of the imposing cavalcade which left there that fine June morning. Maybe they are used to these periodical expeditions by this time, but, of course, I, being a stranger, did not know that, and I object to the shock to my dignity furnished by the ribald and bucolic farewells of a few unimportant bums who had not yet found time to go to bed and the derisive glances of the haughty waitresses of the Harvey House as they condescended to hand us our early-morning meal. However, one must live and learn; and I learned if I didn't live high.

But think of the surpassing importance of this expedition, going bravely forth to the nameless terrors of the Valley of Death to elucidate a great mystery and calm the palpitating bosom of the world! There was Myers, already dubbed "the millionaire" before we got under way, with a shotgun in one hand, an automatic Colt's of murderous caliber protruding from his hip pocket, and attired in a silk shirt and $23 Panama hat, as becomes a man of wealth. And there was Rol King, looking like the bay-window side elevation of the Hollenbeck Hotel, sporting a hat suggestive of a cross between a merry widow and a parachute, and attired in a faultless suit of khaki, fitting closely amidships. It seems hardly worth mentioning, but I can vouch for the fact that his suit was easier after he had come out of the Death Valley reducing mill at the Furnace Creek end two weeks later.

Then there was Scotty himself, attired as usual in a frayed-out pair of pants held up by a belt of string, a blue flannel shirt open at the neck, and a black slouch hat. The ends of two fingers of his left hand had recently been blown off by the explosion of a gun and he bore other marks of hard usage of a more liquid nature. And there was "Jack," with a sand-cap reminiscent of Venice or Atlantic City, and quiet old Brother Bill, with nothing much to distinguish him but his relationship to the hero in front. And I, innocent I, was there, aneroid- and compass-laden, with a thirty-eight caliber cannon in one pocket giving me nervous prostration, a notebook in another, and clad in the regulation khaki with the music-roll leggings of the would-be expert. My outfit was all wrong. Next time I shall know what one needs for such a trip. Just a little hasheesh or chloral, a dash of idiocy, a bathing suit and a sunshade.

They're Off!

And thus we faded away into the northern dust of the desert, Scotty piloting me ahead, Myers and King coming next and Brother Bill and Jack bringing up the rear with the supply wagon. Nothing of any interest happened that day, though the whole party posed once or twice for my camera. Scotty was shy as a young schoolgirl to start with, but soon gave in and permitted the reproduction of his features for the benefit of the waiting world. That night we camped at Indian Springs, thirty-five miles north of Barstow, and the second day pushed on to Hidden Springs and rested there during the third day. It was here that our real adventures began and that I saw the first suspicious circumstances that I had noticed. On the way into camp, two graves were pointed out as those of two men who had been murdered or found dead. They looked suspiciously new to me and so the next day we revisited the spot and, after removing the slabs of rock piled up carefully to resemble graves, we found that the soil had not been disturbed and that the graves were "phoney." I afterwards found that this is an old game and that every effort is made to throw terror into the tenderfoot heart by just such transparent tricks. Somehow, I never was as afraid of a dead man as I am of a live one. But no one is allowed to miss the real graves and the imaginary ones on this desert trip, and there are enough of the genuine article to satisfy me.

Hidden Springs are situated in the mountains south of Wingate Pass, which leads to Death Valley, at an altitude of 3,600 feet above sea level. To the north are the imposing Panamint Mountains, with Telescope Peak's whitened head showing clearly in the brilliant sun, while over to the northeast are the Funeral Mountains, the eastern border of Death Valley proper. In the west the Slate Range stands dim and purple in the fading day.

The Robbers' Roost

At this point we were shown the Robbers' Roost group of claims, situated one and a half miles southeast of the springs on the summit of the range. We were led to believe that this was not the real Scotty mine by any means, but that it could be used in fooling the public while the real location of the great mine was withheld until any possible complications regarding title were removed. In explanation of this suspicious circumstance we were told that a man named A. M. Johnson, manager of the National Life Assurance Company of Chicago, had been mixed up in Scott's mining deals in the past and might cause trouble. We were assured, however, that he had no legal claim and that the proceeding would be merely an extra precaution to throw around the greatest mine the world ever saw. The property is merely a prospect, that might pay to work in a less godforsaken spot and shows about eight inches of quartz that pans well and contains copper values. It is developed to a maximum depth of thirty-five feet, the vein running southwest and northeast in porphyritic granite.

"Johnny Behind the Gun"

There was a great "pow-wow" of desert celebrities at Hidden Springs the day we passed there, and I felt for the nonce like a dime-novel hero myself. I had the honor of renewing acquaintance with "Johnny Behind Gun," or "Johnny Behind the Rock," a character whose real identity is about obliterated in the sobriquets he rejoices in. What gun or rock he got behind or whether the rock or the gun got behind him or not, I was unable to learn, but he recognized me at once and brought back to memory my first trip to the desert eight years ago, when I visited Snow's Canyon in the Argus Range and found him, the only human being within twenty miles, running a little two-stamp mill by burro power and dividing his blasphemous attention between the amalgam plates and the sad-eyed burro, which he belabored with a shovel to goad him to his duty. In those days a trip over the narrow-gauge road from Moundhouse to Keeler, which D. O. Mills said was built "300 miles too long or 300 years too soon," was no idle jest, and when it was followed by a lonesome trip through the deserted town of Darwin and into the forbidding Panamint Valley, one may imagine that Johnny, with his broken English, looked good to me and I should still have insisted upon making his acquaintance if he had been behind the gun then and had he been behind the rock I should surely have pulled him out. I well remember that he invited me to lunch in a cave wherein he dwelt and I also remember that he rescued his pan of bacon from a four-foot rattler as he invited me in. I remember also that the rattler decided for me and that I had no lunch that day. Since then Johnny has had his ups and downs and had just lost $16,000 gambling at Rhyolite when I met him. He confided to me that he "have 'em apex" of the great Keane Wonder vein in a fraction which he still owns between that mine and the claim he lost at the gaming tables. I hope he has; and I know that the saloon keepers and gamblers of Nevada will be glad to hear it, too.

Opera Bouffe Hold-Up

The next day we took up our interrupted trip and descended the declivity to Wingate Pass, said to be the windiest spot on the desert, and known locally as Windy Gap, which runs directly east into Death Valley. After passing Dry Lake we were waved to a mysterious and vaguely indefinite spot up the Panamint slope and regaled with the blood-curdling details of a holdup in which Scotty was the alleged victim. He says he was attacked by two prospectors who were shadowing him to his mine, but there are always two sides to a pane of glass. The other is less romantic and reflects Scotty fleeing from a party (just such fools as we were) he had deserted in the valley, and endeavoring to surround his disappearance with a semblance of decency. It is said that he pulled his rifle from its scabbard at the left side of his saddle and in so doing discharged a ball into his leg. At any rate, he was compelled to make a forced ride to Barstow, sixty-five miles away, with the wound packed in salt. The fact that he reached there proves the grit of the man and speaks well for his nerve. But then no one has ever arisen to say there is anything the matter with his nerve, anyhow. ·

Wingate Pass Ambush

A few miles further on we were shown the scene of the memorable ambush, which closely followed Scotty's ride on a special Santa Fé train from Los Angeles to Chicago and which involved Scott, his half-Indian partner, Bill Keyes, his brothers, Bill and Warner, A. Y. Perle, and A. W. St. Clair. In the shooting that ensued Warner Scott was shot through the leg and Walter Scott was subsequently arrested upon information sworn to by St. Clair. The affair took place on the Inyo-San Bernardino line and the case was thrown out of the San Bernardino County courts upon a demurrer showing lack of jurisdiction in that the assault took place in Inyo County. The case was never decided upon its merits and the interesting evidence was never heard. But it occurs to me that Inyo County missed an excellent chance of ridding itself of the band, and thereby lent some color to the suggestion that its officials were friendly to, if not entirely hand and glove with, Scott. It will be noticed that the latter's operations are always confined to that county and I think they always will be. The sheriff of San Bernardino County has too much important evidence against him to make his work safe within those confines. Incidentally, it is charged that the county line survey monuments were moved to sustain the demurrer, and, from what Scott told me, I think they were. We were shown the fortifications to the south and above the road, from which the rifle shots were fired and I detected evidence that they had recently been fixed up—doubtless for our special benefit. The whole story is a threadbare one now and hardly worth rehashing. One side says that Bill Keyes left the party at Lone Willow Springs and made a forced ride to the scene to shoot an eastern expert who had a certified check for $100,000 in his pocket to pay for the mysterious mine. Scott says the work was of his enemies in an attempt to kill him and that it would be impossible for any man to make such a trip as Keyes is said to have made. I know the country now and I also know that even I could make the trip if a prize of $100,000 awaited my success.

That Bath Tub

The same night we made a dry camp 600 feet above sea level, having descended 3,000 feet in the twenty-four miles made since morning. Our camp was pitched in a dry wash banked by overhanging cliffs of sand and in the dim distance could be seen the forbidding Funeral Mountains with the deep-scarred canyon now known as Scott's. It was here that a cache was found last year by prospectors who had wandered down into Death Valley from Greenwater and the discovery of a bathtub among the hidden plunder gave much food for comment upon Scott's sybaritic proclivities. The romance was totally dispelled for me when I learned that the tub was "lifted" from the Confidence mine and that amalgam plates and everything else that was not nailed down disappeared at the same time.

Into the Sump

On the fifth day we entered the Valley of Death, timing the hour of our start with the rising sun which blazed, like a ball of fire, over the crags of the Funerals at 5 o'clock. By 9 o'clock we had made a further descent of 600 feet and passed the sea-level monument of the United States Geological Survey. These monuments have been placed at a distance of three miles apart throughout the valley and, as I understand it, the lowest reading is minus 378 feet at a point in the borax beds immediately east of Bennett's Holes and near the foot of the steep ascent to the Funerals below Greenwater. As we swung into the north-and-south road up the valley, the heat, which had gradually increased during the two days' descent, became simply terrific and I felt as if I was in a subbasement oven with the lid screwed down tight. And yet the valley offers a certain magnificence of scenery which one could thoroughly enjoy but for the discomforts which accompany it. At most times the heat waves make a clear view up and down the valley impossible, but there are usually mirages of trees and of oceans and of ships, all accentuating one's tongue-hanging condition and the insistent need of a cold bath. To the east are the frowning Funerals in all their forbidding bareness, to the west the magnificent Panamints, with Telescope Peak rearing its head 12,000 feet above you, and in its fringe of snow on the summit suggesting ice cream, iced drinks and every other impossibility that is cool. On the benchland immediately above the sea-level mark I counted nine graves, and still have the bones of a human leg exposed by the shifting sands, which I bore away as a fitting memento of the lowest-down and most damnable spot I ever visited.

I presume that most of the graves contain the remains of Chinamen, who were exclusively employed in the borax industry in the early days. Some, however, still carried the identity given by a single board—usually a portion of a tomato or milk case—and on them I read in penciled letters the sad story of a brave heart that had succumbed with a face towards God's country, after an unequal fight against drought and too much sun—a victim to the unquenchable thirst for gold.

About noon we ate lunch at Salt Wells and drank up our scanty supply of water, pushing on to Bennett's Holes immediately to replenish our canteens at the first water hole in practically fifty miles. There we found the water too foul to drink and so were compelled to push on again to Eagle Borax Works Springs, two miles further north. At that point we made camp and, in order that later developments may be understood, it is necessary to say that our mules were nearly exhausted and had to be persuaded to their work by a well-manipulated chain.

Camp was pitched a few hundred feet south of the ruins of the old borax works in a clump of mesquite which afforded some slight protection from the broiling sun. Copious drafts of water were followed by the serious sickness of all the members of the party but Myers, and I early sought the seclusion of a friendly bush and, with one hand on my head and the other against my diaphragm, communed with myself and wondered if seasickness increased in intensity the further one descended from the level of the sea.

Mules Driven Off

While our sufferings were at the acute stage, Scott, who was also apparently incapacitated, noticed that the mules were not in evidence, and, upon being told by "Jack" that they were last seen north of camp, started out that way. I knew they went south, but was too sick to care at the time, and it was not till an hour later that I even suspected that anything was wrong. Scott, Myers and I then started out to scour the surrounding country, and found one animal placidly browsing in the thick mesquite near camp. The other three had gone, and I am convinced now that they were deliberately driven off by a prearranged plan between Scott and his partner, Bill Keyes, or one of the other outlaws that infest the valley. I remember now that Scott spent some minutes in a mesquite patch north of the borax works directly we reached camp, and I believe that his accomplice was hidden there then, awaiting our arrival. Later I discovered the fresh tracks of a shod horse, and I then knew that Scott had played his old bunco game once more, and that another set of suckers had been caught in his net. He professed to be too sick to follow the trail that night, and it was not till seven o'clock the next morning that he got away on the remaining mule, after promising to be back the next morning.

Seven Days in Hades

And for seven days and nights we remained in that hell on earth, 275 feet below sea level, eaten alive by mosquitoes at night, fighting horseflies as big as bats by day, and amusing ourselves by ordering imaginary iced drinks from an imaginary bartender. I would have stood anyone off for $5 for just one long Clan McKenzie highball with plenty of ice, and I am sure "the millionaire" would have squandered his entire substance for a cold bottle of beer. I don't think King cared much those days whether he drank anything or not; he took a very gloomy view of life, and used enough profanity to last him the rest of his life.

To make matters worse, our scant supply of tobacco gave out on the second day, and for several days thereafter Myers spent a great part of the time in the undignified position of searching for "snipes" on his hands and knees. To while away the interminable hours, we made catapults from strips of packing boxes and rubber bands and waged bloody warfare upon the horseflies. In the last five days the count easily reached 1,000 slain, and there were still some left when we finally departed.

King was seriously sick at times, and Myers and I decided that upon the seventh day we would walk out to Furnace Creek ranch for help. I had previously been one of the rainbow-chasers at Greenwater above us over the Funerals and therefore knew my way. And on the night of the seventh day we started, leaving "Jack" and King in camp to await the arrival of a team which we intended to send down. Of that walk I will say but little. Anyone who imagines that twenty-five miles is a joke has another guess coming, especially when one is compelled to carry a heavy canteen and cross the salt marsh of the treacherous sink. But we finally reached there at seven the next morning so footsore we could scarcely move. We slept on the desert from 3:30 until 4:30 and I shall never, to my dying day, forget Myers when he donned his shoes after rest and essayed to take up the walk once more. I have heard of a cat on hot bricks and I have heard of people walking on eggs but my imagination never conveyed any idea of the reality. We sent an Indian back from the ranch for King and "Jack" and the former arrived late at night with the news that Scott and the mules had come back that morning. He was to follow on the next morning.

And Scott Came Back

And sure enough, the following morning he and "Jack" drove up with a flourish, Scott full of profanity for the mules, which he claimed to have followed back to Barstow. He expressed anxiety to go on with the trip, but when he found Myers and I were just as anxious, he weakened and suggested that it might be better to get an outfit of saddle mules and make a new start from Barstow in about ten days. And then we all knew that the "jig" was up and that we might as well fade away with as much dignity as we had left, out of the jaws of hell into the paradise of Los Angeles. And so we hired a team and struggled back up the interminable wash of Furnace Canyon to the Death Valley junction of the Tonopah and Tidewater Railroad. Maybe you think a Pullman did not look good to us all!

So far as I am concerned, Death Valley is but an unpleasant memory; wild horses could not drag me there again. And I think that any man who will follow the Scotty will-o'-the-wisp is a fool and should earn automatic entry to Matteawan or any other resting place for the criminally insane. He is just a fakir, and one who would be called by another and harsher name if his victims of the past had not been afraid of bringing the laugh down on themselves by exposing him through the channels of the law.

Who Supplies the Cash

It is often asked where Scott obtains the money to make the periodical splurges that have brought him before the public. Lavater says that "where there is much pretension, much has been borrowed." There lies the answer. The money Scott used to pay for the special train to Chicago over the Santa Fé came from a man who still lives in Los Angeles and who hoped to profit by the exploitation of a Death Valley property after Scotty had advertised himself as a mining mystery and, incidentally, as an arrant fool. The experience cost about $12,000, and, at that, Scott refused to recognize his benefactor after he reached New York.

During that trip he managed to entrap others in the East and I know that Obadiah Sands and A. M. Johnson of Chicago and Julian Gerrard of New York, brother of the man who married Marcus Daly's daughter, could throw some illuminating light on the subject. From what I can learn, Scott has received between $50,000 and $100,000 from these sources and in each case has failed to carry out one promise he had made. Protected by the prominence of the fools he has dealt with and their unwillingness to shine before the public as such, he has nursed his bread-and-butter "mystery" until he is nothing short of a public nuisance and a menace to the legitimate mining industry.

Authorities Should Act

I think it is high time state officials took some drastic action towards ridding the valley of Scott and his band, and if they will not do their duty the federal authorities should be called upon. Within the past few years many prospectors have been mysteriously assaulted and shot at and maybe killed. The perpetrators have never been found, but the time has come to rid the valley of the entire band. I believe that their headquarters are in the watered canyons of the Panamints and I also believe that when they are finally rounded up by the strong arm of the law the haul will include Bill Keyes, the half-Indian suspected of the Wingate Pass ambush; Bob Black, an Indian who killed his squaw at Ash Meadows some years ago; and a man named Gilbert, who is said to be wanted for complicity in a bank robbery and murder in Wyoming.

This sketch of the ultimate symbol of the Scotty myth, by Edward Vandeventer, from Sunset Magazine of March, 1926, brings the chronicle of the great con man up to the age of tourism.

SCOTTY'S CASTLE

by Edward A. Vandeventer

HIS PARENTS called him Walter and his last name was Scott, but for more than a quarter of a century he has been world famous as "Death Valley Scotty." He started millions guessing as to the source of his riches in 1905 when he chartered a special train at Los Angeles merely to satisfy a whim for a fast ride and established a speed record to Chicago that never has been approached, and he is still an unsolved puzzle. For while Scotty talks as freely as a brook babbles, he never really divulges any secrets. Today he is superintending the construction of a mansion near the head of Death Valley, in Eastern California, but not even Einstein himself could tell what it is all about.

There are whisperings concerning a huge landing field for airplanes; there is enough cast iron pipe on the ranch to build a water system for a town; there are plans for an ice refrigeration plant in that spot where the white sand makes a mammoth reflector and the sun beats down blisteringly hot during summer's months. Already there is a two-story building of concrete construction, with screened-in sleeping quarters, luxurious bathrooms and expansive dining quarters. There is a garage that houses three trucks and two passenger cars and has sufficient empty space to care for a fire department. There is another enormous building that shelters mules used in the development work. And Scotty is building a plant to generate electricity by the use of power that comes from spring water flowing from higher ground.

It doesn't do any harm to ask Scotty what it all means; neither does it do any good. He was in Goldfield recently and people crowded round him as they always do when he ventures forth from his beloved desert ranch. A plumber, with undue curiosity, tried to find an answer to the riddle. "What is that mansion to be used for when it is finished?" asked the plumber. "You can prepare to move down there soon," came back the reply in the characteristic Scotty manner, "as that is to be a home for crazy plumbers." The crowd laughed and the plumber blushed, and the man of mystery was content, for he had kept his auditors guessing.

A group of young girls with bobbed hair, rouged lips, rolled stockings and other marks of modern feminine youth surrounded the famous prospector and demanded to know why he was constructing an expensive building on the desert sand. "I am preparing that so we can round up the incorrigible flappers and put them where they belong," retorted Scotty.

Now and then he boasts that he will be "sitting on top of the world" and will have more money than any man can spend when he completes his ambitious plans, but that is as far as he will go in divulging his program. His replies to any queries about the use he will make of an airplane landing field are never informative.

Scotty is a master of mystery, but he also possesses a highly developed sense of humor, and never is so happy as when he finds a gullible person who will believe one of his fanciful yarns. He was going recently to Bonnie Clare, Nevada, the nearest railroad point, for some supplies that he had ordered when he met a motor tourist and his wife. The latter asked if he could direct them to the home of the famous Death Valley Scotty. He pointed to the only road leading to his place and they thanked him. On his return Scotty overtook them and began telling wild tales about the man they were seeking.

"If Scotty isn't at home," he said, "we will go into his house anyway and I will cook a meal for you. I know him well and it will be all right."

"If you know him so well," said the woman, "perhaps you can give me some accurate information concerning Scotty. I have been told that he got his wealth by holding up high-grade ore shipments."

With the solemn expression of a judge and in a confidential tone Scotty answered her. "I know this bird like a brother," he said, "and the story sounds plausible."

When the ranch was reached, Scotty invited the travelers into the house and explained that Scotty was not at home. He made them comfortable and began preparing a meal. The woman was hearing and believing enough romance about the prospector to write a novel when an Indian spoiled the joke by stepping into the kitchen and asking a question, "Say, Scotty," he asked, "what do you want me to do with the mules?"

Scotty is not only an unusually interesting character but he is a most likable person. No one could be a more hospitable host. He impresses one with the kindliness of his nature, and the desert country knows him for his generosity. Only those who have merely read of his escapades without seeing him and talking with him entertain the idea that he is a bit light above the ears. Those who have come in close contact with him recognize him as a keen, clever man who knows every minute what he is doing, and is smart enough to keep his purposes to himself. He is always an actor and never steps out of his part.

He is supposed to be about fifty years of age but has all the appearances of a man much younger. He is about five feet nine and a half inches in height and is rather heavy. His head is covered with a mass of bristly hair that seems to have caught its shade from the sands that he has tramped so much. I had expected to see a face baked and cracked by the heat, but was astonished at seeing a skin so fair and smooth that a woman might covet it.

But the eyes of Scotty fascinated me most of all. The blue of the desert sky is mirrored in them. Never have I seen any other eyes like them. They give one the impression that either the pupil fills the entire eye or that there is no difference between the color of the pupil and the color of the iris, and one is not conscious of seeing any white surrounding the blue. . . .

The Scotty ranch is in Grapevine Cañon, Inyo County, California, the cañon leading into the northern end of Death Valley. The ranch is at an elevation of several hundred feet, while most of the valley is below sea level. Scotty built and maintains a good dirt road twenty miles in length from Bonnie Clare, Nevada, on the Tonopah & Tidewater Railroad, to the ranch.

As one drives along that road through barren country he sees the first sign of life when he catches a glimpse of Indian camps on the higher side of the cañon, about one mile from Scotty's house. A few moments later he is impressed by the visualization of the magic of water. For there are the luscious grapes that gave the cañon its name. And there are the fig trees that seem so inviting in the midst of so many miles of desolation. The spring that gurgles far up the cañon has blessed that spot with its constant flow of cool water.

Scotty walks out into the open and immediately he is surrounded by scores of turkeys. His good nature seems to be understood by even the feathered creatures and all the animals. He goes to the cañon side and whistles, and soon a covey of quail can be seen approaching. He steps out of the house with a gun and his two dogs begin barking excitedly as if joyfully anticipating a lark with their pal.

He can keep everything on the ranch but a cook. Recently he went to Tonopah and tried to arrange for three cooks in relays. "I want to know that one is coming while one is going, with one on the ranch," he explained.

There is a belief in Nevada that the hundreds of thousands of dollars used for development of the ranch are furnished by A. M. Johnson, of Chicago, president of the National Life Insurance Company and president of the American Cold Storage Company. He is reputed to be a very wealthy man, and he makes frequent visits to the ranch. One story is that he was injured in a train wreck many years ago and that Scotty, meeting him in Chicago, invited him to the desert country for his health. A hunting trip helped him so much and Scotty made his visit so pleasant that he repeated it, and finally was caught in the spell of the desert.

Only during three months of the year is the weather unbearably hot in Grapevine Cañon. The place is a paradise the rest of the year, and it is said that Johnson desires to spend more of his time there and is having the luxurious home built so he can fittingly entertain guests.

But whether this is the explanation of the elaborate plans that are being carried out, or whether Scotty has some scheme afoot must be left for the future to prove. No one can learn the answer from Scotty or from Johnson.

The Adventure-Seekers

*D*EATH VALLEY'S ILLUSIONS ALSO
attracted adventure-seekers, especially those daring young men in their
gasoline machines, who challenged its deadly image just for publicity's sake.
A mining promoter and con man tells a stirring tale of the first auto trip
across Death Valley in 1906 in a race to purchase a mine. The mine didn't
amount to much, but the publicity was priceless. Then a free-lance adventure
writer tells an incredible, rip-roaring story of a motorcycle dash right
through the heart of the valley, exaggerating the horrors of the place beyond
belief to help promote sales of the bike. Yet with their automobiles and
motorcycles these last adventurers compressed distance and time, robbing the
valley of its remoteness and opening it to tourism for all the rest of us.

FIRST AUTO ACROSS

This classic account of desert motoring, published in the Rhyolite Herald *in June 1906, was written by a talented con man who took the alias of George Graham Rice. Born Jacob Simon Herzig, he began his colorful career by stealing from his father to pay gambling debts. He graduated from reform school to Sing Sing, went on to publish a racing tipsheet, then came to Nevada to start an "advertising agency" touting spurious mines. He wound up headed back to prison again in 1911 and while awaiting trial wrote his memoirs, appropriately entitled* My Adventures With Your Money.

DEATH VALLEY
by George Graham Rice

SHUT YOUR EYES and say "gold hunting." The vision is of an old sun-baked prospector shuffling along behind a pack of dusty burros through an endless desert.

But out here in southwestern Nevada, where mining is newest and most modern, there is another kind of "gold hunting," the kind that is done by the "big fellows." Rather, it should be called mine hunting. The men that engage in it are looking for a MINE. There are mines and MINES. They are looking for a MINE. They know that it needs but one MINE to fix a man for life—and leave something for his descendants.

That kind of a mine hunting is not done afoot behind a file of burros. It's done in automobiles. The men that engage in it keep up an "intelligence department," just as do the war offices of European governments. They have emissaries all over the gold fields—plodding patiently through the desert, "panning" in ravines, upon mountain tops. They have emissaries in the towns, in the saloons, the gambling places—fellows who can engage conversation and have good ears. In the garage close to their office is their automobile—oiled up like a watch, laden with extra tires, gasoline, a "grub" box, and water, the chauffeur lounging near.

Comes the news of a strike. Mr. Mine Hunter grabs up his overcoat, saunters across the street to the garage, steps into the tonneau, and he is off. Beneath the perpendicular sun, beneath the blazing stars, through desert and oasis, mountain or sink, his big machine whirrs—one day, two days, three, if necessary, till he comes to the find. He steps off and examines it. If it looks good he buys it. If not, he goes back, bootless. Bootless thus he often returns, but never impatient. For remember, all he wants is one MINE. It's big, noble hunting.

Nearly every one of these trips is an adventure. The men of the mining districts relate them to each other as, in the Middle Ages, the men who stayed at home told of the hardships and deeds of the searchers for the Holy Grail. The story that is being told here now is the run made by L. M. Sullivan and "Jack" Campbell. From Manhattan, Sullivan and Campbell sprang two hundred and fifty miles, clean across Death Valley, the earth's inferno, into the Panamint mountains on the California side, and pounced there upon a monstrous ledge of rich quartz, the finding of which had been dimly heralded on the wings of rumor. They got there just in time, too. For hardly had they made a preliminary examination and closed the deal, when a big black auto carrying the fortunes of Charles M. Schwab, the steel magnate, whirred into the little camp from the California side—too late.

Just before midnight of June 15, Campbell whizzed through the main street of Goldfield and halted the auto in front of the Sullivan office. Campbell is a mining engineer in charge of the Sullivan properties in Manhattan. The intelligence of the strike had reached him first, and he had come down from Manhattan, 70 miles, in two hours. Sullivan was still in his office, presiding over a meeting of directors. Two words from Campbell were enough, and seizing a box of cigars and his big automobile leather coat he stepped into the machine. A short stop was made at the garage to take on extra tires and gasoline, and then the big machine, an eighty-horsepower Pope-Toledo owned by Sullivan, buzzed out into the open country.

That night's run was uneventful. The road was good. It ran along a plateau that dropped gradually two thousand feet in eighty miles. The two men leaned forward in the tonneau, their teeth crunching upon their cigars; at intervals with short exclamations they urged the chauffeur on. The latter, a long, thin fellow, all humped up as if eternally cutting his way through a recalcitrant atmosphere, drove like a demon. The machine buzzed; at times, the iron flaps covering the engine raised with the friction of the air, and she seemed to fly on extended wings. Above, the stars blazed—the Great Dipper overhead, Orion stalking with flaming scabbard across the horizon in front. On each side, distorted cacti lurked in the shadow like huge tarantulas.

At two o'clock, crossing the Amargosa River, a little stream of bitter water two inches wide, one of the rear tires blew up. The chauffeur jacked the machine up and put in a new one—and they went on. They passed through Beatty like lightning, midst a howling of startled dogs. At three o'clock they were in Rhyolite. They had made eighty miles of mountainous desert in three hours.

There they met Chafey, the young fellow who had flashed the first news of the strike. He informed them that he had sent on a mule team with provisions to Stove Pipe Springs, on the edge of Death Valley. A half-hour stop was made. Breakfast was eaten. A

The Adventure-Seekers

new supply of gasoline was taken aboard, and each man was given a South African canvas bag full of water. Several coal oil cans full of water were also lashed to the shelf behind, for they were entering the country of Death and Desolation.

They started off again with the green sky of dawn behind them and whirred down a dry wash through a canyon of red walls. The enfevered breath of the still invisible valley struck their faces, as if she were hissing warning to them. After a while, the canyon walls opened and Death Valley was below them—a huge bowl, its bottom leprous with some loathsome-hued sediment. They whirred on, down a wash of black flint rock; with each plunge of the machine they entered a layer of air hotter than the preceding, till they panted as at the finish of a mile run. They rolled on, and the mountains rose on all sides—veiled, painted, mysterious mountains. Finally they were at the bottom, one hundred feet below sea level, and stopped at Stove Pipe Springs, a hole in the sand from which a little black water oozed.

The mule wagon which Chafey had sent on ahead was there, driven by G. N. McCullough, a desert prospector of years' experience. They loaded up with the water from the spring for the machine, hoarding the better water for drinking, and then they went on across the valley of Death.

A half mile on, they reached the sand dunes and the big machine stuck, its wheels whirring impotently through the elusive stuff without catching.

"We can't make it," said the chauffeur.

"We've GOT to make it," answered Sullivan and Campbell in one breath. Before them, blue with the distance, rose the Panamints with its mine, the MINE that they were after.

The three men got out. With a shovel they cleared the sand heaped up before the wheels; they placed gunny sacks beneath the tires; then, putting their shoulders against the tonneau, they pushed and strained while the chauffeur applied full power. The wheels whizzed, caught the sacking, the men strained and toiled. The machine gave a jump—one foot, two feet, three! It stuck again. More shoveling, more placing of sacks under the wheels, more pushing and straining. The machine jumped six feet and then stuck again. For two hundred yards, foot by foot, they went thus across the dunes. Then the sand grew deeper and their best efforts unavailing.

"Can't make it," said the chauffeur.

"Got to," said Sullivan and Campbell.

Before them, far, mysterious as a veiled woman, the Panamint Range rose with its promise of golden splendor.

They sat down upon the baking sand to consider the matter.

"The mules!" exclaimed Campbell at length.

"You've got it," said Sullivan.

With ropes they tied the wagon to the front axle of the auto. McCullough took the reins. "Yip! Yip! Yip!" he yelled, urging the animals with voice and gesture, while the chauffeur put on full power and the men pushed from behind. The machine vibrated, it jumped up and down in its tracks. There was a crash, and the mules started forward at a gallop, dragging McCullough with them, while the auto remained in place, immovable as a rock. The whiffle-tree had broken.

With the handle of a pick, Campbell and Sullivan improvised a new one. Then they hitched the mules directly to the auto. There was a sharp struggle. The mules tugged, the men pushed, the wheels whirred through the yielding sand. The auto began to move, an inch, a foot. The men panted. The wheels began to take hold, the machine gave a jump, and rolled forward.

For a hundred yards it went. Then the mules stopped, exhausted, and the men rolled over, half dead. The perpendicular sun fell upon them like drops of molten lead. The shimmering sand caught the heat and threw it back to the sun, which promptly poured it down again, till earth, sky, and air pulsated with a blinding glow. But ahead, far, mysterious, the Panamints rose with their purple promise of riches.

"Let's go on," said Sullivan.

They went on. For seven miles, by hundred-yard stretches, they heaved the machine over the sand. And finally they struck hard ground.

They left McCullough there with the wagon and the mules and a supply of water. They got into the auto and buzzed on across the shimmering alkali, a hundred feet below sea level, through an atmosphere that scorched. And ever before them the Panamints rose, veiled and inscrutable.

The machine struck a downgrade and whizzed along. At the bottom of the grade, a faint, green mustiness was visible. The machine approached it with vertiginous speed. Suddenly, with an exclamation, the chauffeur leaned forward and put on both brakes. There was a thump, a screech of tortured steel, the machine skidded and jumped, then came to a full stop, like a cow pony that throws itself on its haunches. The front wheels were buried in the treacherous soil.

With infinite labor, they pulled her back out of it. They examined the ground and found that the road led through an alkali swamp. Over the oozy depths, a crust that seemed hard but broke to weight stretched like a shimmering white lie.

Chafey went up on a little knoll to reconnoitre. The heat waves, rolling like gigantic breakers, caused strange illusions. On the top of the knoll, Chafey seemed to be limping as if his left leg were cut off at the knee. Then he began running in an extraordinary fashion, around in a circle. The rest of the party called him back, afraid. He assured them that he had been walking peaceably along the ridge. They were in the land of delusions, and everything was false.

They held a conference, and then decided upon taking a wild chance.

With only the chauffeur in it, the auto was backed far up the grade it had come down. The rest of the men spread along the path through the marsh, ready for any emergency. Sullivan dropped his handkerchief for a signal, and the machine started down the hill.

Right away, the chauffeur put on full speed. The steel flaps in front opened like wings. Silently at first, like a shadow, she whizzed down; then, as she caught the full impetus of power and grade, she began to buzz in a crescendo that rose till she roared like a bombshell. Down she came aroar, like a meteor from the skies. An involuntary cry came from the men in the marsh as she bore down upon them. She cleared the first hundred feet as if with one spring. She slowed, hesitated, yawed from side to side, then, the wheels catching a bit of harder ground, jumped forward again, through an oozy place, the wheels bespattering the skies. The men watched her, breathless. She struck a succession of hard spots between mud holes. Each time the wheels, catching the hard spot, jumped her over the next soft one, and thus, by a series of mad leaps, she went almost across, the chauffeur rising and falling upon his seat like the rider of a dromedary. On the further edge, a few feet from safety, she seemed to mire for good. She stopped, the wheels whirring madly through the slime. But the men alongside, frenzied, threw their coats, their hats, their shirts beneath the wheels, and slowly, inch by inch, she at length rose upon the hard ground.

Everything afterward was easy in comparison, though enough to daunt wills forged of baser metals than those of Sullivan, Campbell, and Chafey. An examination of the machine showed the frame that supported the engine to be cracked. It was braced with a drill and a shovel handle. Five miles from Emigrant Springs the party ran out of water, and the machine refused to go without it. Leaving Sullivan and the chauffeur with the small canteen that remained, Campbell and Chafey hiked on afoot with the empty water bags. With the desert sun pumping the water out of their bones, it was a desperate race, and their tongues were swollen almost out of their mouths before they reached the little pool of stagnant water. They filled all the bags and returned to the machine. Again in working order, the auto pumped slowly up the remainder of the grade and at midnight rolled into the little camp at Emigrant Springs.

Even then it was not time to rest. Afoot the party climbed over the hills, and just at sunup, they were standing upon a monstrous outcropping of gold-bearing quartz, the MINE so desperately won. Taking samples here and there, they returned to camp, "panned" them, and there and then, Sullivan, Chafey, and the prospectors closed the deal. Hardly had this been done when the puff-puff of an auto drew them outside of the tent. Slowly, painfully, a crippled automobile was rolling in from the other side of the mountains. Campbell recognized the man in the auto, a confidential agent of Charles M. Schwab, the great steel magnate. The race had been won, and just won.

A RACE FOR LIFE

This exaggerated tale of a midsummer motorcycle dash by an adventuresome free-lancer was published in Wide World Magazine *in October 1922. John Edwin Hogg actually made his run in the cool of December 1919 and talked of returning in an airplane to search for lost mines. But he couldn't get enough fuel into the valley for the occasion, so he turned to hunting wild burros in the Panamints on his motorcycle.*

IN DEATH VALLEY
by John Edwin Hogg

THIS ADVENTURE, which came within the scantiest margin of adding two more names to the long list of unfortunates whose bones have bleached in the shimmering, heat-scorched wastes of Death Valley, really began in Chicago. A business trip had taken me to that city, where I was in conference with the advertising manager of a great motorcycle factory with whom I had previously enjoyed pleasant business relations.

The advertising manager appeared to be worried. "We've got to do something," he said, "to counteract this competitive propaganda about our motors overheating." The factory was building motorcycles of the conventional air-cooled type, and, having had a great deal of experience with their product, I knew that the talk about motors overheating was purely what the advertising manager termed it—competitive propaganda. "If you can suggest some plan to offset this attack we are ready to pay you well for it," continued the advertising man, and in these words I saw my opportunity.

"Why not send a couple of machines through Death Valley in August?" I suggested. "Death Valley, you know, is reputed to be the hottest place on earth, and if we can explore it by motorcycle during the warmest month of the year it should supply the desired advertising proof that your motors do *not* overheat."

When I lightheartedly made this suggestion I was thinking more about the money the task might bring than the actual feasibility of carrying it out. Had I known then of the days of awful torture that were in store for myself and companion of the trip, and the scanty—almost Providential—margin by which we were able to drag ourselves back to civilization from that blazing inferno, no amount of money would have taken me into Death Valley. The advertising manager, however, thought my idea an excellent one, and he named an attractive figure for the work. I knew the trip would be fraught with certain hardships, but, having had years of experience in the desert, I accepted the job with enthusiasm.

Upon my return to California the essential detail of finding a suitable companion for the midsummer dash through Death Valley was soon disposed of by getting in touch with Wells Bennett. Bennett is several years my senior, but I might have combed the world without finding a man better qualified for such a foolhardy venture. For many years he has been a professional motorcycle racer, and is the holder of no less than a dozen of the most coveted road records.

To understand the nature of our journey, a few words of description are necessary. Death Valley is shown on any good map of California. It lies in the east central portion of that state, close to the Nevada boundary. It is about a hundred miles long, and varies in width from ten to eighteen miles. Hemmed in by titanic mountain ranges which tower to more than eleven thousand feet, every inch of the valley's floor lies below sea level. It is actually two hundred and eighty feet below the ocean level at its lowest point, and is one of the most complete deserts on the face of the earth. With the exception of a single oasis, appropriately known as Furnace Creek, Death Valley is decidedly hostile to human existence. Its average annual rainfall is less than three-tenths of an inch, and in summer it swelters under temperatures up to a hundred and forty-five degrees (F.), with sun temperatures much higher. Added to this terrific heat there is the heavy atmospheric pressure of negative elevation to be reckoned with, for Death Valley is the lowest depression on the face of the Western hemisphere, and the lowest on earth with the exception of the Dead Sea region of Palestine.

The valley acquired its name during the gold rush to California in 1849, when a party of immigrants lost their way while crossing the Great American Desert. They wandered down through the maze of canyons in the Funeral Mountains, which bound it on the eastern side, and failed to find the pass leading out of the valley through the Panamint Mountains to the west. They ran out of water in the terrific heat, and of the original party of some sixty-three members all but three perished miserably from heat or thirst. Since that time, although the valley has long been considered unfit for human habitation, tales of great mineral wealth concealed there have lured countless prospectors to their doom. Never a year goes by that Death Valley does not claim its quota of victims. The lure of gold takes them in; then heat, thirst, blistering sands, bottomless salt-bogs, shimmering mirages, and springs of clear sparkling water charged with deadly mineral arsenic and cyanide affix the signatures to the death warrants of these victims of the Valley of Horrors, who are swallowed up never to be heard from again.

Our journey from Los Angeles to Barstow, the last outpost of civilization, a distance of a hundred and eight miles, was merely an uneventful motorcycle tour. At Barstow the real hardships of the desert began. Of our journey across the desert to the extreme southern end of Death Valley, around the east side into Nevada, and back again to the east side of the valley, I will speak but briefly; for the adventures of that portion of the trip pale into insignificance compared with those that were to befall us later. To approach the valley from the east, in accordance with previously carefully made plans, we had to journey three hundred miles through the desert around it. This was a trip of four days in a temperature around a hundred and twenty degrees, during which time we never set eyes upon a human being. For roads we had virtually nothing. We simply engineered our way across the desert, across dry lakes, up washes, over ranges of burned-out desert mountains, and down the other side to the next range. We made our way from one water hole to the next, the supplies of drinkable liquid being anywhere from thirty to eighty miles apart. Our entire stock of water, food, and motor fuel had to be carried in the sidecar, which had been carefully equipped and attached to my machine for the purpose.

Eventually we reached the borax mine at Ryan, which is located in the Funeral Mountains eighteen miles from the floor of Death Valley, and at the end of a narrow-gauge railway connecting the mine with the markets of the world. In our journey around the valley most of our traveling had been done through desert country well above three thousand feet elevation, so we had not suffered severely from such desert temperatures as are encountered at lower or negative elevations.

It was noon when we arrived in the wash directly underneath the borax mines, where we stopped to take advantage of arrangements previously made to replenish our supplies of food, fuel, and water. There Mr. W. L. Faulkner, the superintendent, evidently sympathizing with us in what he termed "a most hazardous undertaking," invited us to have lunch with him. Having lived on dried and tinned foods for four days, his hospitality was greatly appreciated. He showed us every possible courtesy, and by two o'clock we were on our way down Furnace Creek Wash.

The trip from Ryan to Furnace Creek Oasis took us from an elevation of four thousand three hundred feet to one hundred and seventy-eight feet below sea level. This descent was made in eighteen miles down a trackless wash, and with every foot we descended it seemed that the temperature came up to meet us. In going down the wash we knew that we were going into the blistering inferno of Death Valley, and literally destroying the bridge behind us; for, with the steepness of the gradient and the depth of the sand, we realized that we could never drive the machines out by the route over which we had entered. Furthermore, any thought of getting out of the valley without the machines would be the utmost folly, because in that heat it is impossible for one to carry sufficient water to make his way out on foot.

Bennett, riding "solo," was able to travel faster than I could with the sidecar outfit, which demanded careful maneuvering among the rocks of the canyon floor. He rode ahead until he went out of sight around a curve in the walls, and I did not see him again until I got down almost to the floor of the valley. When I found him he was stretched out under the base of a ledge, where he had taken refuge from the sun. By this time the sun was getting low over the western mountains, and we realized that some measure of relief from the heat was only a matter of a few more hours. A more vivid realization, however, was in my mind.

If this was a sample of Death Valley heat, what could we expect the following day? We didn't need a thermometer to tell us that the heat was terrible, but, thinking to determine the actual number of degrees, I got out our instrument-box, which included a Fahrenheit thermometer with a scale up to a hundred and thirty-five degrees. As I removed the instrument, the mercury was clear up at the top of the tube, and even before I had time to examine it, there was a sharp "Ping!" as the end of the tube and contents went off into space. The thermometer had simply blown up! We knew that the actual temperature was in excess of one hundred and thirty-five degrees from the fact that the thermometer had exploded, but with the shattering of the glass went our hopes of gathering accurate scientific data concerning Death Valley temperatures.

From the point where Bennett had stopped to rest to Furnace Creek Ranch was a distance of about six miles. Furnace Creek Ranch is the only point of human habitation in the whole of Death Valley, and is, without exception, one of the most extraordinary irrigated farms on the face of the earth. It is a work of man under the pressure of necessity. Near Furnace Creek Ranch there are undeveloped deposits of borax which are believed to offer an inexhaustible supply. The Pacific Coast Borax Company laid claim to these deposits with the view to their future exploitation, but in order to comply with the law, and retain possession of the only supply of water for many miles, certain development work has been compulsory. Furnace Creek Ranch, comprising sixty-five acres of irrigated land under cultivation, is the result. It produced garden stuff, chickens, eggs, and meat, which are wagoned out of the valley up Furnace Creek Wash to the mine at Ryan. The personnel of the ranch consists of several

Piute Indians, who are inured to the terrible conditions under which they live, and a white foreman, who enjoys the unique distinction of being the only white man who has been able to survive a second summer in the place. Mr. Oscar Denton, the present foreman, has occupied his position for the past eight years. He succeeded three foremen who died from the heat during their first summers in the valley, and two others who went insane.

The Indians at Furnace Creek Ranch had never seen a motor-cycle before. They evinced little interest in my sidecar outfit, but Bennett's "solo" machine was something clear beyond their powers of comprehension. When they saw him approaching, waving from side to side as he plunged through the sand on two wheels, they scattered in every direction. They seemed to regard him and the machine as something supernatural, and after running for cover they refused to leave their hiding places until Mr. Denton came out, shook hands with us, and called the Indians out by speaking to them in their own language.

Denton was delighted to have two white men visit him. He told us we were the first white men he had seen for thirty-one weeks, and invited us to stay with him as long as we cared to and to make ourselves at home. During our introductory conversation with the ranch foreman, we had been standing under a cottonwood tree taking refuge from the sun. Suddenly Bennett held up his hand to indicate silence. "Listen," he said, "what are those church bells I hear?"

"Church bells!" exclaimed Denton. "Why, my dear boy, there isn't a church within two hundred miles! It's the heat working on you, and if you don't want to die, I suggest that you get in the water, clothes and all, immediately."

My own brain was buzzing with the heat, and I could feel the blood pounding in my temples until it felt as if someone were rapping me on the head with a mallet. Thereupon, we both acted upon the foreman's suggestion. We merely removed watches and other trinkets from our pockets, and then got bodily into the nearest irrigation ditch. That stream of water looked wonderfully cool and refreshing, but as I splashed into it, I let out a yell, and my first impulse was to jump out as fast as I could, for the water nearly scalded me.

As a matter of fact, the water which supplies Furnace Creek Ranch is brought down into Death Valley from two large springs in the Funeral Mountains. It comes through seven miles of open ditch and steel pipe, and in making this journey it is heated by the sun until, when it runs into the irrigation ditches at the ranch, it is at a temperature of about a hundred and twelve degrees. The effect of getting into the water, however, was exactly what Mr. Denton said it would be, for the atmosphere of Death Valley is probably the driest on earth, containing less than one-hundredth of one percent moisture. It is dangerous to human life because the dry atmosphere is constantly drawing moisture out of the body at an almost greater rate than it is possible to restore it. Coming out of the water into the heat and dry air, we felt wonderfully cool, and thirty minutes later the heavy woollen clothing we wore was as dry as if we had never been in the water. Meanwhile the sun had set and the temperature descended to about a hundred and twenty-five degrees. We learned later from Mr. Denton that the temperature upon our arrival at the ranch had been a hundred and forty-two degrees. He has a weather observation station at the ranch, from which he reports Death Valley weather conditions and temperatures to the United States Weather Bureau at Washington. The temperature that afternoon had been within three degrees of the highest ever recorded.

At the ranch foreman's suggestion we decided to spend the night at the ranch. After supper that evening we sat out on the veranda in the comfort of an ingenious water-power fan which the ranch foreman built for himself. There was a moment of silence, and then Denton asked: "What on earth ever brought you boys down here into this hell-hole?" Our mission was explained in a few words, which apparently satisfied his curiosity. For several minutes the ranch foreman was thoughtful. Then he spoke again, saying: "I don't want to douse cold water upon your plans, but if you'll take a word of well-meaning advice you'll leave this valley tomorrow night by the route over which you came in. If you can't get up the wash with your machines, I can send them out with one of my Indians on a wagon. I don't believe you realize what a blazing inferno this valley is! You may not think it, but the heat nearly got both of you this afternoon. If you think it is hot here, just wait till you get out yonder in those salt marshes."

After listening to Mr. Denton's argument we expressed our determination to go south through the valley, and to get out at the south end as we had originally planned. At this the ranch foreman shook his head. "Boys," he said earnestly, "if you have anything to live for—and I suppose you have a great deal—you'll take my advice. If you really want to die, you'll save yourselves a lot of needless torture by stepping out there in the cemetery and finishing yourselves off with your pistols. I'm not trying to scare you, and I admit I admire your nerve, but if you go south through the valley your bones are going to bleach out there. You'll never make it, I tell you—you'll never make it! I've seen too many men die down here already. I've pulled them in out of the salt marshes, and I've dug too many graves out back of this ranch. I've found them dead out here in the yard after they'd staggered in too late for water to save them. I've found 'em dead with canteens of water hangin' round their necks. They die of heat, I tell you—it isn't thirst that kills!"

For the next hour Denton went on telling us tales of Death Valley. His ranch is to the valley about what St. Bernard's Hospice is to the Alps of Switzerland. He told us stories of men he'd found along the very route we intended to travel, of nightmare mirages, the infernal heat, men bogged down in the salt marshes, and other stories so gruesome and horrible as to literally turn one's hair. In the midst of this conversation the lamp which illuminated the veranda spluttered and went out for lack of oil. Denton excused himself to go and fill it, and Bennett and I took advantage of the opportunity to discuss the situation between ourselves.

"What do you think about it, Wells?" I asked him.

"I think he's giving us good advice," replied Bennett, "but I've come down here to see this job through, and I'm for going ahead with it. How do you feel about it?"

"For me," I replied, "there is no alternative. Possibly I've bitten off more than I can chew, but I have the company and my reputation to consider, and there is no turning back now."

"That suits me," said Bennett. "I'll ride until my machine falls to pieces under me, or until I am baked by the sun. But I'd rather die fighting than to be a quitter, so suppose we shake on it."

Thereupon we shook hands, and there was something about Bennett's determined handshake that convinced me he meant it.

A moment later Denton returned with the relighted lamp. "Well, boys," he said, as he approached us, "have you decided to go back up Furnace Creek Wash?"

"No, Mr. Denton," I told him, "we're going south through the valley tomorrow."

For a moment the ranch foreman was thoughtful. Then he said: "Very well, then. I admire your pluck but deplore your judgment. Since you are determined to go I reckon you may succeed, but I wouldn't give a tinker's curse for your chances. If you *must* go, I want to be of such service to you as I may. I know the valley thoroughly, and I'll sketch you a map showing you the best route. I can guide you to the waterholes, and steer you clear of the ones that are poisonous." With that he produced a paper and pencil and began to draw. An hour later he gave us the map, with a lot of valuable notes on it and some verbal comment, without which, I am confident, I would not be alive to write these lines today.

At Denton's suggestion we deferred our start through the valley until after supper next evening. There was to be a full moon that night, and by traveling by moonlight we should escape the terrible heat of the day while getting over the worst portion of the journey.

Fortune seemed to be favoring us, for the following day dawned slightly cooler. At four o'clock in the afternoon the temperature stood at one hundred and thirty-eight degrees—four degrees cooler than it had been at that time the day before. By eight o'clock in the evening, when the moon rose over the Funeral Mountains, illuminating the snow-white floor of the valley, the temperature had fallen to a hundred and twenty degrees. We shook hands with Denton and toured away into the deathlike silence, with only the sharp barking of our motors to cheer us. We knew only too well that we were gambling, with our lives as the stakes, against the proper working of two internal-combustion motors. If one or both machines went out of business there wouldn't be a burglar's chance of our getting out of the valley alive.

During our sojourn at Furnace Creek Ranch we had made a careful study to ascertain our requirements of water in such terrific heat. We found that six quarts per man per hour was about a minimum for supporting life with any degree of comfort. Thus, with thirty-six quarts of water in the specially-built tank in the sidecar, we could expect to last about three hours while making the dash from one water hole to the next. With the utmost conservation we might be able to extend our time to six hours, but obviously any serious delay due to mechanical difficulty would be at the peril of our lives.

To persons living in a temperate climate and accustomed to drinking only a quart or so of liquid every twenty-four hours, six quarts of water per hour undoubtedly seems a physical impossibility. Subject yourself to a temperature of from a hundred and twenty to a hundred and sixty degrees, however, and one's life may be measured by the amount of drinking water obtainable. This may be accounted for by the fact that normal human blood temperature is under a hundred degrees. It stands to reason, therefore, that if one's blood temperature were ever to approach that of the surrounding atmosphere a fatal fever would be the almost immediate result. Perspiration, and the reduction of temperature effected by its evaporation, is thus the only means which Nature has provided to stave off death. Great quantities of water must be drunk to supply the perspiration, and if the supply is curtailed death is obviously only a matter of minutes. That is why it would be utterly impossible to carry enough water to escape from Death Valley on foot.

The Adventure-Seekers

Six miles from Furnace Creek Ranch we came to the Frying Pan Salt Marsh at the point where Mr. Denton told us we were to cross it to the other side. The marsh at this point is three miles wide, and once across it we would be within eighteen miles of Bennett's Hole, which would be our next chance for water. If we could get to Bennett's Hole by sunrise we could camp there in the shade of a mesquite thicket, near water, before journeying on to the next water at Owl Hole, twenty-nine miles farther south. That salt marsh, however, came very near adding our bones to the bleaching skeletons of Death Valley—just as Mr. Denton had warned us.

The salt marshes of Death Valley are not marshes in the usual sense of the word. Salt mazes would be a better name for them. They are great areas where seepage water is drawn out of the ground by capillary attraction. This water, evaporating at a terrific rate, leaves the salt and minerals in it forming a maze of salt pillars resembling the stalagmites of a cavern. The marshes are perfect forests of these curious salt pillars, as hard as concrete and projecting upward anywhere from ten to thirty-six inches. The only way in which we could get the machines across the marsh was by hewing a path—a job comparable with cutting a three-mile path through concrete posts. Mr. Denton had contributed an axe and a pick to our outfit, and with these implements we went to work. We labored from nine o'clock that evening until almost sunrise the next morning, chopping down the salt pinnacles and casting the fragments aside.

Working against time, the heavy exertion in that awful heat compelled us to make serious inroads upon our precious water supply. We worked stripped to the waist, and constantly fighting off clouds of bloodthirsty mosquitoes, which attacked us most unmercifully. Long before the first rays of daylight began streaming up over the Funeral Mountains, both of us looked like raw beef and felt as if we had been bathed in nitric acid. Our work was hampered by the necessity of making frequent trips to the water tank, and to save as much time as possible we kept moving the machines forward as fast as the path was cut. By sunrise we had the path broken to the sand on the other side of the marsh, and as we pushed the machines ashore we drained the last drop of water out of the thirty-six-quart tank. There was scarcely enough fluid to wet our tongues. We were eighteen miles from a fresh supply, with no telling how long it would take us to get there, and the grave possibility of finding the water hole dry when we did arrive. Our only hope lay in being able to negotiate that eighteen miles in record time.

Even as we mounted our machines to ride away from the salt marsh our mouths and throats had begun to dry to the point where it was only with difficulty that either of us was able to speak. There was no time to be lost. In a voice that sounded like the rattling of dried beans in a pod, I admonished Bennett to ride ahead to the water hole and return with a canteen of water if I failed to show up within a reasonable length of time. In another second Bennett's motor was roaring and he was throwing sand high in the air with his rear wheel as he tore out across the desert with his machine zigzagging like a fancy skater on thin ice. Before he had gone a hundred yards the mirages began to play and the atmosphere around me had begun to waver with the heat. The great peaks of the Panamint Range to the west and the purple-tinted Funeral Mountains to the east were vibrating like mountains of rubber twisted by a hurricane. For a moment Bennett appeared as a Colossus riding a miniature motorcycle. Then, almost instantly, this apparition would be reversed, and he would appear as a Lilliputian astride a machine as big as a railway locomotive. The salt marsh we had left behind had become a magnificent silvery lake. It appeared as a beautiful expanse of clear cool water, with trees, shrubbery, and tall majestic palms fringing its shore. By this time the sun was well up over the eastern mountaintops, and its rays felt as if a million searchlights had been focused upon me.

The rubber grips on the handlebars of my machine were soon so hot it was agony to hold to them, even with the heavy leather gloves that I wore; but knowing that my life depended upon driving the machine to water, I gritted my teeth and opened the throttle. The rear wheel of the machine was spinning so fast in the sand that the speedometer driven off it was utterly useless. At times the hand went around to indicate sixty miles per hour, but probably I wasn't traveling more than twenty-five. The mileage dial, of course, was running up false mileage—probably three for every one that I moved forward. There wasn't a trace of a trail to follow, other than the track Bennett had left in the sand; and assuming that he was traveling in the right direction I plunged ahead after him. There could be no sparing the machine now. It had to get me to that water hole or be smashed to pieces in the attempt. Its proper functioning meant life; its failure spelled a swift and horrible death!

The floor of the valley along this route was none too smooth, and our course was broken by numerous washes, loose boulders, and thickets of stunted desert brush. Over this course I drove like a madman, with the agony of thirst and the fear of death upon me. I tore through the washes by sheer force of momentum, sliding sideways around obstructing boulders, and plunging through brush as high as

The Adventure-Seekers

my shoulders, with no more regard for it than if it had been so much grass. For mile after mile the machine stood up under the terrific abuse without ever a falter. The punishment I received from the saddle was almost unendurable. As I plunged through the washes it seemed at times as if the rear wheel would surely be driven through my spinal column. Would the machine and the tires hold out? That was the question that stood between me and death.

I was still following Bennett's track at this wild pace when I drove into a sand pit where it seemed as if the earth gave way under the machine. The sidecar outfit went from a speed of probably thirty miles per hour to an absolute standstill, almost as if I had brought up against a concrete wall. I went straight off over the handlebars, landed on one shoulder, and turned about three somersaults in the sand. My delight, on picking myself up, to find all my bones intact overshadowed for the moment my impending death from thirst. The wheels of the sidecar had "stalled" in the sand, but the motor was roaring with the throttle wide open. Running back and shutting off the motor, I came to a sickening realization that something had failed about the transmission. My hopes revived somewhat when I discovered it was nothing more serious than a broken drive-chain. It would take but a moment to make a repair, I thought; but upon getting out my tools I found there was not a tool in the roll that could be handled, even with my leather gloves. They felt as if they had been taken out of a baking oven. By this time my tongue had swollen and dried until it felt like a bath towel rolled up and stuffed down my throat, and my upper lip was distended until it obstructed my nostrils. Even as I fumbled with the tools, trying to handle them with a cloth, I began to hear church bells and the music of a distant orchestra. Then everything around me commenced to whirl and the sunlight turned black. I felt dreadfully sleepy, vomited violently several times, and then went to sleep, still fumbling with the hot tools and the still hotter drive chain.

It seemed as if I had been asleep for hours when I awoke to find myself lying in the shade of a mesquite tree. Bennett was standing over me with a canteen. Every cell in my body was figuratively crying out for water. I tried to speak, but couldn't utter a sound. After several desperate efforts I managed to gasp—"Water! For heaven's sake, Wells—water!" With that Bennett stooped over me, and poured a few drops from the canteen into my mouth. Never have I tasted anything that seemed so good as those few drops of liquid! With the moistening of my tongue and throat I could speak with less difficulty. "Give me a drink!" I breathed. "I'm on fire all over!"

"There! There!" he replied. "You're coming out of it all right. I'll give you more in a minute, but I don't want to kill you with the first drink."

Every minute or two after that he would press the canteen to my lips and give me a few more drops of the life-giving fluid. Soon I had recovered my voice enough to be able to talk, and I got to my feet feeling somewhat sick and weak. It was then that I learned from Bennett that we were at the oasis at Bennett's Hole. Bennett had arrived there some twenty minutes ahead of me. He had fished a dead coyote out of the spring, cleaned it thoroughly, taken several drinks, filled a canteen, and then gone back to the edge of the mesquite thicket to look for me. He saw me approaching over the desert, and I was within a quarter of a mile of the oasis when he saw me go over the handlebars. Seeing me get to my feet, he expected me to mount the machine again and ride in. A few minutes later, however, he saw me sink down in the sand. Running out to where I was, he found me unconscious and had carried me to the oasis, all but crumpling up himself before he got there.

Even in the shade of the mesquite thicket which surrounds the spring at Bennett's Hole, the heat was almost unendurable. In these circumstances the logical thing to do was to stop where we had shade and water and continue our journey by moonlight. Bennett cooked a little food, and after having breakfast I began to regain my usual strength. My thirst, however, was still inexorable, but after haunting the water hole for several hours I obtained sufficient relief to be able to wet my clothing, spread my blanket in the shade, and go to sleep. When I finally woke up again it was to find Bennett cooking supper. We ate, and by that time the sun had gone down behind the Panamints, so that we were able to go out and bring in my machine. My experience of the morning, however, had made me almost useless. The terrific heat had seared my palms even through the leather gloves, and the backs of my hands were so badly blistered that when the gloves were removed the skin came off with them.

Leaving Bennett's Hole after the moon arose, the going was chiefly through heavy sand. Bennett, with his "solo" motor, and his extraordinary skill as a rider, got along well, but with the heavily loaded sidecar I was less fortunate. Two miles south of Bennett's Hole we encountered sand through which the sidecar was unable to move, and in attempting to force the machine through, the drive-chain parted again. We repaired it as quickly as possible, but hadn't gone half a mile before it snapped once more. The experience was repeated again, and again, and again. With the delays due to constantly breaking the drive-chain, we realized that sunrise was going to catch us less than halfway to Owl Hole, which was our next chance for water and shade. If we failed to get there in time we should again run out of water, with our chances ten to one for being roasted alive.

After making about the tenth repair to the drive-chain, we had used up our last spare chain-link. If the chain broke again we were done! In a last desperate effort to save the chain, we got out the tow-rope and attached one end of it to the sidecar axle and the other to Bennett's machine, with the view of giving the sidecar some assistance from the "solo" motor. Roped together in this fashion, I used the Klaxon horn of my machine to signal to Bennett, and with both motors roaring we tore off through the sand. The scheme of towing the sidecar wheel worked out even better than we had anticipated, and for the next ten miles we plunged southward over the floor of Death Valley. When we stopped it was because the towrope broke. I shut off my motor instantly, and signalled Bennett to stop, for fear of again breaking the drive-chain.

We were still fully fifteen miles from Owl Hole when the first rays of daylight began streaking up over the Funeral Mountains. If fortune favored us, we should make that distance before the sun began to burn us up, but with the slightest delay we faced the identical predicament of the morning before. Realizing this, we lost little time in getting under way, but hadn't gone a mile before the towrope parted again. This time it was the stand of Bennett's machine, to which the rope was tied, that pulled out. We repaired it with hay wire, but at the expense of sacrificing a whole precious hour. By this time our water supply was down to only about ten quarts, and the sun, with its scorching rays, was upon us.

Getting under way once more, we drove like madmen, with the faint hope that if disaster overtook us, we might have a ghost of a chance of getting near enough to the water hole to make the balance of the distance on foot. In this, however, our hopes were blasted, when Bennett's machine, unable to stand the abuse it was receiving, stripped a locking-key on the motor driveshaft. We had spare keys for making the necessary repair, but the job could not be accomplished in less than an hour, and by that time we should be withered by the sun. We were still twelve miles from water and shade. We were not out of water yet, but our supply was altogether inadequate to entertain a hope of seeking our salvation afoot.

The mirages had now begun to play again, and our doom appeared to be sealed when Bennett chanced to look toward the foothills of the Panamints, along the brow of which we were traveling. "What is that spot on the hillside yonder?" he asked, pointing in that direction. I could make out the spot too, but wasn't sure whether it was real or just mirage. I reached for my field glasses, and with them made out that the spot on the hill was the entrance to a dugout—evidently built by some prospector during the winter months. It offered us shade, at least, and with what water we had left we might be able to live through the day and make our way to Owl Hole after nightfall.

With Bennett pushing the sidecar, I gave the motor as much power as I felt the drivechain would safely stand, and we made our way to within a few hundred yards of the dugout. There we stuck in a sand wash, and, unable to endure the heat another minute, both of us grabbed a canteen of water and ran toward the dugout. The sole occupant was a five-foot rattlesnake, which foolishly announced himself by rattling as we entered. A single bullet from my pistol put an end to him, and we threw his still-squirming body outside as we moved in to take possession. The furniture of the dugout, which was fairly roomy, consisted of two soap boxes, a piece of burlap on the floor, and an improvised stove made from an old oil tin. It remained for Bennett to make the discovery which unquestionably saved our lives. He lifted the burlap from the floor, thinking only to ascertain if it harbored another rattlesnake. Under the burlap was a trapdoor of rough boards, and in a pit beneath it a sixty-gallon barrel half-full of stale water. We trundled the barrel out of the hole, struck the bung, and sampled the water. It was as black as ink and smelt nasty— but it was water! By disinfecting it with potassium permanganate, which we carried as a remedy for possible rattlesnake bites, we could drink it by holding our noses, and it wasn't half bad when made into coffee. The temperature inside the dugout was like that of an oven, but, even then, it was probably forty or fifty degrees cooler than in the sun outside. We spent the day in the dugout, and managed to get in about six hours' sleep in spite of the heat.

After sundown we filled our canteens and then put the barrel back in the pit for some other poor wanderer who might need it. Then we returned to Bennett's machine, and in about an hour had it repaired, ready to travel again. It should be mentioned here that the enamel on both machines had begun to blister and fall off in pieces as big as a man's hand. It had been oven-baked at the factory, of course, but the Death Valley heat brought it off just as it had taken the skin off the back of my hands. Our faces by this time were literally cooked. Our lips were cracked and continually bleeding, and both of us were showing the effects of the hardships we had endured by the loss of considerable weight. Of course, we had not shaved since leaving civilization, and the whiskers, with our sunbaked faces, protruding cheekbones, and swollen lips, made us a hard-looking pair indeed.

A few miles south of the point where Bennett's machine had gone wrong we came upon firm, gravelly soil—a welcome relief from the heavy sand we had been fighting. We were able to discard the towline, and our speed began to improve. We got to Owl Hole about an hour after getting Bennett's machine in running order, loaded up all the water we could carry, and pushed on. Our next water hole would be Cave Spring, at the extreme southern end of the valley. This was a journey of ninety miles from Owl Hole, and the longest stretch we had to cover between water holes. By this time we were getting into the higher elevations of Death Valley, our aneroid showing the floor of the valley just below Owl Hole as being only fifty feet below sea level. This higher ground offered us some relief from the terrific heat, and we calculated that if we could make the next stage of the journey to Cave Spring that night, we should be able to get out of Death Valley through Cave Canyon Pass the next day. This plan was all very fine in theory, but in practice it went awry. Little did we realize then the horrors that were in store for us the following day!

We made fairly good progress until the first rays of daylight began to show. As nearly as we could tell, we had covered about fifty miles of the distance from Owl Hole when we came to a place where a great shelf of rock protruded from the wall of a canyon that came down to the floor of the valley from the foot of the Owl Mountains, the range forming the southern rim of Death Valley. The shelf offered complete protection from the sun, so we decided to make a dry camp there until after sunset. There was no water closer than Cave Spring, still forty miles away; and since we could never hope to make that distance before the heat of the day overtook us, camping for the day where we had shelter from the sun seemed by far the best plan. I drove the sidecar under the sheltering ledge, and unloaded such of our equipment as we needed. We were walking about under the ledge, looking for a flat place to shake down our beds, when a huge rattlesnake popped his head up from behind a boulder, and began to rattle. In an instant both of us had jumped back with our pistols drawn. "Bang! Bang! Bang!" went Bennett's automatic, and with the third shot the snake crumpled down behind the rock where he had appeared. We fished him out stone dead. We went about making our camp, after throwing the dead snake aside, and thought nothing more of the incident. After breakfasting we crawled on to our blankets. By this time the heat was stifling, but both of us were soon asleep, and we never opened an eye until the long shadows of our ledge on the opposite canyon wall told us the sun had almost set again. We got up, and I set about preparing supper, thinking to eat before we began traveling again. I put coffee in the pot, and handed it to Bennett, requesting that he add the water to it. A moment later, as I was stirring corned beef in the frying pan over the fire, I heard a volley of oaths emanating from Bennett's direction. He was standing beside the sidecar stamping his feet on the ground and cursing. I ran towards him, calling out, "What's the matter, Wells?" For a moment he stood there with his lips trembling; then he spoke in a most despondent voice, saying, "Well, old man, we're done! And it's all my fault, too! We're going to die, and you ought to have the satisfaction of killing me, because I'm the cause of your death!"

With that he pointed to a small round hole in the body of the sidecar, and a moist spot on the sand under the vehicle told the rest of the story. One of Bennett's bullets, fired at the rattlesnake, had apparently glanced from the rocks. It had struck the sidecar and gone through our water tank within a quarter of an inch of the bottom. The machine had been tilted slightly to that side, and every drop of our precious water supply had run off into the sand!

I was staring blankly at the bullet hole in the sidecar body, endeavoring to think what possible action could save us from certain death, when I was interrupted by Bennett. "Well, why don't you shoot me?" he demanded.

"I'm not going to shoot you, Wells," I told him. "But for you, I should have been dead the day before yesterday; and I certainly have no desire to kill you now. Come, don't let us cry over lost water. It's gone, and we can't help it."

Without further ado we threw our outfit into the sidecar and were soon under way again. We still had a scant three quarts of water in the two canteens, but obviously that was not enough to offer any hope of getting to the water hole in Cave Canyon before death from thirst overtook us. Another desperate race to water might be essayed, but it seemed such a forlorn hope, with the water forty miles away on the other side of a range of mountains over which no road existed, that it was scarcely worth considering. According to our reckoning we were then thirty-one miles from the mouth of Cave Canyon, with the prospect of a nine-mile climb upward through the canyon from fifty feet below sea level to an elevation of five thousand eight hundred feet before we should be out of the valley and near water! My chances of making it with the sidecar were not even those of a snowball in a blast furnace.

Turning these disheartening thoughts over in my mind, I signaled to Wells to stop. "Wells," I told him, "there is just one chance in a million for us to get ourselves out of this. You take the two canteens, with what water we've got, and beat it for Cave Spring. Ride as you have never ridden before, fill the canteens, and return to me as fast as you can. I may be dead before you get back, but it's our only chance. I'll keep plugging along as best I can. The water in those canteens ought to take you to Cave Spring at the rate you can travel. I can probably last to the mouth of Cave Canyon before I dry out, and if you have any kind of luck at all you ought to be able to get back to me before I'm dead."

At first Bennett refused to listen to this plan; it seemed so pitifully hopeless. "I'm afraid you'll go out with the heat and shoot yourself before I can make it," he said.

"Very well," I replied, "if that's what's worrying you, take my pistol with you."

Only on this condition would Bennett consider the proposal, and so I handed him the gun, holster, belt, and cartridges, which he strapped about him. I could even see a ray of humor about the incident as Bennett rode away looking like a "two-gun bandit," with a pistol slung on either hip. Little did we realize at that moment that his having two pistols would actually be the means of snatching us both from the very jaws of death.

Giving his motor the full throttle, Bennett roared southward through the valley. For the first mile or two he bounded along through the sand like an enormous jackrabbit. Then he went out of sight around a thicket of mesquite, and I was alone once more in Death Valley, apparently without a ghost of a chance of ever getting out alive. For a full hour I forced the machine southward, floundering through washes, clumps of desert brush, and around boulders. My tongue and throat were fast drying out, and I felt utterly hopeless and miserable. I tried to sing, thinking to keep up my spirits, but with the dryness of my throat the best I could do was a guttural croaking. I chewed a pebble in the hope of stimulating the flow of saliva, but my salivary glands seemed as dry as the sand of Death Valley itself.

The moon came up over the eastern mountains, and by its silvery light I followed the track that Bennett had made, praying hard that the motor would keep turning. I ceased attempting to estimate the distance and the length of time I had traveled, for that only kindled false hopes. My thirst was becoming more terrible every minute, and looking at my watch only made it worse. On, on, and on into the night I rode, trying to think of all the pleasant incidents of my life and endeavoring to forget that I was facing my doom in

Death Valley. It was difficult work, for the fear of death and the torture of thirst were upon me. At last the motor stopped for lack of fuel, and as I began transferring petrol from the reservoir in the sidecar, I ventured to look at my watch. It was ten o'clock. I had traveled for three hours without stopping. Surely, I thought, I must be getting close to the mouth of Cave Canyon! Almost fearing to look, I began to scan the mountains to the right, and there, almost at my side and with Bennett's wheel tracks leading into it, was a black, yawning chasm. It must be Cave Canyon, I thought.

When I remounted the machine, preparatory to driving into the canyon, my thirst had become almost unendurable. My ears were singing and my head was whirling until it was only by the most supreme effort of willpower that I kept from tottering off the saddle. I was peering into the black depths of the canyon, wondering just how far I would get up it, when I was almost dumbfounded to see a tiny black object go scooting out between the walls, and start straight across the floor of the valley. I watched the thing intently, and had almost concluded that it was a delusion due to my troubled brain when it took the form of a small automobile. I stopped my motor and listened. No, it was not a phantom, because I could hear the sharp cracking of its unmuffled exhaust. There was a lone man on the front seat, and he plunged out across the valley as if the Evil One himself was chasing him. In another moment the car was out of sight, and I sat there mentally cursing myself to think what a fool I had been not to catch up with the driver of the car and get water from him. I could not shout, and I had no pistol with which to attract attention. The chances were ten to one that the man had driven past me without even knowing I was there.

I was about to press the starter of my motor again when another black object bolted out of the canyon. "Certainly, I am seeing things," I thought. In another minute, however, I realized that what I had seen was real. The second black object appeared to be smaller than the first. Then it began to take form, and I came to a sudden realization that it was Bennett on his motorcycle. How he could have got to Cave Spring and back again in the length of time he had been gone was simply incomprehensible—but there he was, coming across the desert towards me. Two minutes later he was beside me and was pressing a full canteen of water to my lips. He was smiling from ear to ear and appeared to be in high spirits. "Here's the water," he cried. "Drink all you want, for I've got thirty-six quarts more about a mile up the canyon." Where he had secured the water was a mystery, and until I had regained my voice I was unable to ask him.

At last, observing by my gesticulations that I was perplexed to know where he had obtained the water, Bennett told his story.

He had been delayed by a clogged fuel-line while making his way up Cave Canyon, and was working on the machine trying to remedy the trouble when he heard an automobile coming down. At first he could hardly believe the evidence of his senses, but a moment later a man driving a "flivver" came into view. From this point the story is best told in Bennett's own words: "When I saw the man, I thought, of course, that he would give me water if he had it. I have traveled a great deal in the desert, and until half an hour ago I never met a man who would not have given me the shirt off his back if I needed it. That's the spirit of men when they meet each other in the desert. But this fellow was different. I suppose it's because he was just a low-lived 'snake.' When I hailed him he wasn't going to stop— and he didn't stop, either, until I pulled my gun and sent a bullet singing past his ear. Then I made him stick his hands up and get down out of the car. When I asked him for water, he pretended he didn't understand English, so I started talking to him in Spanish— what little Spanish I know. I know that water in Spanish is 'agua.' I kept saying 'agua, agua, agua' to him, but the scoundrel just kept shaking his head. I began looking through his car, and when I found that the dirty hound had a twenty-five-gallon tank of water in the machine I came mighty near shooting him full of holes. I ought to have killed him, but I didn't. Well, I was rummaging through his car looking for a canteen or something to put the water in when that brute jumped on my back, and we rolled over and over fighting for the gun. I still had the gun in my hand when I saw that he had the advantage, and was about to wrest it from me. I beat him at his little game, however, by firing the five remaining cartridges out of it. Then he got the gun, but he had no shells. Apparently he realized the gun was empty, for he tried to club me over the head with it. Thank God I had your gun! I fended him off with my arm as best I could until I could wriggle around and pull your gun on him. The skunk evidently didn't know I had two guns. Well, I got the drop on him and that settled it. I backed him over against the car and made him fill seven six-quart canteens out of the tank in the tonneau. Then I made him get back in the car and beat it. I fired a few shots after him to speed him on his way, and the last I saw of him he was going down the canyon as if he were trying to establish a speed record. I cached the six cans of water up in the canyon, and came back down with this one can to find you."

From his limited conversation with the man, Bennett had

learned that he had come out from Barstow and was heading for the Carbonate Mine, about forty miles to the east on the other side of the extreme southern end of Death Valley. With twenty-five gallons of water, the quantity Bennett had relieved him of would not inconvenience him in the least. By the time Bennett had finished telling his story, I had recovered my voice to the point of being able to laugh with him over the incident. My companion's only regret over the affair was that he hadn't killed the snake. "I ought to have killed him! I ought to have killed him!" he kept muttering.

"Never mind, Wells," I said. "It's just as well you didn't. But, mark my words—a skunk like that has no business on the desert, and sooner or later somebody *will* kill him!"

Bennett had been keen enough to memorize the man's car-license number, which furnished us with some interesting information upon our return to civilization a few days later. From the state motor vehicle license bureau we learned the man's name and that he hailed from the Ibex Mine, just to the east of Death Valley in the Aramagossa Desert.

After having secured water, the ascent of Cave Canyon was by no means the ordeal we had anticipated. We arrived at Cave Spring about an hour after daylight, where the elevation of nearly six thousand feet gave us welcome relief from the terrific heat we had been living in. Three days later, with faces that were so heat-cracked, blistered, and gaunt-looking that they resembled head-hunter trophies almost more than human countenances, we arrived home in Los Angeles. Bennett tipped the beam twenty-five pounds lighter than when we started into Death Valley, and I had gone down in weight an even twenty-two pounds. By the end of two weeks after our return to civilization, however, we had regained our lost strength and were apparently none the worse for the ordeal we had been through.

Meanwhile, my report of the trip had gone to the factory, and in response I received their congratulations as well as the check which the successful completion of the work entitled me to. Almost in the wake of the postman who brought the check came Bennett. He was greatly excited and had a newspaper clipping in his hand which he handed to me. It was the story of how a prospector by the name of John B. Reynolds had staggered into the sheriff's office at Barstow to give himself up for having killed a man at the extreme southern end of Death Valley. The prospector had run out of water and his burros had died from thirst. He had wandered for more than a day, crazed from the heat and thirst, when he met a man with a small automobile, who had refused to give him water or aid him in any way. In desperation the prospector killed the man and took what water he needed from a twenty-five-gallon tank in the man's car. He then made his way into Barstow, where he gave himself up to a deputy sheriff. Papers which the prospector had removed from the dead man, and which were turned over to the sheriff's office, established the identity of the slain man as the very man who had refused Bennett water and whom Bennett had robbed of sufficient to save our lives at the point of my pistol! He had received the just deserts of the cur who fails to understand human nature in the desert, where the brotherhood of man is probably stronger than anywhere else on earth. According to the newspaper clipping, Reynolds, the prospector, was placed under arrest and then taken before a justice of peace for trial before a jury hastily summoned by the coroner. Ten minutes later the jury rendered a verdict of "justifiable homicide."

Two months later the manufacturers of a well-known air-cooled automobile, having heard of our dash through Death Valley in August by motorcycle, invited me to carry out a similar task with one of their machines the following August. The offer was a most attractive one, but no money on earth would again be the slightest temptation for me to undergo the agony of heat, the torture of thirst, and to take chances on my life by the scanty margin that permitted Bennett and myself to escape. In rejecting their offer I said: "Now that I have been through Death Valley in August, it is a thrilling adventure to look back upon, but all the wealth of Wall Street would not induce me to attempt repeating it. That Mr. Bennett and I are living today I attribute only to some act of Divine providence, or to the fatalist theory that our time hadn't come. We lived through the journey only by the fact that we had most extraordinary luck—luck with tires, machines, water, and everything else. The same combination of good fortune could never be expected again, and without it our lives would have been forfeit."

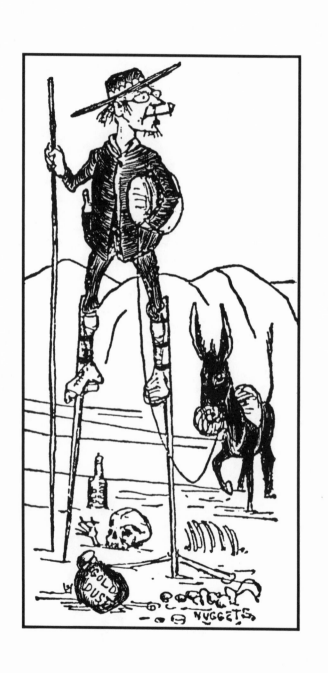

Solar Armor & Other
Tall Tales

*A*S COMIC RELIEF TO ALL THE
horrific lore of the valley, there also cropped up from time to time some
wonderfully tall tales to stretch belief far beyond the breaking point.
Comstock editor Dan De Quille led the way, concocting a tale of "Solar
Armor" for the local columns of the Territorial Enterprise one dull summer
day in 1874. It was so well received that he wrote a sequel to stretch the
yarn just a little farther. The editors of Greenwater's Times and Miner
conspired many years later to foist a truly marvelous "Substitute for Water"
on their credulous readers. Then a Reno Gazette reporter revealed the secret
of the Amargosa's "Canteen Fish." But the tallest tale of all was that of a
Los Angeles Times scribe who told of the epic exploits of Colonel Jewks in
his quest for the treasure of the "Petrified Argonauts" in a deadly sea of gas
that covered the floor of Death Valley.

This classic hoax by Dan De Quille, nom de plume of Virginia City Territorial Enterprise local editor William Wright, first appeared as an anonymous news item under the heading of "Sad Fate of an Inventor" in the July 2, 1874, issue of that paper. It was widely copied by both credulous and incredulous editors as far away as London and was even picked up by the Scientific American. It was such a hit that Dan couldn't resist further elaboration in a follow-up on August 30, entitled "A Mystery Explained."

SOLAR ARMOR
by Dan De Quille

SAD FATE OF AN INVENTOR

A GENTLEMAN who has just arrived from the borax fields of the desert regions surrounding the town of Columbus, in the eastern part of this state, gives us the following account of the sad fate of Mr. Jonathan Newhouse, a man of considerable inventive genius. Mr. Newhouse had constructed what he called a "solar armor," an apparatus intended to protect the wearer from the fierce heat of the sun in crossing deserts and burning alkali plains.

The armor consisted of a long, close-fitting jacket made of common sponge and a cap or hood of the same material; both jacket and hood being about an inch in thickness. Before starting across a desert this armor was to be saturated with water. Under the right arm was suspended an India rubber sack filled with water and having a small gutta percha tube leading to the top of the hood. In order to keep the armor moist, all that was necessary to be done by the traveler as he progressed over the burning sands was to press the sack occasionally, when a small quantity of water would be forced up and thoroughly saturate the hood and the jacket below it. Thus, by the evaporation of the moisture in the armor it was calculated might be produced almost any degree of cold.

Mr. Newhouse went down to Death Valley, determined to try the experiment of crossing that terrible place in his armor. He started out into the valley one morning from the camp nearest its borders, telling the men at the camp, as they laced his armor on his back, that he would return in two days. The next day an Indian who could speak but a few words of English came to the camp in a great state of excitement. He made the men understand that he wanted them to follow him. At the distance of about twenty miles out into the desert the Indian pointed to a human figure seated against a rock.

Approaching, they found it to be Newhouse still in his armor. He was dead and frozen stiff. His beard was covered with frost and —though the noonday sun poured down its fiercest rays—an icicle over a foot in length hung from his nose. There he had perished miserably, because his armor had worked but too well and because it was laced up behind where he could not reach the fastenings.

A MYSTERY EXPLAINED

The Sequel to the Strange Death of Jonathan Newhouse, the Inventor of the Solar Armor

A fortnight after our account of the sad affair was published we received a letter in regard to the matter from one David Baxter, who states that he is justice of the peace and ex officio coroner at Salt Wells, a station in Inyo County, California, situated at the head of the Sink of Amargosa River, at the north end of Death Valley. Mr. Baxter states that he held an inquest on the body of the deceased, Newhouse, in due form, and that the verdict rendered was as follows: "We find that the name of the deceased was Jonathan Newhouse, a native of Knox County, Ohio, aged 47 years; and we further find that deceased came to his death in Death Valley, Inyo County, California, on the 27th day of June, A.D. 1874, by being frozen in a sort of coat of sponge called a 'solar armor,' of which he was the inventor and in which he was tightly laced at his own request, said 'solar armor' being moistened with some frigorific mixture, with the precise nature of which we are unacquainted."

Mr. Baxter further states in his letter that he had before him as witnesses the men stopping at the camp on the borders of Death Valley where Mr. Newhouse was last seen alive. These men produced what Mr. Baxter had not before heard mentioned, namely: the carpet-sack of the deceased, which he had left at their camp. In this was found, besides a few light articles of wearing apparel, several bottles and small glass jars, containing liquids and powders or salts of various kinds, with the nature of the most of which no person in the settlement was acquainted. One of the largest bottles was labeled "Ether," known to them to be a very volatile liquid and capable of producing an intense degree of cold by evaporation.

From this they were able to give a shrewd guess at the nature of the contents of the other vessels. Although it was at first stated— and generally believed until after the contents of the carpet-sack had been overhauled and the inquest held—that deceased had used water only in filling the little India-rubber sack used in supplying moisture to the armor, one of the witnesses, Mr. Robert Purcell, testified that he had observed Mr. Newhouse at a spring about fifty yards from camp half an hour previous to his donning the armor, and recollects distinctly to have seen him handling one or two of the bottles and jars found in the carpet-sack, though at the time he thought nothing of it and did not approach very near the deceased, as he did not wish to be thought inquisitive.

Besides the bottle containing the ether, there was another in which was a liquid labeled "Bisulphide of Carbon." There were small glass jars containing what appeared to be salts. They were labeled "Ammonic Nitrate, Sodic Nitrate, Ammonic Chloride, Sodic Sulphate, and Sodic Phosphate."

Mr. Baxter is firmly convinced that with these chemicals, either alone or diluted with water, the degree of cold was produced which caused the death of the unfortunate man. He thinks that in his attempts to reach the fastenings of his armor on his back, when he began to experience a painful degree of cold, he unavoidably compressed the India-rubber pouch and thus constantly ejected more and more of the freezing fluid into the head-piece of his armor. As he stiffened in death, his arm under which the sack was suspended naturally pressed more strongly upon his side and thus caused a steady flow of the fluid. Mr. Baxter is of the opinion that the frost and icicle found on the beard and depending from the nose of deceased were formed from the water mingled with the more volatile fluids comprising the frigorific mixture.

He states as a remarkable fact—and it is strange that this was not mentioned by the gentleman from Columbus, Mr. Abner Wade, who gave us our first brief and imperfect account of the affair—that the men who went out with the Indian to find the remains of Mr. Newhouse came near having their hands frozen in handling the body when trying to place it upon the back of a horse. The freezing mixture oozed out of the spongy armor upon their hands and gave them intense pain. Finally—after they found they could handle the body in no other way—they were obliged to cut the lacings to the armor, when, after an infinite deal of pain to their hands and fingers, the armor was peeled off the body and left lying in the desert, where it probably still remains.

One of the men, Alexander Martin, suffered for about three weeks from the freezing his left hand received and he came near losing the middle finger, gangrene supervening at the root of the nail.

Viewed in the flood of light which Mr. Baxter throws upon the strange death of Mr. Newhouse, we think there can be but one opinion in regard to it, which is that he fell a victim to a rash experiment with chemicals with the nature of which he was but imperfectly acquainted.

In conclusion, it only remains for us to state that Mr. Baxter informed us that it was his intention to send the bottles and jars of chemicals to the Academy of Sciences at San Francisco; also, the solar armor, in case he could recover it. Whether or not he has done so we cannot say. For several weeks we have closely watched the reports of the proceedings of the learned body named, but as yet have seen no mention made of either the chemicals or the armor.

A SUBSTITUTE

This yarn was started by the editor of the Greenwater Times and was stretched a little farther by his rival on the Greenwater Miner. No copies of the originals survive, but the story was copied in other papers and is reprinted here from the Rhyolite Bullfrog Miner of May 10 and 24, 1907.

FOR WATER

ACCORDING TO REPORTS from Greenwater, another prank of nature has been discovered in the Death Valley country, in which she has provided in her own way a substitute for water in that desolate region where so many have perished from thirst.

If the sufferers had only known as much as the animals which are governed by instinct, it is barely possible that no lives would have ever been lost in that portion of the desert. But men did not know how to look for it, and they lost their lives while their animals continued to live.

The story of the discovery of nature's new kind of water, which is in condensed form, is told by the *Greenwater Times* as follows:

"Seven miles from Greenwater in a westerly direction has been discovered a peculiar substance owing to the fact that it contains 60 percent moisture. It is a very white formation, much resembling lime and what is called sulphide of sulphur, but the fact is that it is an unknown material which even the chemists of this camp have passed up.

"It was first found by following a well-beaten path by wild sheep and other four-footed animals, and there was such a mystery about it that it caused a critical investigation. C. W. Patrick, more curious than any, resorted to every known device to determine its worth. He had trailed his burro to this place and found him feasting on its substance, and he took with him to camp some of it, and in testing it by fire he learned that the dry, white limelike substance contained 60 percent moisture and it was this material supposedly where the wild animals had quenched their thirst and where they had been supplied with a substitute for water in the absence of any liquid form in that forbidden part of the desert.

"Mr. Patrick has been exhibiting his find and he demonstrated the fact by lighting a match under the substance, and by a contact with the flame it quickly melts away and leaves water in its stead, a most peculiar circumstance, mysteriously true, and reliably, a seeming impossible transformation of rock into water."

(To which the Greenwater Miner *added:)*

A Water Mine

THE DISCOVERY of a water mine on the Death Valley slope by C. W. Patrick of Greenwater is opening up the possibilities of Death Valley to agricultural purposes, and an effort is being made to interest the United States government in the matter. The new mine consists of a ledge entirely exposed and giving assays of from 60 to 70 percent water. When heated, the rocks give off this water in streams, which may be regulated by the amount of heat applied to the rocks. A company is about to be organized to develop the new discovery, and water will be provided for the irrigation of the entire floor of Death Valley through this source. A sample broken from the ledge exposed and brought to Greenwater caused wild excitement in the camp. The rock was placed on exhibition in one of the leading saloons and provided several quarts of water when heated.

The development of the property is delayed at present on account of the necessity of erecting reservoirs to hold the water when heated and run from the rocks. When this is done the promoters expect to pipe it to Death Valley, where they will sell it for irrigation purposes. As yet no farms or homesteads have been taken up in the valley on the strength of the proposition. Land is plentiful and cheap in that vicinity and when irrigated will probably produce wonderful melons and tropical fruits.

CANTEEN FISH

This undisguised hoax appeared in the Reno Evening Gazette
of June 15, 1916.

OF AMARGOSA

JONAH'S WHALE, flying fish that sing, and other Waltonian finny wonders are excelled by Nevada's latest discovery, the canteen fish of the Amargosa desert.

According to F. L. Bixbey, federal irrigation expert now in the employ of the university, and J. G. Scrugham, dean of the College of Engineering, this fish must be classed as the ninth wonder of the world.

They have recently returned from Leland, in the Amargosa desert, where irrigation experiments are being made along the Amargosa River which is supposed to lose itself in the desert and again reappear miles away.

"Fish in this river, the natives tell us," said Mr. Bixbey today, "have great trouble in keeping up with the river which dries up every afternoon," he continued. "Nature has provided them with canteens attached to their tails and in the morning they fill up these canteens. When the river dries up in the afternoon they tie themselves in a circle like a hoop snake and roll over the desert in search of where the river will reappear again."

"The water in the canteen keeps them sprinkled in the afternoon. Of course these fish rolling around make a lot of dust and strangers think it is a sandstorm but it is just the canteen fish looking for the lost river."

PETRIFIED

This leg-pulling "report" of the farcical exploits of Colonel John Jewks was originally published as "Death's Valley Opened," in the Los Angeles Times of January 19, 1890, for the supposed benefit of a visiting French savant. The identity of "Kelp," its author, remains a mystery.

ARGONAUTS
by Kelp

A Half-Century of Horror Cleared Up—The Adventures of an
Explorer—The Sea of Gas—Across the Deadly Valley on Stilts—
Vast Wealth—Petrified Skeletons

AMERICA IS INDEBTED to foreign authors for much valuable information about herself. Hardly a year passes but some distinguished
writer passes through on his way to Asia, and his impressions a few
months later are given to an appreciative public. It has become a
matter of journalistic courtesy for the press of this country and citizens at large to aid these authors as much as possible, and *The Times*,
while desiring to respect that professional modesty which prevents a
paper from blowing its own horn, is forced into the position of stating what it has done in this connection.

For some months past there has been in this county a distinguished member of the Institute of France, a gentleman who is
known in scientific circles all over the world. This savant is preparing an elaborate work on Death's Valley, to be published at an early
day. He found in Los Angeles so much information concerning it
that a visit to the place was hardly necessary. *The Times* was informed
of the matter some time ago, learned that the scientist wanted maps
of the valley and accurate measurements of the depth of the deadly
gas; samples of sticks eaten or corroded by contact; drawings of
bodies and teams seen in the valley from the cliffs above—and determined to aid him in procuring the bottom facts.

The New York *Herald* had its Stanley; the *Times* had its Sch-
watka; the *Cosmopolitan* its race around the world. Why should not
the Pasadena edition of the Los Angeles *Times* have its representative
in Death's Valley, and give the results to this noble-hearted and
gifted foreigner? There was but one difficulty: Who could be found
to face the terrors of the now famous valley, that for years had been
the destruction of thousands? It is enough to say that the man was
found in the guise of Col. John Jewks, late general manager of a Chicago gas company. *The Times* learned that Col. Jewks could inhale

more gas and live than any man in Southern California. The Colonel wanted excitement, so it was settled, and two months ago he started.

Yesterday the expedition returned, and the Colonel's report is given for the benefit of the savant who is now in Los Angeles and the general public. "Yes, sir," said the Colonel, to a *Times* reporter; "I am back, and I claim to be the only man who ever went through Death's Valley and didn't die; and, moreover, the valley is open to the public for the first time in the memory of man."

"The valley is well known; it has the reputation of having caused the death of over 3,000 persons in this century. Hundreds of trains wandered into it and stood there petrified, or rather vitrefied, turned into metal monuments."

"Did you bring any of these out with you?" asked the reporter.

"No, I did not," replied the Colonel, "and I will tell you why. To begin at the beginning, I made my will and started two months ago. I have been in the gas business all my life, and by habit have got so used to it that I can breathe it for some time without injurious effects; that's why I thought I could make a go of it. I went to Barstow by rail, and on the 10th day of November started with a burro for the valley across the desert. I was 10 days on the trip, and on the 11th I sighted what they call the black cloud, which is, I discovered, nothing but buzzards hovering over the valley, watching the bodies and not daring to go down. They look from a distance like a black cloud, and are so described in some geographies; just make a special point of that as a new discovery. Death's Valley is," continued the Colonel, "about 10 miles wide by 15 long, and is surrounded by a range of lofty mountains. Before daylight of the 12th I was on the summit and, with the burro, looked down onto one of the most frightful scenes in the known world. I could see the whole thing— inviting and beautiful if you didn't know it, but a horror if you did. What looked to be a beautiful lake I knew to be gas. With my glass I saw over 500 wagons of all kinds, bodies of horses, men, women and children—all as natural as life, just as if it was a picnic party. And that's how so many got trapped; they see it all, think it a beautiful place to camp, ride in, and are suffocated.

"My plans were to cross in different directions and photograph the scenes, measure the gas layers and see where it came from. So, after a good night's sleep, to the windward, I buckled on a pair of stilts I had brought, and with my gasometer and photographic outfit lashed to the mule, started down. I descended 2,000 feet before I struck the level, and then took a gopher out of my pocket which I had brought for the purpose and dropped it upon the ground. The

Solar Armor & Other Tall Tales

gas was there, as the gopher died in 10 seconds. I took another gopher and stooped down; at my waist it was all right, but at my knees it began to gasp, so I determined that the height of the gas at the outer or radial edge, or, to use the technical term, at the outer edge of its impingement, it was five feet deep. Care was now necessary, as, should I stoop or fall and get my head below this, I would be a dead man. I moved on with the greatest precaution, but, as slowly as I walked, some of the gas came up and almost suffocated me.

"I carried a long stick, and, lifting it up, the moment the end which had been in the gas struck the atmospheric air, it burst into a blue flame that under the spectrum showed violet lines. In a moment the flame went out and I found the stick encased in a white metallic substance; in fact, the fiber had disappeared.

"Moving on carefully, I approached a train, an old-fashioned prairie schooner, and tying the burro to the wheel prepared to photograph the scene. Here was a family sitting. The man was smoking a pipe, the mother in the act of stooping down, the children lying in various positions—all looking from the action of the gas as if they had been turned into white metal. Near here was a bag which had burst open, and piles of gold and silver poured out through a break. Without thinking, I stooped to pick it up, but the gas met me, and measurement showed it to be three feet deep here. I leaned against the wheel and took off my stilts and tried to fish up some of the money; then one of the gophers I had in my coat pocket began to struggle, and I jumped onto the cartwheel to save it, and bethought me of my watch. I pulled it out; it had stopped at 10:30, the gas had destroyed the works."

The Colonel showed the reporter the watch. It had no works, the space being filled with a substance resembling cotton.

"I worked over two hours trying to reach that wealth, but had to give it up. I visited over 30 trains of immigrants and looked upon hundreds who would have been 49ers had it not been for this deadly valley. There was not a living thing excepting self, the burro and black cloud of buzzards a mile overhead. I found, [and here the Colonel brought out a map covered with figures] that the gas was lowest in the exact center of the valley, it being but two feet deep there; but it was more deadly. A gopher introduced here died in just one second, without a struggle. From this point I found the depth gradually increased inversely as the distance from the center to the mountains, and that its power decreased inversely in the same proportion. In other words, at the center, where the gas was three feet deep, a gopher died in one second; while at the base of the mountains, where the depth was eight feet, it took 10 seconds. In this way, by multiplying the time it took to kill the gopher at the three-foot place by the time it took to kill one at the five-foot base, I obtained the specific gravity of the gas and the volume, which I estimated at 6,000,000,000,000,000 meters."

"Gas meters?" asked the reporter.

"Certainly," replied the Colonel, courteously. "In five days I mapped the entire region, and located the depths as you see on the map.

"Every night as I retired to the surrounding peaks to sleep and feed the burro, I pondered upon some method to secure the property, in sight but so unattainable. The only way was to remove the gas; but how? Would it burn? The next day I took in an ordinary beer bottle and brought it out filled with gas. Touching a match to it, it flamed up like ordinary gas, and developed such a heat that it melted the bottle. Well, young man," said the Colonel, taking off his sombrero, "to say that I was delighted goes without saying. I saw myself going back to Pasadena rolling in wealth.

"Well, the next three days I employed in hauling sticks and grass to the summit of the steepest peak, and finally I had a combustible ball 20 feet in diameter. You perceive my idea; it was to light the ball, start it down, and so ignite the lake of deadly gas. I waited until the night of the 30th, and as soon as darkness set in I applied the match, and the enormous ball blazed up. A simple touch, and it went rushing down into this terrestrial hell. I sat on the back of the burro and watched it bound from rock to rock, until finally it sprang into the abyss, and—" Here the Colonel rose and led the way to the back yard.

"Do you see that burro?" The reporter did. The burro was pure white and resembled the last one in at the late tournament. "Do you see this?" and the Colonel raised his sombrero. "When that ball was touched off, that burro and my hair were as black as coals; 18 seconds later they were as white as the riven snow. My reason totters when I tell it," continued the Colonel, pacing the floor, "but the moment the ball struck the lake of gas the world seemed afire; a mass of flame 10 × 15 miles shot upward with a roar. I felt a mighty heat, noticed an indescribable odor of burning feathers, and knew no more. I was aroused by being struck by something, and came to, to find my burro white as snow and dead, and singed buzzards falling all about; so I estimated that the flame had shot up a mile in height to have reached the birds. The first thing in the morning I cast my eyes in the direction of the valley. There it was, but not a wagon or the remains of a single object. I hurried down, released several gophers and they ran off. The gas had disappeared. I took off my

Solar Armor & Other Tall Tales

stilts, walked about, laid down; not a trace of the deadly poison remained; but every trace of human beings had disappeared. The fierce heat had melted the gold and silver, and destroyed every trace and vestige of what has been so long a horror."

"Death's Valley is open to the world, then?"

"Yes, sir," replied the Colonel; "it is perfectly safe; the gas cannot accumulate again, I have estimated, under 1,000 years."

"There was one point," said the reporter, "I did not understand."

"What was that?" asked the Colonel.

"How did the burro breathe the gas?"

"Ah! I am glad you mentioned that point," said the explorer. "I muzzled his nose in a gunnysack and he breathed through his ears. Necessity is the mother of invention."

Such are the simple facts collected by *The Times* expedition. When they appear in the new work by the eminent savant among us full particulars will be given. The Colonel has been offered an extended engagement to lecture on Death's Valley, and will probably go East soon.

EPILOGUE

AND IT'S NOT OVER YET, all this yarn-spinning and lore-making about Death Valley. This very night, around a table in Tecopa or at a bar in Beatty, a traveler will hear some new flight of fancy about continental drift or underground testing, or perhaps an old wheeze about the lost Breyfogle given some new twist. And in the vast and empty desert dark, the illusions will grow and comfort and persist.

BIBLIOGRAPHY OF SOURCES

A PLACE IN THE MIND

"The Horrors of Death Valley," *New York World*, September 16, 1894.

"Treasure Basin of the World," by Clarence E. Eddy, *Death Valley Magazine* (February 1908) pp. 28–29.

THE FORTY-NINERS

"The Argonauts of Death Valley," by John Wells Brier, *Grizzly Bear* 9:2 (June 1911) pp. 1–4, 7.

"Good-bye Death Valley!" by William Lewis Manly, from his *Death Valley in '49*. San Jose: Pacific Tree and Vine Co., 1894, Chapters IX and X, pp. 131–61, 197–217. Facsimile reprint, Bishop: Chalfant Press, 1977.

LOST LEDGES

"The Lost Ledge," by John Ross Browne, from his *Adventures in the Apache Country, A Tour Through Arizona and Sonora with Notes on the Silver Regions of Nevada*. New York: Harper & Brothers, 1869, pp. 512–22. Facsimile reprint, New York: Promontory Press, 1974.

"Breyfogle's Lost Ledge," by Standish Rood, from his "Lost Ledge," *Whittaker's Milwaukee Monthly* 4 (August and September 1872) pp. 41–46, 89–94.

"Charles Alvord," by William Lewis Manly, *The Pioneer* 10 (May 15, 1895) p. 8 and (June 15, 1895) p. 4. Reprinted in *The Jayhawkers' Oath and Other Sketches*, edited by Arthur Woodward, Los Angeles: Warren F. Lewis, 1949.

"Searching for the Lost Goller," by Milo Page, from his "Searching for Lost Mines: The Goller Mine," *Sierra Magazine* 2 (February 1909) pp. 3–11.

TWENTY-MULE TEAMS

"She Burns Green, Rosie!" and "The Twenty-Mule Teams," by John Randolph Spears, from his *Illustrated Sketches of Death Valley and Other Borax Deserts of the Pacific Coast*. Chicago: Rand, McNally & Co., 1892. Chapter IV "Tales of the White Arabs," pp. 55–63, and Chapter VII "Freighting on the Desert," pp. 83–104. Facsimile reprint, Morongo Valley: Sagebrush Press, 1977.

DEATH IN THE VALLEY

"The Lost Wagon Train," by Robert E. Rinehart, *Los Angeles Times*, August 16, 1908. Reprinted in George Wharton James, *Heroes of California*. Boston: Little, Brown and Co., 1910.

"Victims of Death Valley," by Orin S. Merrill, from his *"Mysterious Scott," The Monte Cristo of Death Valley, and Tracks of a Tenderfoot*. Chicago: Orin S. Merrill, 1906, pp. 103–10. Facsimile reprint, Bishop: Chalfant Press, 1972.

"Murder in Camp," by M. R. MacLeod, *Skidoo News*, April 25, 1908.

"A Bogus Grave," by Clyde J. McDivitt, *Randsburg Miner*, March 22, 1906.

RAINBOW CHASERS

"Prospecting Death Valley in Summer," by Paul DeLaney, from "A Trip Across Death Valley in Mid-Summer" and "Rattlesnakes and Spooks of Death Valley," *Death Valley Prospector*, November and December 1907.

"Southwest from Bullfrog," by Rufus Milas Steele, *Pacific Monthly* 18 (October 1907) pp. 465–69.

"Half a Century Chasing Rainbows," by Frank "Shorty" Harris, *Touring Topics* 22 (October 1930) pp. 12–20, 55. (As told to Philip Johnston).

DEATH VALLEY SCOTTY

"Scotty, King of the Desert Mine," by Charles A. Taylor, from his *The Story of "Scotty"* . . . *Walter Scott* . . . *King of the Desert Mine*. New York: J. S. Ogilvie Publishing Co., 1906, pp. 5–6, 17–44.

"Scotty's Ride," by Earl Alonzo Brininstool, *Los Angeles Examiner*, July 12, 1905.

"Chasing Rainbows in Death Valley," by Sydney Norman, from his book of the same name. Los Angeles: Los Angeles Mining Review, 1909, 35 pp.

"Scotty's Castle," by Edward A. Vandeventer, from "Death Valley Scotty, Mysterious Son of the Desert," *Sunset Magazine* 56 (March 1926) pp. 22–25, 72–73.

THE ADVENTURE-SEEKERS

"First Auto Across Death Valley," by George Graham Rice, from "Modern Mine Hunting with Automobiles," *Rhyolite Herald*, June 29, 1906.

"A Race for Life in Death Valley," by John Edwin Hogg, *Wide World Magazine* 50 (October 1922), pp. 58–72.

SOLAR ARMOR & OTHER TALL TALES

"Solar Armor," by Dan De Quille, from "Sad Fate of an Inventor" and "A Mystery Explained," *Territorial Enterprise*, July 2, August 30, 1874. Reprinted in *Comstock Bonanza*, edited by Duncan Emrich. New York: Vanguard, 1950.

"A Substitute for Water," from *Greenwater Times* and *Greenwater Miner*, quoted in the Rhyolite *Bullfrog Miner*, May 10, 24, 1907.

"Canteen Fish of Amargosa," *Reno Evening Gazette*, June 15, 1916.

"Petrified Argonauts," by Kelp, from "Death's Valley Opened," *Los Angeles Times*, January 19, 1890.

FOR THE HISTORY OF DEATH VALLEY SEE:

Death Valley & the Amargosa: A Land of Illusion, by Richard E. Lingenfelter. Berkeley: University of California Press, 1986. 664 pp.